Voices from

VIETNAM

Voices from
VIETNAM

Richard Burks Verrone
and Laura M Calkins

David and Charles

For my parents, I. Richard and Carol C Verrone
and for Julie

Richard Burks Verrone

For my parents, Dan and Nan Calkins
and for Sharon

Laura M Calkins

A DAVID & CHARLES BOOK
David & Charles is a subsidiary of F+W (UK) Ltd.,
an F+W Publications Inc. company

First published in the UK in 2005

Narrative copyright © Richard Burks Verrone and Laura M Calkins 2005
Extract copyright © Vietnam Archive, Texas Tech University 2005

Distributed in North America
by F+W Publications, Inc.
4700 East Galbraith Road
Cincinnati, OH 45236
1-800-289-0963

A catalogue record for this book is available from the British Library.

ISBN 0 7153 2032 7 hardback

Printed in the USA
for David & Charles
Brunel House   Newton Abbot   Devon

Commissioning Editor   Ruth Binney
Desk Editor   Lewis Birchon
Art Editor   Ali Myer
Designer   Lisa Wyman

Visit our website at www.davidandcharles.co.uk

David & Charles books are available from all good bookshops; alternatively you can
contact our Orderline on (0)1626 334555 or write to us at FREEPOST EX2 110, David &
Charles Direct, Newton Abbot, TQ12 4ZZ (no stamp required UK mainland).

CONTENTS

The Republic of Vietnam

Demilitarized Zone

Route 9

Cam Lo
Cua Viet
Dong Ha
Quang Tri City
Mai Loc

Khe Sanh

Camp Evans

Hue

Phu Bai

Yankee Station

A Shau Valley

I CORPS

Da Nang

Hoi An

Tam Ky

Route 14

Chu Lai

Quang Ngai

Dak To

Route 1

Central Highlands

Kontum

Pleiku
Plei Me

An Khe

Qui
Nhon

Route 19

Ia Drang Valley

Tuy Hoa

Ban Me Thuot

Route 21

Gia Nghia

WAR ZONE C

II CORPS

Nha Trang

Phuoc Binh

Da Lat

Cam
Ranh
Bay

The Fishhook

An Loc

Nui Ba Den
(Black Virgin Mountain)

Route 14

III CORPS

Phan Rang

Iron Triangle

Tay Ninh

Bao Loc

Route 1

Cu Chi
Parrot's
Beak

Lai Khe

Phuoc Vinh

Ben Suc

Tan Son Nhut Air Base

Xuan Loc
Phan Thiet

Mekong River

Plain of Reeds

Saigon

Bien Hoa

Ha Tien

Chau Doc

Long Tau Canal

Long Xuyen

Dong Tam My Tho

Long Binh

Phu Quoc
Island

Sa Dec

Vinh Long

Vung Tau

Dixie Station

Rach Gia

Can Tho

Bassac River

Mekong River Delta

Ben Tri

GULF OF
THAILAND

Route 4

Soc
Trang

IV
CORPS

Quan Long

Bac Lieu

SOUTH
CHINA SEA

Ca Mau
Peninsula

N

Vinh Te Canal

Saigon River

Vietnam War Area of Operations

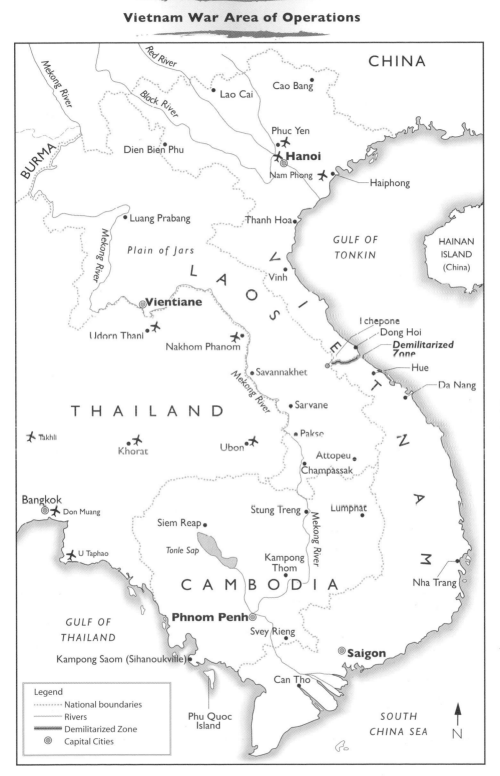

CHINA

Mekong River

Red River

Black River

Lao Cai

Cao Bang

Phuc Yen

BURMA

Dien Bien Phu

Hanoi

Nam Phong

Haiphong

Luang Prabang

Thanh Hoa

GULF OF
TONKIN

HAINAN
ISLAND
(China)

Plain of Jars

L A O S

V I E T

Vinh

Mekong River

Vientiane

Udorn Thani

Nakhom Phanom

Tchepone
Dong Hoi
*Demilitarized
Zone*

Hue

Savannakhet

Da Nang

Mekong River

Sarvane

T H A I L A N D

Takhli

Pakse

N
A
M

Khorat

Ubon

Attopeu
Champassak

Stung Treng

Lumphat

Bangkok

Don Muang

Siem Reap

Tonle Sap

Mekong River

Kampong
Thom

Nha Trang

U Taphao

C A M B O D I A

GULF OF
THAILAND

Phnom Penh

Svey Rieng

Saigon

Kampong Saom (Sihanoukville)

Can Tho

Legend
.... National boundaries
―― Rivers
▬▬ Demilitarized Zone
◎ Capital Cities

Phu Quoc
Island

SOUTH
CHINA SEA

N

FOREWORD

When I think about the war in Vietnam, what I witnessed and experienced in four tours, I see the faces and hear the voices of the soldiers and Marines I marched and lived with as a war correspondent. From the beginning – the first battalion of Marines who landed in March of 1965 – to the end in April of 1975, those are the memories that never leave me.

From my first patrol, with a Marine battalion commanded by a Lieutenant Colonel named P.X. Kelly, to a Huey ride in the darkness into a place in the Ia Drang Valley called Landing Zone X-Ray and an Army battalion commander named Hal Moore, to a hundred marches in the hot sun or the cold rain, my memories are of great young Americans doing a hard, thankless and dangerous job for their country.

Men and women like those I knew have a voice, and they get to have their say, in *Voices from Vietnam*. They speak about what happened to them, what they remember about the most important time of their lives. These authentic voices, culled from interviews with the individuals, speak across the years about what Vietnam was really like. Their voices, their stories, are told in this book, which offers a window into the reality of war – on the battlefield, on the front lines and behind them, from the grunts to the officers, from those at home who supported the war to those who protested against it.

Much has been written about the Vietnam War. Scholarly studies dissect the war from every angle, present arguments, analyze motives, try to lay blame and underscore high-flown interpretations of what happened there and back home in a divided and angry nation. This book is different. It talks about the war as it was lived by those who were there – Americans, their allies, and Vietnamese. *Voices from Vietnam* tells us more about the Vietnam that I remember than any academic work ever could.

On this 30th anniversary of the fall of South Vietnam, the voices of those who fought the Vietnam War and those who felt its impact back home are with us, testifying to their experiences.

We owe a debt of gratitude to The Vietnam Center at Texas Tech University, with its Vietnam Archive and Oral History Project, for establishing a permanent and accessible home for all materials relating to the Vietnam War. In *Voices from Vietnam*, Richard Burks Verrone and Laura M Calkins of the Vietnam Archive's Oral History Project have produced a work that utilizes this unique collection and contributes to the history of the war while also informing and enlightening us, and those who come after us, about our war.

Voices from Vietnam will take you back in time to the story that was and is the Vietnam War.

Joseph L Galloway
January 1, 2005

Co-author: *We Were Soldiers Once . . . and Young*
Co-author: *Triumph Without Victory: The History of the Persian Gulf War*

THE LIVING MEMORY OF THE VIETNAM ERA

Where does one turn for insights into the humanity and inhumanity that emerge in times of war, for glimpses of the bitter and the sweet that arise when nations, ideologies, and armies collide? Our best sources are the voices of those who were there, who experienced the day-to-day events of war. Memory is imperfect, but somewhere in remembrance also lies truth. It is that truth that we have tried to portray in *Voices from Vietnam*.

So much has been written about Vietnam, yet confusion about the war still exists. Our aim for this work is to help clear the muddy waters a bit, to allow readers to see more acutely what happened in Vietnam and America during that tumultuous period when America fought its longest and most controversial war. We cannot capture all voices from that era, nor can we hope to address every issue arising from the war. This book does not represent everyone or every experience. It will not answer every question. It is our hope, however, that this book will encourage others to continue to ask the questions that need to be asked.

The Vietnam Archive at Texas Tech University in Lubbock, Texas, holds the world's largest non-governmental collection of materials on the Vietnam conflict. We are proud to be part of this effort to collect and preserve all items that document the Vietnam era. We encourage all those who have such materials to consider making the Vietnam Archive the permanent home for their photographs, letters, and all manner of documents and keepsakes, knowing that they will be safe and accessible for future generations. We also urge anyone with any connection to the conflict to contact the Oral History Project, so their experiences can be preserved and made available for research, as well as being honored, remembered, and understood.

The Vietnam generation is aging and will be gone one day. The window is closing on the opportunity to capture these voices for the future. Indeed, to obtain the vital insights into the Vietnam era that only personal stories can convey, we must make earnest efforts now. The histories yet to be written depend upon whether we act, or allow time to steal the precious stories away.

Alone, we could not execute the enormous task of recording the stories of the Vietnam generation, nor could we have produced this volume. We are grateful for this opportunity to acknowledge and thank our talented, dedicated, and supportive colleagues, including: Dr James R Reckner; Stephen Maxner; Mary Elizabeth Saffell; our technology guru Justin Saffell; all our cheerful colleagues at the Vietnam Archive – Mary Ruth Thurmond, Ty Lovelady; Victoria Lovelady; Kevin Sailsbury; Kyla Osborne – and our terrific Oral History transcription team: Shannon Geach, Laura Darden, Brooke Tomlin, and Jessica Harrell. We also thank Ruth Binney for her guidance and hard work in bringing this project to fruition.

Each person who speaks in this volume participated in the preservation and oral history interview programs of the Vietnam Archive at Texas Tech University. Without their willingness to share their memories, all that follows would remain cloaked, hidden from view, locked in memory but nowhere else available to those – now and in the future – who have questions, who seek answers, who want to know what it was like to be a part of the Vietnam generation. To them we owe the highest gratitude for their courage to tell their stories.

Any errors are ours alone.

Richard Burks Verrone
Laura M Calkins

Lubbock, Texas
March 2005

1
EARLY DAYS 1954–65

THE UNITED STATES AND THE FRANCO-VIET MINH WAR

American interest in the military conflicts in Vietnam dates from World War II. President Franklin D Roosevelt, contemplating the postwar situation in Asia, anticipated that the local nationalist movements that had defied occupying Japanese troops throughout Southeast Asia since 1942 would in large measure define the political future of the region. Some of these nationalist groups had links to Communist parties, particularly that in China, but wartime circumstances and a shared enmity toward Japan had led American, British, French and Dutch forces to seek cooperative arrangements with nationalist leaders in their respective Asian colonies. In Japanese-occupied Indochina, for example, a Free French movement persisted despite the fall of Paris in May 1940, and the US military had developed links to the Viet Minh, Vietnam's main anti-French, anti-Japanese popular front organization. Based in northern Vietnam, the Viet Minh had organized an underground military opposition to Japan's occupation forces. It was led by a dynamic politician named Ho Chi Minh, who had lived for some time in France and China and was active in the international Communist movement. Ho hoped for American support in resisting a postwar French reoccupation of Vietnam. To curry favor with the Americans he promised that the Viet Minh would help rescue downed American airmen flying missions to Southern China. Roosevelt himself urged the French to relinquish political control over their colonial territories in Indochina, including Vietnam.

The prospects for American–Viet Minh cooperation quickly faded. After President Roosevelt's death in 1944, American resistance to the re-establishment of France's colonial empire relaxed. Japan's surrender in August 1945 threatened to leave much of coastal Asia from Korea to Cambodia without any form of government at all. The British, French and Americans decided together that Allied troops had to be sent to these areas to accept the Japanese surrender, to preserve whatever remained of the economic assets of the region, and to prevent political anarchy, from which only Communists and other leftists would benefit. British forces entered

Saigon in September 1945, along with token American and French units; they anticipated the arrival of more French troops in the near future.

Ho Chi Minh, meanwhile, recognized that Japan's surrender presented him with an unparalleled opportunity to seize power. He traveled to Hanoi, and on 2 September 1945, he declared Vietnam's independence, citing the American Declaration of Independence in his speech. As leader of the new 'government,' which he termed the Democratic Republic of Vietnam (DRV), Ho also unleashed his own Viet Minh forces against pro-French Vietnamese leaders and landowners who might assist the return of the French or attempt to unseat him. Nguyen Xuan Phong, who later became South Vietnam's Ambassador to the Paris Peace Talks in the early 1970s, recalls the impact of this period on his own family:

> There was also the case that we had the period [when] the Viet Minh were able to have power for a few months there [in late 1945]. Of course they imprisoned all the landowners, whomever had any kind of function under French rule, and then some. So my maternal grandfather was jailed because he was a village chief. Luckily my uncle, that is the younger brother of my mother, knew the Viet Minh chiefs or leaders they had – they were schoolmates one time and they are friends – that uncle [of] mine went to see his schoolmate, say[ing] "Why [did] you put my father in jail? He was a harmless man, he hadn't done anything cruel." So he was released after a few days . . .

By 1946 the French had mustered sufficient troops to reoccupy much of Indochina and, with its forces back in control of the cities and ports, France tried to harness the Viet Minh by opening talks with Ho Chi Minh. Although some points of agreement were found, there was no fundamental accommodation between the aspirations for continued colonial control harbored in Paris and the aspirations for Vietnam's complete independence held by Ho Chi Minh. Armed hostilities between the French and Viet Minh erupted at Haiphong in December 1946.

Meanwhile, President Harry Truman's administration had assigned high priority to maintaining a non-Communist government in metropolitan France, which was recovering from years of war and foreign occupation. Despite lingering American disapproval, however, France embarked upon a policy aimed at full reinstatement of its colonial authority over Laos, Cambodia and Vietnam. The United States, focusing its efforts on preventing the further expansion of Soviet influence in Europe and of

Chinese Communist control on mainland China, turned a blind eye to developments in Vietnam.

In Vietnam itself, the Viet Minh made the most of popular resentment against the return of the French, enlarging both its political apparatus and its military wing. While the Viet Minh remained based in the rural north, its recruiters were active in southern Vietnam as well, where the French presence was most noticeable. The Viet Minh was also active amongst urban intellectuals, who recognized the disparity between French ideals of political liberty and French colonial policies. Nguyen Xuan Phong recalls that,

> [The intellectuals] wanted to be, to shake off the French rule, colonial rule. That was everywhere. That was the general feeling. We didn't like the French on our back, although we enjoyed the kind of life that they offered but . . . we may say that in the cities and the countryside there was a relative impression of peace. There was no war, maybe some action from the Viet Minh here and there . . . but relatively speaking you see, the resistance movements were nothing to match against the French forces, which were called expeditionary forces, and they were back [in Vietnam]. But there was a beginning of a feeling of resistance and actions of resistance against [the] return of the French . . .

As the Franco-Viet Minh war broadened during the late 1940s, the Viet Minh began to make greater inroads in southern Vietnam. As Nguyen Xuan Phong recalls, students like him were the targets of Viet Minh recruiters, and eventually his own family was divided by the growing appeal of the Viet Minh's call for independence from France:

> In the late 1940s there were agitations in the Vietnamese schools . . . [The Vietnamese students at the school] were circulating photographs of Ho Chi Minh side by side with Lenin, Karl Marx . . . Mao Zedong, Stalin . . . I was one of those boys who distribute[d] those photographs too. We were caught, of course, and my father was called and I was in principle expelled. So my father took me home, spanked me a lot. "Why do you do things like that? Don't do things like that." "I don't know, guys gave me those things, then they just disappeared . . ." So he managed somehow to explain and then I was returned to the school . . . It was also interesting for me to try and think of my uncles and other relatives who went north in the 1940s and joined the Viet

Minh ranks. They remained there, but they had contacts through the family in the native villages. They were up there and we were down south, so each side had its own ways of life I suppose. It was not much of a choice, in the end nobody had a very conscious act of choosing . . . You were caught in a certain context and you remained there and then you respond[ed] to circumstances.

International developments during 1950 changed the complexion of the political and military situation inside Vietnam. By that time the expanding Viet Minh military had scored numerous successes against the French, and Paris had begun increasing the number of troops in Indochina. In early 1950 the Chinese Communists completed their rout of their Nationalist opponents and extended their geographical control to the China–Vietnam border area. They also began to supply Ho Chi Minh's forces with weapons and equipment. Ho Chi Minh embraced this aid, and announced his adherence to the international Communist movement by exchanging diplomatic representatives with Moscow and Beijing. To meet this new Communist threat, the French requested American military support to 'contain' the Viet Minh Communists. The Truman Administration, newly embroiled in the war in Korea, created a US Military Assistance and Advisory Group (MAAG) which was set up in Vietnam to process equipment transfers to French troops. At the end of 1950 the US committed $133 million in economic and military assistance to the French and French-backed locals in Vietnam.

American policy in Vietnam under President Truman and, from 1953, under his successor, President Dwight D Eisenhower, was driven by a strategic concept known as 'the domino theory', which held that territories abutting a Communist-run nation were most vulnerable to Communist subversion and infiltration. At is simplest, the theory proposed that in order to 'contain' Communist expansionism it would be necessary to defend those countries that shared borders with a Communist nation; to fail to do so would invite subversion and the fall of that country, and eventually the one adjoining it, and so on across whole regions of the globe. The Viet Minh's growing relationship with the Chinese Communists indicated to Washington that Vietnam would be the next domino. In June 1952 the US sent another $150 million in military assistance to the French.

French officials recognized that Washington's fear of Communist aggression was an excellent tool for leveraging yet more American support for France's project of preserving its colonial-style authority in Indochina. In the summer of 1953, while promising to grant greater independence to its new 'post-colonial' client governments in Laos, Cambodia, and Vietnam, France also let it be known that only a greatly enlarged military aid package from the US could sustain its troops in the field against the Communist-led Viet Minh. The United States agreed, and in 1953 it approved another $385 million worth of planes, weapons, ammunition and equipment for French forces in Vietnam.

The Viet Minh leadership realized that America's growing support for the French might well crush its military organization. It prepared an all-out battle to force the French from Vietnam for good. In November 1953, when French forces were airlifted to a remote valley town in northwestern Vietnam named Dien Bien Phu, Ho Chi Minh and his principal military strategist, Vo Nguyen Giap, saw their opportunity. The French position at Dien Bien Phu depended wholly upon resupply and reinforcement from the air. Giap's plan was to surround Dien Bien Phu and strangle it, using anti-aircraft weapons to harass supply planes and artillery to pound the entrenched French position. The plan worked to perfection.

By March 1953 the French had committed some 12,000 of their best troops to the defense of Dien Bien Phu. Fearing that the entire garrison would be slaughtered, the French sought emergency aid from the United States. President Eisenhower discussed several possible remedies for the French position, but decided to do nothing to change the situation at Dien Bien Phu. The post was surrendered to the Viet Minh in May 1954, just as a major international conference on Indochina's future opened in Geneva. Foreign Service Officer Joseph Mendenhall, who in the late 1950s served on the Vietnam desk at the US State Department in Washington, remembers the circumstances surrounding the Geneva Conference:

> The French, by 1954, unless they got outright military
> intervention on our part, in support of their battle of Dien
> Bien Phu, were resolved to throw up their hands. The existing
> French government collapsed. Mendes-France took over as
> the Premier in France, and initiated the process which moved
> toward the Geneva Conference on Vietnam, Cambodia and
> Laos in 1954 . . . There were quite a number of countries which
> took part in that conference: France, the UK, the US, Russia,
> Communist China, and obviously the Viet Minh and the non-
> Communist government in Saigon, the one which had never fully
> acquired independence, but which was by now recognized by
> the US and many other countries . . . This conference in Geneva
> occurred in the summer of 1954. It soon became clear that all

the French really wanted to do was pull out [of Indochina] and the Eisenhower administration, with Mr Dulles as the Secretary of State, did not want to be directly associated with the fall of any new territory [to] Communist political control. After all, they had seen what had happened to the Democrats when the Communists took over China and they did not want to be tarred with the loss of Vietnam.

THE PARTITION OF VIETNAM

The international conference at Geneva finally concluded with an agreement to partition Vietnam into two sectors: Ho Chi Minh's Communist-run 'Democratic Republic of Vietnam' in the north and a pro-Western, non-Communist 'State of Vietnam' in the south. The United States declined to endorse the agreement, and set about instead ensuring that the southern sector of Vietnam would be oriented toward the United States, rather than toward the now-retreating French. As Joseph Mendenhall remembers:

All the United States did with respect to [the Geneva] agreement, was to issue a unilateral statement stating that we would not use force to upset any of these agreements . . . The United States decided to support a man who was a non-Communist – but who had been in exile because of his opposition to the continuation of a lot of French control as far as the new Vietnamese state was concerned – to support him as the new Prime Minister, and that was Ngo Dinh Diem. He was then in exile in New Jersey. Diem did take over the government then, with US support. A few months after he took over, he decided that he wanted the remaining French military in South Vietnam withdrawn, and he wanted to look to the United States for military assistance. Now, under the armistice provisions that'd been signed by the French and the Viet Minh, no new foreign military troops could be introduced into either half of Vietnam. The strength of any foreign units that were there [already] had to be maintained at the existing figure. We already had, at the conclusion of those agreements, some three to four hundred US military in South Vietnam administering our assistance agreements with the French, so we were legally permitted to retain that number in South Vietnam and we maintained that number for quite a number of years subsequently, because we did try to adhere to the agreement. We did have three or four hundred other temporary military personnel in Vietnam to recover the equipment that we had furnished to the French . . . [so] the total American military [strength] in Vietnam during the entire Eisenhower Administration was between eight hundred and nine hundred.

There was, however, one provision of the Geneva protocols that allowed the US military to intervene temporarily in Vietnam in 1954. Mendenhall explains:

There was a subsequent agreement . . . [that] allowed for anybody in either [the northern or southern sector of Vietnam] who wanted to move to the other area to do so within a ninety-day period. Nine hundred thousand North Vietnamese left to go south in one of the most, at that time I think, massive refugee movements in [recent] history.

Named Operation PASSAGE TO FREEDOM, this refugee transportation initiative involved scores of vessels of the US Navy, most of which were called from duties in the Philippines or Japan. Jack Majesky, a Naval officer on the USS *Menard*, one of the ships involved in the operation, remembers his captain framing the refugee mission clearly within the Cold War context:

He came on the old loudspeaker and . . . it was like going to see a John Wayne movie. He [was] saying, "Hey, we're headed down there where the Commies are, those sons of bitches," and so forth and so on, and, "There's no telling how dangerous this is going to be, and we're going to Condition 3 [high alert] and we'll be on that until further notice, and we're going to fight back," and it was one of those deals . . . I don't remember anybody coming and saying, "Well, hey, we're going down there and we're going to pick up a bunch of people in the north and we're going to take them down to the south."

Few US Navy ships had ever called in Indochinese waters. Another Navy officer, Robert Mix, remembers the confusion that accompanied the early days of the assignment:

We were trying to look to where we could land ships because nobody had ever been to Haiphong before and we knew nothing about the layout of the land and how we were going to get all

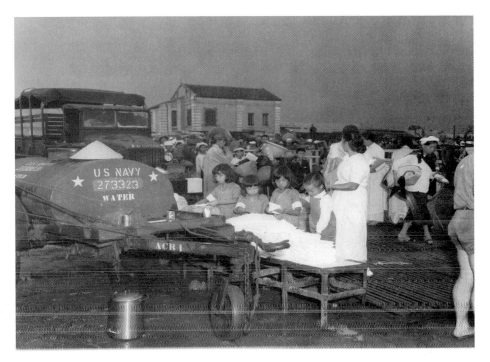

In Operation PASSAGE TO FREEDOM, North Vietnamese civilians relocating to the South after the partition of Vietnam at the 1954 Geneva Conference were transported by the US Navy, which also provided humanitarian assistance to the refugees.

these people on to the ships . . .We were trying to find out who we should contact with the French, whether we should be in contact with the embassy, whether we should be in contact with MAAG or with the North Vietnamese or with the South Vietnamese or the [Catholic] church . . . From [the Philippines] we went into . . . the Red River Delta there in the Tonkin Gulf where all those beautiful islands are. Oh God, they're beautiful. That's where we anchored and started making contact then with the locals.

The Vietnamese who boarded the US ships were, in effect, refugees from the soon-to-be installed Communist government of Ho Chi Minh. A large percentage of them were Catholics. Their priests, many of whom had been educated in France or in French schools, warned the Catholic minority about their likely fate under Communist rule, and led many thousands to the evacuation point at Haiphong. One American naval officer, Leo Andrade, recalls the operation this way:

These refugees, at least the initial ones, were all from the hinterland. They all came from back in the hills, and they were led by their priests. Vietnam or Indochina was one of the few places in Asia where Catholicism really took hold, other than the Philippines. So, the leaders of this group were priests. I'm sure there were some officials of the Indochinese. I don't remember any Frenchmen there, although that was the language that you had to speak in . . . Well the captain, as I recall this, he asked for volunteers to act as interpreters and I had had some French in high school and college so I raised my hand, but it was soon obvious that that wasn't going to work . . . I just wished that I was more skillful at it. But we found a guy on board the ship who's named appropriately 'Frenchy', and he was a French Canadian, so he spoke I guess French with a Canadian accent to the Vietnamese who spoke French with a Vietnamese accent. But, they managed to communicate . . . [The Vietnamese refugees] were all sizes and shapes and ages . . . They weren't dressed in western dress for the most part; they didn't appear to be impoverished or starving or anything like that. Now, I don't know how long that trip was but it was a few days from the north to south and the weather was awful, and of course the [USS] *Menard*, being a troop transport, we had these big holds where the troops [normally] were and the bunks were stacked five or six high, and that's where we put everybody for the most part . . . There was a general sense that this was a humanitarian thing and we wanted to do what we could for the refugees.

The Americans' approach to the refugees differed on each ship that participated in the operation. Robert Mix remembers how on his vessel the shipboard movements of the Vietnamese were restricted:

The refugees would not be allowed to be down in the ship's quarters and berthing areas. They were primarily to be housed on top side or . . . on LSTs [Landing Ship – Tank], in the large hold in the LST, in areas like that, and they were to cook their own meals, and they had makeshift latrines and all of this type of facility. They were not to use the ship's facilities. We didn't know who the good guys and the bad guys were. We didn't want to contaminate the ship and we didn't want to have problems with sabotage or anything else.

Other ships provided a more hospitable atmosphere. Ray Bell remembers that on his ship,

> Me and some other guys from the ship's fitter shop built the
> toilets and stuff. We split barrels to make toilets for these people
> . . . We split barrels, welded them end to end, and then put
> boards across for people to sit on, ran a fire hose in one end and
> left it running and then a drain lane out over the side of the ship
> for the waste to go out. We built a privacy shield around these
> the first trip, but so many of us couldn't talk Vietnamese and
> so many of them couldn't talk English, we couldn't tell them
> where the bathrooms was at and things and they was going to
> the bathroom in corners, all over, and so the next trip we took
> the privacy shields down and they started using [the latrines],
> except the boards we put across for them to sit on, they would
> step up on them and squat down over them in an Asian fashion
> . . . I can remember feeding them in the chow line . . . They took
> some garbage cans and steam cleaned these garbage cans and was
> cooking this rice and stuff in these garbage cans. It was kind of
> sad. You just had to feel so sorry for these people, the conditions
> they was coming from, and scared of us but still wanting to take
> a chance to try to get something better for themselves.

The refugees disembarked at Saigon. Many received additional American-financed welfare assistance at purpose-built 'reception centers', which provided food, clothing, and some medical care. Some refugees were certainly recruited during this period as interpreters and informants by American intelligence officials. Meanwhile a few of the American Navy officers participating in the refugee transport mission were given leave to enter Saigon. These visitors included Leo Andrade, who recalls the ambience of the city in 1954:

> We were told that it was a relatively dangerous place and I don't
> think we had general liberty . . . Saigon at one time was known
> as the 'Paris of the East'. It was really a pretty spot, at least the
> places that we went to. There were a lot of French military and
> a lot of French Foreign Legionnaires, a pretty intimidating
> group of people if I ever saw one . . . They were the biggest
> and most ferocious-looking people I've ever seen. They were
> really something else. They had a lot of outdoor cafés, typical

of what you might see in Paris. We were forewarned that we should be very cautious because there were bombs being thrown occasionally and those outdoor cafés were a good target for that.

While the US Navy helped transport Catholics and other non-Communists to the South, many Southern Communist activists left their homes for the new Communist zone in North Vietnam. One of those who left the South in 1954, Nguyen Phat Le, remembers that time:

After the ceasefire we were told that since we had not won a complete victory, we had to accept a temporary division of the country, which would be reunited by general elections in two years. People in the South agreed to be regrouped to the North because they hoped that in two years the country would be reunited and afterwards they could return to the South. If they had known that there would not be unification after two years, they would never want to leave their homeland in the South to go to the North. During the period before the regrouping, Communist cadres carefully and cleverly mobilized the people from Saigon to Ca Mau to visit and say goodbye to those who were leaving for regrouping to the North. The visit and farewell was very emotional. We were told that those who would be regrouped to the North and those who would stay in the South had the same glorious and important task. Later I learned that only political cadres and those who had not seen the North were to stay in the South and all the [Viet Minh] military troops had to go to the North.

The Geneva Agreement of 1954 called for national elections to be held throughout Vietnam in 1956 – both in the North and in the South – as a means of reunifying the country under a single, popularly elected government. Joseph Mendenhall of the US State Department remembers why, with American support, the President of South Vietnam, Ngo Dinh Diem, declined to prepare for or hold the elections in July 1956:

As far as the election provisions were concerned, Ngo Dinh Diem, who had not signed anything at Geneva, decided in 1956 that the elections should not be held in South Vietnam because the preponderance of the population in Vietnam was in Communist-controlled North Vietnam and he knew that no

Communist regime had ever conducted a free election. So if elections were held in both the North and the South in '56 on the question of reunification of Vietnam, obviously the Communist view in the North would prevail, because the great majority of the population were in that zone. Again, this became an issue later during our war in Vietnam, that we had not carried out the elections [in 1956] because we issued a statement of support of Diem's position. We had only committed ourselves earlier, as you recall, to avoid the use of force to upset those agreements. We did not use force; we simply issued a statement in support of Diem's position.

For urban intellectuals in South Vietnam, the idea of elections to reunify the country was an appealing prospect, and Communist propagandists and training cadre would later use the issue of the failure to hold elections to generate opposition amongst intellectuals to the government of Ngo Dinh Diem. Nguyen Xuan Phong, however, remembers that in 1956, the very concept of elections was alien to most Vietnamese:

What would be the value or the meaning of such elections to the Vietnamese people at that time? Were they aware what it would mean to have the general election? In the traditions and customs, the ways of life of the Vietnamese people, elections – what would that mean? Most of them wouldn't understand what the ballot is. So that [is] why I call it mechanical democracy: you can take them to the polls and you make them put a piece of paper in the box, but that was it.

THE BEGINNINGS OF AMERICAN AID TO SOUTH VIETNAM

The Eisenhower administration's support for the Diem government in Saigon included a broad program of military, economic and diplomatic assistance. In 1954 the US Secretary of State, John Foster Dulles, included South Vietnam as one of the states to be protected by a new American-led multilateral defense organization, the South-East Asia Treaty Organization (SEATO), the Asian analog of the better-known North Atlantic Treaty Organization (NATO).

Private American interests, which viewed Diem as a beacon of progressive Western values in Asia, poured money into assistance programs in Vietnam, while American officials provided Diem with intelligence information that helped him dispose of several internal enemies anxious for his demise.

South Vietnam's President, Ngo Dinh Diem, visits the Holy Family Hospital in Qhi Nhon. He cultivated the political support of South Vietnam's influential Catholic minority, including those who moved to the South when the Communist-led government of Ho Chi Minh took control of the North in 1954.

Indeed, between 1955 and 1961 the US devoted more than $1 billion in aid to the Diem government. Diplomat Joseph Mendenhall notes that this money was spent on a variety of initiatives:

> We had an extensive economic aid program, among other things, for the support of the 900,000 refugees who had come down from North Vietnam in 1954 . . . And also with many projects in the economic sector, among other things, the construction of two highways in central Vietnam, from the coast into the interior highlands. When I say 'highways', I don't mean paved, but they were being constructed, hopefully, on an all-weather, non-paved basis to enable increasingly easier access to the Central Highlands. And economic programs in many fields including support of the big import program to counter [any] inflationary

developments and to try to ensure that there was no waning of political support of Diem for economic reasons, because we were still [one] hundred percent in support of Diem at that juncture.

As impressive as the economic development package was, it was still the case that over three-quarters of the total US expenditures in South Vietnam during the 1955–61 period – more than $750 million – went to Ngo Dinh Diem's military and internal security forces. American military advisers redeveloped the French-era Vietnamese army, then including 250,000 men, into a smaller, better trained 150,000-man force. Americans built new installations, training facilities and supply depots for the new Army of the Republic of Vietnam (ARVN). The United States paid the salaries of its men and officers, and provided it with everything from uniforms and ammunition to tanks and planes. Although the American investment in South Vietnam made the Diem government viable in the short term, the ironies of the situation were not lost on Nguyen Xuan Phong:

It was inherent in the context of that [time] that the more help the Saigon people got from the US, the worse it was for them . . . It was not possible for the Saigon government to appear good to the Vietnamese people without the American presence [and] capability to help them stand up; but the more that you help them stand up with the American means, the worse they appear in the eyes of the Vietnamese people.

The goal of the American military assistance program was to make South Vietnam invulnerable to an attack launched by the Communist government of Ho Chi Minh based at Hanoi. American officials knew that Ho's goal had always been a unified, independent Vietnam under Communist control, and they believed that if South Vietnam had a strong military trained and equipped by the US, Vietnamese Communism could be contained indefinitely in North Vietnam. The American strategy, in effect, was to make the division of Vietnam permanent. As Nguyen Xuan Phong remembers, many Vietnamese saw the American 'containment' policy as an affront to national unity:

For the Vietnamese people, that division of [the] country was completely fictitious . . . Why should the people be divided? And then Ho Chi Minh played on that right away: "Vietnam is one, the Vietnamese people is one."

The American plan did not fully account for two other factors. The first was the Communists' decision to launch a campaign of subversive attacks and guerrilla warfare, rather than a main force invasion, against South Vietnam. The second was the rising popular discontent in the South, aroused by President Diem and his regime's use of brutal tactics to control dissent.

The Communists' campaign of violence began to take shape in 1957. By design, it avoided confrontations with ARVN forces, and concentrated on vulnerable 'soft targets,' as Nguyen Xuan Phong recalls:

> They tried to devise ways to fight the American-backed regime
> in South Vietnam . . . not throwing their tanks against South
> Vietnam, but [using] insurgencies. That was the beginning of
> assassinations, harassment and terrorism in the villages, cities
> and hamlets of South Vietnam. It was sheer acts of terrorism;
> they blew up movie houses, market places, because these were
> the only way for them to fight. I do not believe that Ho Chi Minh
> and [Vo Nguyen Giap, the Viet Minh commander at Dien Bien
> Phu] were conscious and were geniuses who say, "I invent a new
> type of war." They were blocked into a certain context and they
> developed ways and means appropriate to them, within their
> reach, to carry on their struggle.

These attacks were carried out chiefly by local southern Communists who had remained 'underground' in South Vietnam at the partition of the country in 1954. Le Cao Dai, a physician with the Communist North Vietnam Army (NVA) in the 1960s, recalls that,

> Even after the [move of some Communists] in 1954 to the North
> . . . the political mass of [the] South Vietnam Communist Party
> in the south was very strong, especially in the countryside.

The Communist Party leadership in North Vietnam also controlled the actions of the thousands of southerners who had moved to the North in 1954. As Nguyen Phat Le, one of those 'regrouped' to the North in 1954, remembers, these southerners were anxious to return to the South and escalate the struggle to topple the Diem government:

> I missed my parents very much. Sometimes I cried during the
> night. I did not stay with my parents very long because I left my

house to join the revolution early, but my parents had raised me
and given me precious education during my childhood. But time
cured my homesickness. I became used to it after a few years,
and besides I was grown up and busy with daily work. I had no
time to think of my family. I think since I was about 25 years old
I had nothing to cry about, because I had no more tears. [We]
wanted to return [to the South] as soon as possible. Once [the
Communists' senior military commander] General Vo Nguyen
Giap was asked when we would go south and if our country
could be reunited in two years. His answer was that we had no
time limit to carry out the revolutionary task.

In 1959, the Communist leadership in Hanoi determined that the time
had come to escalate the challenge to President Diem. The Communist
networks in South Vietnam were slowly reinforced with trained insurgents
returning from North Vietnam via the growing complex of routes from
North Vietnam through Laos and Cambodia. At the same time attacks
on local representatives of the Diem government intensified. By 1960 the
internal security situation in South Vietnam had substantially deteriorated,
with some 2,500 assassinations of village heads and local officials reported
that year.

Meanwhile President Diem, while relying upon growing American
economic and military support, failed to engender popular support for his
government. Many rural Vietnamese saw him as an aloof ruler, as Nguyen
Xuan Phong recalls:

The mentality of those peasants in the countryside was, "What
kind of a ruler [do] we now have, after the French? . . . We were
supposed to have general elections, didn't have general elections,
now we have a ruler, Ngo Dinh Diem." I think that Ngo Dinh
Diem did not really impress the peasants in the countryside. [He]
was still removed as a ruler was supposed to be in the Far East,
something very far away, very high up. But what would matter
to the large majority of those people in the countryside was:
was he able to bring a better life to them? Would they be able to
plow their plot of land better? Would they be able to feed their
children better?

At the same time, Diem's government was also alienating urban workers
and intellectuals. In particular, his brother Ngo Dinh Nhu and Nhu's wife

concentrated power and decision-making in family hands. They issued executive orders to control the press, the legislature and government offices down to the village level, and secretly arranged for the elimination of Diem's opponents. The dissatisfactions created by these policies were, as diplomat Joseph Mendenhall recalls, already a major concern for American policy by 1957:

> Diem was running a very tightly controlled, autocratic
> government. And a lot of the educated . . . intellectuals felt
> that they should play somewhat of an increasing role in this
> and they weren't being permitted to play any role because
> Diem and his brother Nhu were controlling all aspects of the
> political situation. So it's primarily in that class that the dissent
> was arising.

US officials in Saigon pressed President Diem to make reforms, but they also protected him from coup plotters and from the growing Communist insurgency. In 1960 a US military reassessment of the Communists' guerrilla operations led to a shift in training priorities for Diem's ARVN forces. The earlier emphasis on conventional warfare training was shelved in favor of more intensive instruction in counter-insurgency techniques. Edward Nidever was one of the US Special Forces officers sent to South Vietnam in 1960 to retrain South Vietnamese forces to combat Communist guerilla operations:

> The situation was that Diem would send people [in] battalions,
> regiments at a time, out in the field. They never saw anything.
> They needed a couple other officers to command units in-
> country to lead formerly [French]-trained Ranger companies
> in how to do small ambushes on the Ho Chi Minh Trail and
> [Cambodian] border. These were South Vietnamese Ranger units,
> which were not like Diem's [ARVN] units that went out and
> never saw anything. Our mission was take these [Ranger] units,
> go out in squad- or platoon-size [groups]; we went with them
> and set up ambushes on the Ho Chi Minh Trail . . . [We had] a
> little orientation, not much. The people [in Saigon] really didn't
> know what the hell was going on in the field. [They said,] "This
> is where you're going. Here are maps." Mostly from the military
> side . . . Nothing from the psychological, political side at all. All
> we knew was, here's what we had to do. Here's what Diem wasn't

doing. Here's what we had to correct . . . We were told to train these people . . . Our mission basically was to motivate them. You also did this by going along with them. When you start going out in a squad size, 10, 11, 12 people and you're there too, you're saying, "Anything you do is going to affect me." . . . We went out to find caves, tunnels, set up ambushes, surprise people so they don't know you're coming in . . . We did capture [Communist] Vietnamese records even at that time that said "Hey, if the United States comes in, all we have to do is hold out for an extended period of time. The United States cannot, will not, support a long, drawn out situation. The longer you hold out, the quicker the United States goes away."

As part of their strategy for long-term struggle, Communist forces had begun to develop a complex system of footpaths, bike trails and roads leading from North Vietnam into the South, going through the borderlands of Laos and Cambodia. This trail system, which Americans dubbed the 'Ho Chi Minh Trail,' became the principal conduit for supplies and infiltrators moving into South Vietnam. Edward Nidever remembers the mission he was given in 1960 on one part of the Ho Chi Minh Trail near South Vietnam's border with Cambodia:

Understand what the trails were like even at that early stage. You had large rice plantations. You had rubber plantations, etcetera. The roads, if you call them 'roads,' they were mud roads. Most of the roads were cut by the [Viet] Cong all over different places. So, you're not going to take Jeeps or anything else through. They would [only] be able to handle their man-carried stuff over these things. We would set up along someplace where it was a good ambush site, where you could see who was coming . . . But you usually could tell very quickly what was going on. If they ran, they were [Viet] Cong . . . You set up in very small units a fire zone to somewhere where they would be walking or riding. I say riding because most of them were on cycles . . . You could carry more that way . . . [One day] we were going down a trail into a rubber plantation area from a rice area. Boom, one shot rings out. The dust jumps up in the road in front of me and I'm hit in the leg. Just that simple. We dressed in their clothes so we looked like one of them. But of course, we had white faces . . .

THE KENNEDY ADMINISTRATION AND VIETNAM

In 1961, as the numbers of Viet Cong in the South continued to grow, President John F Kennedy ordered a substantial increase in the amount of American counter-insurgency assistance to Diem's government. South Vietnamese troops, led by American advisers, launched widespread counter-insurgency operations against the Viet Cong. Meanwhile, the Diem government had for years been implementing the 'strategic hamlet' program. Under this initiative, which was inspired by Britain's successes in controlling the Communist-led insurgency in Malaya a decade earlier, people from scattered villages were concentrated in newly constructed hamlets, each with defensive perimeters. The objective of the plan was to deprive the Viet Cong of village-level support, thereby isolating them from the population and rendering them more vulnerable to military attack by ARVN forces. Nguyen Xuan Phong notes that in many cases, the strategic hamlets made the local villagers more vulnerable to terrorist tactics:

> [The hamlets gave] a kind of security which was no security because, with the concrete and with the barbed wires, then the enemy used the rockets. They didn't have to send in the troops . . . it was a reign of terror for the people inside those strategic hamlets to receive rockets at [virtually] any time. That was really a terrifying thing for the ordinary population to receive Viet Cong rockets. [They were] used not to destroy the strategic hamlets, but to impress on the mind of the people that the Saigon government would never be in position to provide . . . the security that they claimed.

Under President Kennedy's leadership, the US doubled its military aid to Diem's troops between 1961 and 1962. As more and more American advisers and technicians were sent to Vietnam, the US military faced the prospect of a larger and longer commitment in Vietnam. Nonetheless, Kennedy inspired confidence in the future. US Air Force pilot Richard Duckworth remembers the enthusiasm of American pilots and crews for their new assignments in Vietnam:

> Well, then everybody thought Kennedy was a hero . . . So we were getting ready to go into Vietnam and nail those little [Communist] son of a guns. I mean, they couldn't stand up to our technology! My God, there was no way, see!

An ARVN unit learns swamp fighting techniques near Soc Trang in the Mekong Delta. American military advisers helped train South Vietnamese troops beginning in the late 1950s; President Kennedy greatly increased the number of such personnel during the early 1960s.

Among the new American technologies being deployed in Vietnam was a new generation of defoliant chemicals. By 1962 US planes were spraying defoliants along the major roads in the Saigon area to deny Viet Cong units the cover of roadside underbrush. One of the Air Force's advisers in South Vietnam, John Hodgin, remembers how these flights began:

> We couldn't fly unless we had a Vietnamese on board, who was [supposed] to be the person that was flying the airplane and we were advising them. Although, since the Vietnamese pilots were so scarce, there never was a pilot. They always sat in the back. At the last part, it was just some young soldier who had never flown on an airplane before and they usually just threw up . . . The first mission we had [in February 1962] was to practice the spray run down, just south of Saigon on Highway 15. Our commander, who was Captain Marshall, and Captain Robinette and myself as the navigator flew down there and practiced the spray runs. They were going to test it to see whether it really worked or not. Flying that low was interesting and a little scary, [but] I got used to it.

The defoliation mission made military sense, but it handed the Viet Cong another stick with which to beat the Diem government and the Americans who assisted them. As American diplomat John Condon recalls,

> The people of the countryside saw the effect, and there was an effect on the humans also . . . [The] Viet Cong said, "You want to live under this people?" That's all the Viet Cong said. [They] called [the locals] out of the village and said, "Would you like to live with the people that do this to your trees?"

The expansion of American military aid in the early 1960s made South Vietnam's senior military commanders more independent of President Diem and his tight-knit circle of advisers. Several generals became involved in plots to overthrow Diem. The regime became even more unpopular during early 1963, when South Vietnamese troops at Hue in central Vietnam fired on a crowd that had gathered to protest against government orders banning the display of flags celebrating Buddha's traditional birthday. Buddhist priests nationwide mobilized in a chorus of criticism against Diem's government. They conducted hunger strikes and held public meetings in Saigon and Hue. On 11 June 1963, a Buddhist monk set himself on fire at one of Saigon's main intersections, and American newsmen, who had been informed in advance, were on the scene to record the event. US Army aviator John Givhan was one of the American advisers in Saigon that summer:

> I thought [Vietnam] was unorganized chaos . . . Even the news we got over there, through *Stars and Stripes* [the US government's military newspaper], [said] you had Buddhists demonstrating downtown, you had Buddhist monks burning themselves, you've got a very unpopular president in Diem, even among most of his own people. There he was a Catholic and the Catholics only made up about 10 percent of the country. You got 90 percent Buddhists who hated Diem. It didn't take me two weeks after being over there to [begin] thinking, "What in the hell are we doing over here?" and "How in the hell are we ever going to turn this thing around?" It didn't take a rocket scientist to realize we can't even pee, hardly, without getting in a helicopter! We don't control any of the roads. It was a civil war . . . Something's just not right here . . . Most all aviators realized there was something real bad wrong with this whole scenario.

Since mid-1963 Diem's opponents in the South Vietnamese military had been sounding out American diplomats and intelligence officials in Saigon about America's likely reaction should Diem be removed from office. Army pilot Givhan remembers the atmosphere in Saigon:

> There was constant rumors of coups and all that type of thing
> . . . A week to ten days before the coup [that ousted President
> Diem], we . . . actually hauled ARVN troops from out in the
> country, from various units, to Saigon . . . I remember asking this
> ARVN lieutenant, who spoke broken English, "What's going on?"
> And he kind of smiled and he pointed towards downtown Saigon
> and then he ran his finger across his neck.

On 1 November 1963, under extraordinarily complicated circumstances, President Diem was ousted from power and assassinated; his brother Ngo Dinh Nhu was also shot dead. John Givhan recalls the day that Diem was killed:

> When Diem was assassinated, the place, Saigon, the whole area,
> was in just utter chaos. As a matter of fact, the airfield at Tan Son
> Nhut was actually strafed by a Vietnamese Air Force aircraft more
> than once. Several rounds actually came through the roof of our
> operations building out at Tan Son Nhut because you'll keep in
> mind that during the coup there were Vietnamese good guys on
> both sides, pro- and anti-Diem. So the 120th [US Army Aviation
> Company] were briefed. We actually had standby orders in case
> everything really fell apart, to fly our helicopters out to an aircraft
> carrier supposedly on station [in the South China Sea] off of
> Vung Tau . . . Of course, that really got our attention because we
> were faced with the immediate threat that the good guys may not
> even be on our side any more, you know what I mean?

Suspicions that the US Central Intelligence Agency (CIA), the US Embassy and US military officials were directly involved in the coup abounded, although the precise developments that preceded the generals' move against Diem remain obscured. John Condon, a State Department official who served in Saigon, remembers how a message of American approval might have gone through to the anti-Diem generals:

> The Vietnamese generals acted pretty much on their own, or with

the encouragement of individual CIA agents acting on their own. I mean, it happens; I have practiced it myself. It is possible indeed that some CIA agent acting on his own beliefs, with the best of intentions of course, had a friend among the military, among the generals, and [he] sort of indicated that, perhaps, if that is what you want to do, you know best. That was enough for the generals that had already considered the idea to allow themselves [to think] that they had a clear light [to launch the coup].

LYNDON JOHNSON AND THE DECISION FOR WAR

President Kennedy's assassination on 22 November 1963 followed that of Diem and Nhu by just three weeks. When Lyndon B Johnson subsequently assumed the presidency he quickly reasserted America's determination to support South Vietnam and to commit more US resources to the fight against the Vietnamese Communists.

Meanwhile, Communist insurgents began operating in greater concentrations and over wider areas. By some estimates, they already controlled 40 percent of the country's land area.

In the Mekong River delta, where the Viet Cong (VC) had long controlled much of the Ca Mau peninsula, American military operations escalated in 1964. Helicopter pilot John Givhan remembers an operation there in which American helicopters flew ARVN soldiers into battle:

Okay, here we go towards this landing zone without – and I emphasize without – [any] Air Force pre-strike of the LZ [landing zone], no artillery pre-strike of the LZ, and no helicopter gunship escort. For a combat assault mission, that was something that was just absolutely a no-no . . . I remember having this sinking sense of foreboding that this is not good. Anyway, as we approach, we started slowing down air speed and approaching the LZ . . . and for the first time in my career in Vietnam I see VC running along these dikes setting up weapons. The VC were behind dikes firing at us openly. I mean, it was like the gunfight at OK Corral . . . At about 400 feet, we were climbing out . . . I'm sitting there, flying one second, and the next second my right calf and most everything below my knee just disappears . . . I remember looking over at my co-pilot . . . and this is that few-second interval before the shock and the pain just hits you like a whammy – and he said, "I'm blind." He had his visor down on his helmet and I reached over and flipped his visor up. The reason he was blind was meat and all that stuff from my leg was plastered all over his visor.

American officials were increasingly concerned that the Viet Cong were receiving new manpower and new weapons from the North. To gauge the rate of infiltration of Communist forces to the South, American aircraft based in Japan and South Vietnam began conducting more surveillance missions, as US Air Force pilot Joe Boyer remembers:

In August of '64 [I] flew into Saigon and we stayed in a hotel in downtown Saigon . . . Our missions were refueling the fighters that escorted the reconnaissance aircraft flying missions up through North Vietnam – RF101s. The F100s were refueling them or escorting them. We refueled all of them . . . We'd orbit way up there about the DMZ [demilitarized zone], maybe even over North Vietnam. That was before they got so many sophisticated anti-aircraft missiles and radar, and we would refuel [the aircraft] and wait on them. They would make their runs low level, supersonic I guess, and when they would come back, we'd refuel them where the 101 could go supersonic back to Saigon and quickly process his pictures . . .

The surveillance photos revealed a growing flow of both military forces and supplies from North Vietnam to the South. One of the southern Communist cadre regrouped to the North who returned to the South in 1964 on the Ho Chi Minh Trail, Nguyen Phat Le, remembers the trip:

I reported to the camp to prepare for going south in 1962, but I actually departed for the south in 1964. I remember it was on Sunday, all of us reported for departure, including artillery units, tank units and chemical weapons units (because by that time the US had already started to use chemical weapons in South Vietnam). By that time, the regrouping center had already been moved to the former base of 330 Division in Ha Dong Province . . . The leader was a native of Nghe An but he had served in the South during nine years of resistance against the French. I was the deputy leader and there was also a political officer . . . Covered trucks took us from Thanh Hoa Province to Dong Hoi on National Highway 1. The trucks were covered to avoid people's suspicions. We stopped only at deserted places. When we arrived at [the] Vietnam–Laos border, we rested for one day. We took off [the] North Vietnamese military uniform and put on black pajamas to disguise ourselves as southern farmers. We were asked to check carefully all our possessions to make sure that we did not keep anything that related to North Vietnam or other Communist countries. We were invaders who tried to disguise ourselves as liberators. We left the trucks and walked on foot to infiltrate the South. It was not an easy trip because we did not walk on the roads or trails but crossed the forest with 30-kilogram bags on our shoulders. First we crossed Ben Hai river and climbed up a very high and dangerous mountain called 1001 hill. It was the most difficult part of our road to the South.

When we reached the peak of the mountain we rested. We could see the sun in the morning, but in the afternoon it often rained. It was wet and humid. I thought with my health condition I could not make the trip . . . We walked about eight hours a day, but since we had to climb the mountain and cross the forest, we did not get very far. When we got tired we rested. For food we were supplied by waiting (stopping) stations along our way. These stations were set up by those who had gone before us. Sometimes we were short of food and water . . . The further we got the worse problems we [were] faced with, because we had already used almost all of the food we brought along. We also were closer to the danger of the enemy's military operation. We could stop and rest anywhere along our way if the area was clear and safe . . . Sometimes we walked for three days and nights and suddenly the guide came and said, "Stop and rest here"; then we stopped and rested right in the forest. There was no shelter for rain or bed to sleep on . . .

On my way to the South I was not sick but I stepped on a stake set up by local guerrillas. My foot was swollen and got infected. I had to stay over at a stopping station for treatment along with other friends. My group consisted of 45 men but only seven or eight of them arrived at the final destination. Some of them died. My friend, Captain Tran Chanh Ly, died suddenly of malaria while we were resting at one of the stopping stations. Each of us had a medicine box [that] contained common usage medicine made in China and a lot of anti-malaria tablets. A great number died of malaria but there was no official statistic report about this because the Communists always kept secret their losses to maintain high morale for their forces. We found out information about these matters only through close friends . . .

When we passed by Pleiku and Kontum, we went through thatch fields. We had to disguise ourselves to avoid being discovered by enemy planes. Sometimes a jet plane flew right over our heads. In these areas we saw droves of wild oxen but we did not dare to shoot. When we arrived in Khanh Hoa region, we met a group of teenagers who were sent to the North to study; they were cadres' children. Some other times we met other groups going in the opposite direction; they did not go to the North but to Central Vietnam to observe [the] fighting situation . . . My group was not attacked by South Vietnamese forces but other groups were attacked by ARVN's Rangers. On my way I did not see any marks of bomb [explosions] except for the area south of Central Vietnam. In other words, the bombing did not affect the infiltration in 1964. I arrived in Tay Ninh Province [in South Vietnam]. I rested two days at the reception station. I left the North on 24 May 1964 and arrived in Tay Ninh [in] August; I did not remember the exact date. One thing I would like to mention here about our trip to the South is that love and care of one comrade to the other did not exist among us; each individual tried to preserve his own life and did not care for the other comrades.

As more information about the location and usage of Communist infiltration routes from North to South reached Washington, President Johnson became more alarmed about the prospect of South Vietnam's survival. To stem the flow of supplies to the Viet Cong, a secret campaign of bombing the Ho Chi Minh Trail in Laos and the local Communist forces, known as the Pathet Lao, was undertaken using the aircraft of Air America, an airline company owned and financed by the CIA. The US Air Force also explored the possibility of expanding its operations in the area, as pilot Ray Merritt remembers:

[In] November of 1964, our squadron was tasked to send ten airplanes to Da Nang Airbase . . . on the trial basis to see if the [F-]105 could be adapted and used in Southeast Asia . . . We were only there about two weeks, as I recall . . . I can remember going over into the Laotian area to act as cover . . . in case the MiGs came down from North Vietnam or even China; wherever they might come from. Again, some Laotian fighters, bombers [were] doing some bombing work in Laos, which at that time, nothing much was said about that. I don't even know if the American public knew. Of course, probably, the pilots were Laotian pilots, [and] probably Air America [was] doing the training of the Laotians . . . They were flying T-28 aircraft and that doesn't carry too many bombs. But they were attacking probably the Pathet Lao there and some positions in the southern part of Laos.

President Johnson shelved plans for more American military action in Vietnam until, in early August 1964, he received reports of skirmishes between American naval ships and North Vietnamese patrol craft off North Vietnam's coast in the Gulf of Tonkin. The administration concluded that the US had to retaliate, and Johnson quickly ordered US aircraft to bomb targets near Vinh, North Vietnam. Within days the US Congress overwhelmingly endorsed a resolution giving the President the authority to use military means to repel armed attacks against American forces and 'to prevent further aggression' in the Vietnam theater. The President, however, mindful of the upcoming election, declared that he did not seek a 'wider war' in Vietnam.

After winning re-election in November 1964, Johnson quickly returned to the problem of shoring up South Vietnam. The consensus of most of his advisers was that additional air strikes against North Vietnam were needed to stop the increasing flow of men and *matériel* to the South. On 24 December 1964 a bomb exploded in an American barracks in Saigon, while another coup in Saigon in January 1965 highlighted South Vietnam's domestic political instability. When Viet Cong fighters attacked another US Army barracks, this one in the Central Highlands at Pleiku, on 6 February 1965, President Johnson decided to reply with force. He ordered a series of bombing missions against military targets just north of the partition line between North and South Vietnam. US Air Force pilot Ray Merritt's first mission over North Vietnam, flown in an F-105, very nearly did not come off:

We had some orders sending our squadron . . . to an airbase in Thailand, Korat . . . to prepare for flying over North Vietnam . . . This was late February [1965]. This was going to be the first US Air Force mission into North Vietnam. We briefed for this mission . . . Of course, we had all this stuff laid out on our map: where the DMZ was, where we could fly, where we couldn't fly. It

was very, very tight control on what you could or could not do, if
and when we went into North Vietnam.

We briefed for this mission, we went out in the airplanes, sat
basically a cockpit alert with all those things on, ready to push
the button to start for about minimum two hours . . . waiting
for a release to go against this target . . . Finally, we were called
back in and [command] said, "Okay, mission's cancelled. Brief
same mission tomorrow, same time, same station." . . . We did
this the second day. We sat in airplanes and waited to release
and nothing ever happened. We were called back to the briefing:
"Your mission's scrubbed." . . . Finally, on either the third or
fourth day, we got released to take off and go bomb this target
. . . Anyway, the first four aircraft of F-100s were first to cross the
target with what they call "flak suppression" – dropping CBUs,
cluster bomb units, anti-personnel weapons, little teeny bomblets
. . . To deliver CBUs . . . it's a low level, high-speed pass across the
target. I mean, down to one, two, three hundred feet.

We were warned that there were automatic weapons up to
medium densities, 57mm anti-aircraft weapons, around this
particular target. It was a very easy target to see: a few buildings
and a lot of boxes and things like that standing around. It was
designated as an ordnance supply point. First four airplanes,
the F-100s, went across, one of them was shot down. That sort
of delayed us while we tried to figure out where he went: was he
going to be able to be rescued? Did we have to go over and help
the rescue rather than continue the bombing mission? I later
found out that the pilot was captured and was a prisoner, [the]
first Air Force prisoner [of war].

Our four airplanes went across the target in formation . . . and
our number two airplane was hit with small arms, automatic
weapons-type fire. We continued releasing our weapons now.
The weapon that we had . . . comes out of a canister and it has a
parachute. It floats down and as it hits the ground, it explodes;
it has a trigger device that explodes it. They're not very big,
maybe [the] size of a softball. Somebody forgot to take into
consideration that there were a lot of trees around this place.
As we went across, we could see little white parachutes all over,
hanging in the trees. These little bomblets . . . had not exploded
. . . We were done; we were headed back anyway. We went out and
covered for our downed pilot and he was picked up. Here now,

out of eight airplanes across the target, two of them were shot down . . . We never did re-bomb that target.

Meanwhile, Viet Cong units had attacked an American installation at Qui Nhon on 10 February 1965. Johnson – advised that 'defeat was inevitable' if he did not commit American military forces to the defense of South Vietnam – ordered a much broader program of gradually intensified air attacks against the North, in an operation codenamed ROLLING THUNDER. Pilot Ray Merritt recalls that its purpose was

> . . . to apply pressure up to a point without getting involved into a full, go-to-hell war. Targets, Rolling Thunders, [were] primarily against the transportation means between North Vietnam and South Vietnam . . . We're trying to bomb the jungle, so to speak; to stop the flow of goods coming south.

At the same time the President approved the deployment of US Marines to protect an important air base at Da Nang. Within weeks, the use of napalm as well as conventional bombs had been approved, and by April 1965 American aircrews, with token participation by the South Vietnamese Air Force, were flying over 3,000 bombing sorties a month against North Vietnam. That same month, the US Joint Chiefs of Staff met with Defense Secretary Robert McNamara and other senior administration officials in Honolulu, and approved a plan for placing up to 40,000 American ground combat forces into South Vietnam. American diplomat John Condon, who was assigned to the US Embassy during this period, remembers the unease he felt about the American military escalation. As Condon recalls, he explained his views to a professor from Harvard, Henry Kissinger, who was visiting Saigon:

> We had . . . an hour and a half for discussion, but my
> main point was . . . we wanted this war more than the
> South Vietnamese wanted it . . . Then I proceeded to put
> it in more sophisticated terms so that we were taking
> initiatives, we were taking the place of the South Vietnamese,
> we were undermining their will to do the things their own
> way and on their own, and I thought that was not the way
> to do it . . . It doesn't promise for success in the future. We talked
> a great deal, but in the end, in order to illustrate the point, [I said
> that] a father who is forcing or making his child eat more than

eat more than the child wants to eat is in trouble, because he's
at the mercy of the child.

By the spring of 1965, US ground, naval and air forces were engaged in
South Vietnam. Fighting in alien terrain, against an enemy operating in
his own backyard, American military personnel found themselves ensnared
in a civil war with international dimensions. This costly and protracted
unconventional war would be unlike any the US had ever fought before.

2
GOING TO WAR

Just after 9:00am on 8 March 1965, US Marines from the 3rd Battalion, 9th Marine Expeditionary Force based at Okinawa, Japan, stormed ashore at Da Nang, South Vietnam. Tasked by Washington to guard the air base at Da Nang, the Marines were the first official ground combat troops committed to the defense of the Republic of Vietnam (RVN) and thus represented a new and much larger commitment by American policymakers. The US was now involved in a ground war in Vietnam that would ultimately cost it over 58,000 lives and cost the Vietnamese hundreds of thousands of lives.

MILITARY SERVICE AND THE DRAFT

How did the American servicemen and women get to South Vietnam? Were they volunteers or were they drafted into the military by the US government? What did they go through in their military training prior to going to Southeast Asia? As one can guess, it was a different experience for everyone who served. The US instituted the Selective Service Act in 1948 and through its extensions over two million men were inducted into military service between 1965 and December 1972, when President Richard Nixon ended all draft calls for the war. The Selective Service System operated about 4,000 local draft boards throughout the country. Quotas for the number of inductees were set at a national level by the Department of Defense, and men were drafted according to projected enlistments and needs. The Department of Commerce and Labor defined and controlled draft deferments in terms of critical occupations and essential activities.

However, local draft boards had significant latitude in selecting men for service, thus creating inequities in the system. Such inequities were easy targets for those who disagreed with American policy in Southeast Asia. John Lawitt, who was subject to the draft as a student in Connecticut and in New Mexico, saw the draft in a way that was common to the anti-war movement:

> . . . I saw military conscription as a great evil. It'd be one thing if

people volunteered and wanted to go into it, another thing when you force people to go [because] I had no second thoughts about what I viewed to be the wrongfulness about the Vietnam War. I saw World War II as a necessary fight and realized that I would have joined; I would have enlisted, I would have been one of the people that had enlisted after Pearl Harbor. I didn't have the consciousness about the Second World War. I believed that there were wars that were just and necessary . . . this [Vietnam] I saw as a war for politicians and for the exploitation of the Vietnamese people to stop an ideology, at least in that part of the world, that was never a threat; and in fact, I saw US government activities as bringing about that ideology despite itself because I thought that the United States could've done much more and had much more of an influence in Vietnam to stop Communism if that was necessary by building bridges, not bombing them.

Lawitt went on to burn his draft card in protest during an anti-war march in Philadelphia in 1968. He then applied for and was accepted at the University of Bridgeport, Connecticut, in order to obtain a student deferment, one of the Commerce and Labor Department's essential activities.

If a man could not secure a deferment, he knew his fate. Bill McCullum, an Armored Troop Carrier (ATC) engineman in the US Navy in Vietnam from August 1968 to July 1969, remembers his predicament in 1967 in Brooklyn, New York:

To tell you the truth, I really never thought much about it [serving in the military]. I mean I thought about going into the military because unlike today, back then we had the draft and it was a foregone conclusion that you were going to be drafted or you were going to enlist.

Gary Jackson, from Oregon, and who served in the US Air Force (USAF) from 1962 until 1971, believed that his service in the military was simply a matter of time:

. . . by the time we [got] out of high school we're subject to the draft, and almost everybody did either get drafted or took care of their military obligation some other way. So I assumed at some point I would be in the military, and it was just a question of, would I go in before I got out of college and if I stayed until after college then I'd go to some officer training. I didn't particularly have a branch of the service scoped out, it was just kind of, everybody understood they were going to do some kind of military service.

Another experience with the draft was actually volunteering for military service to avoid being drafted. Individuals who went this route often cite the fact that they could exercise some control over their military fate. They also state that sometimes they were talked into joining the military by a recruiter so that they were 'guaranteed' a particular branch and job within that branch, something they could not get if they were randomly drafted. Andy Roy, who ended up serving three tours of duty in Vietnam from 1967 to 1969, describes the experience he had in May 1966 when he was 18 and facing the draft:

> . . . seeing that there was a war going on and, to an 18-year-old, you believed the things, that war builds men, war matures you, you prove yourself. It was time for me to go down and sign up for the draft and I happened to go past the recruiting office on the way. I went down, signed up for the draft, came back and there was a table with a whole bunch of pamphlets out in front of the recruiting officer and I just started casually looking through them and saw a pamphlet on infantry and saw a pamphlet on paratroops and started thinking that well, you know I really don't have any future right now and actually I'm going to get drafted pretty soon and I wanted to go off to war to prove all those things that an 18-year-old sometimes wants to prove to themselves. At the time there wasn't really very much negative feelings about the war either. I went into the recruiting office, talked to the recruiter and volunteered for a three-year hitch on the conditions that I be trained as a parachute infantryman and that they sent me to Vietnam, which they were more than willing to guarantee.

On the other side of the spectrum, there were those who believed the draft was not a bad thing for the US and wanted to serve in the military, even knowing they most likely were going to fight in a war thousands of miles away from home. Sometimes the desire to serve came from a strong sense of patriotism. Sometimes service came as part of a lifelong dream, or because of family tradition.

There were also those who found themselves fighting in Vietnam because they joined their university Reserve Officer Training Corps (ROTC) programs, thus committing themselves to active duty service after graduation. Jack Wright went into the Army ROTC knowing that the draft would get him in the military anyway:

> I went in the first two years because of the world situation we were facing at that time. I decided, well, I'm going to go ahead and apply for the advanced courses, the advanced ROTC. If I've got to go in the service, it looks like that's what is going to happen anyway [via the draft], [I] might as well go in as an officer. I applied and was accepted. I went through the last two years of ROTC and was commissioned.

Marshall Paul, a native of Lubbock, Texas, recalls that even at the height of the draft in 1967 and 1968, many young men remained unaware that enlistment in the National Guard, the reserve branch of the US military under the jurisdiction of the Department of Defense and state governors, would place them beyond the reach of the draft board:

> [When a classmate] joined the National Guard, I was so naive I thought, "I've misjudged this guy all this time, he's really patriotic, he's doing this for his country." Because it was a time of crisis, and we were at war and I thought, "The guy's all right, I really, I've really been wrong about him being a jerk." And even after I went into the military, it was years before I figured out that the National Guard was the way you got out of going to Vietnam. This guy's parents had figured out while we were still in high school: join the National Guard while you're in high school and you won't have to go to Vietnam. And that's what Steve did. I never figured that out.

But there were some who wanted to join the military out of a sense of duty, knowing full well that they would probably serve in Vietnam. Some even hoped that they would be sent there. Marshall remembered that:

> I just assumed that everybody wanted to do their duty, and all of the protesting we saw in the news was something that was happening somewhere else; some other part of the country, [and] that in this part of the country, we took care of our

responsibilities . . . Late on the radio one night . . . [there] was a
recording made by a grunt in Vietnam. And it was made during
the night, during a night firefight . . . I thought this guy sounded
like he was stuck out there, and nobody else wanted to help.
And I thought "Why should all of us stay here? Uh, I'm not in a
position to judge national policy; I could give a shit less about
national prerogatives." What I was concerned about was that
people were being sent places and nobody [was] helping them
. . . I looked at the way my life was and not having a lot of support
among people I wanted to belong to, and I was beginning at that
time to see how superficial they were. And I looked at the war
and I thought the war could be a source of comradeship. And so
I enlisted, I joined the Army before I even graduated from high
school. And I was 17 at the time.

Once the men were in military service, no matter how they arrived there,
they all went through training before they went to Southeast Asia.

TRAINING

When men arrived in Vietnam to fight, most had gone through rigorous
training in the US to prepare them for their duties in their particular
Military Occupation Specialty (MOS). Basic training introduced individuals
to military life and weeded out those who could not handle it. It was
in the advanced training phase that soldiers, airmen, and seamen learned
their specialty, the job they eventually would perform in Vietnam, and
this was when many men learned that they actually were going to the
war in Vietnam. Those who were going to fight the war on the ground
in Vietnam, the US Marines and the US Army, describe their advanced
training as a time when they learned to work on more specific small-unit
tactics, on particular weapons systems, and more conditioning. Mike
Bradbury, a US Marine at Camp Pendleton in California in 1966, describes
his advanced training as much more specific in nature and directed more
at the squad level:

We would . . . go out on maneuvers, they would teach us
squad tactics and some of the stuff we had seen on film in
the classrooms . . . and they would have bad guys out there to
ambush us with blanks and stuff and everybody would hit the
deck and then you would return fire and everything and then you
would have judges out there to judge how you did; you would

be critiqued and say ok, well you guys, should have moved one squad over there and [there were] a lot of forced marches.

Advanced training was where most men learned about what to expect in Vietnam. Some of their instructors were Vietnam veterans who spoke about what they had already seen in the war. Bradbury continues:

> They [the instructors] told us about booby traps, about things to look out for, [for example] if you're looking at villages and even kids, just how they react, they told us when you're going through a village, and it's deserted or something and you see something that might [make] a good souvenir, don't pick it up because it is booby trapped . . . They prepared us, you know, about different sounds to look for and [for the] night. They said when you're out there looking at night, there [are] a lot of psychological things and they said when you're [on] a night ambush, or just on a perimeter, don't fix your eyes on anything particular because you're looking at a bush, [and you] start looking at this one particular bush, pretty soon that bush . . . starts looking like a man to you. So you start cranking off fire and then they know where you are . . . They talked to us a lot about . . . the things to avoid, things to look for, and just things to be wary of.

Tom Esslinger, a Marine in Vietnam in 1967 and 1968, recalls that his instructors did their best to try to prepare them for the war:

> You just can't be prepared, I don't think, for the atmosphere and the situations that we found in Vietnam. They tried and they did a good job of trying. But training is not the same as the real thing.

Support personnel, such as aircraft and vehicle mechanics, who went to Vietnam had exposure to instructors who had been in Vietnam as well. Some, like Timothy Lockley, an aircraft Crew Chief and Maintenance Supervisor on C-130 airplanes, had virtually no discussion of what to expect:

> I can't remember any of them [instructors] mentioning anything about Vietnam, all through basic or through tech school I can't remember anything about Vietnam whatsoever.

Joseph Donald, a C-130 mechanic in Vietnam, had instruction in basic training on exactly what to expect:

> They trained us. We were taught all the hazards even down to
> not kick a tin can or pop can . . . We got a lot of training, which
> included sexual orientation, first aid. We got a lot of things . . .
> I was pretty well prepared mentally. See, if you're not prepared
> mentally that's when I think people get hurt. You've got to be
> willing to do a job and not get caught up in the hoop-lah of what's
> going on. Even though we had a lot of demonstrations going on
> at that time, anti-war type. We were briefed more on that than a
> lot of things we were briefed about Southeast Asia. Even though
> we were given all the shots and we were told about all the different
> diseases, the plague, the cholera. We were told not to drink water.
> You were just trained to use common sense. As long as you used
> your common sense it was ok. War is never pretty. When you go
> into an isolated area, you've got to expect the worst.

During advanced training, aviators learned to fly the planes and helicopters that they would use in country. All pilots who flew in Vietnam went through extensive training before they went to Vietnam and all describe a variety of experiences. One common thread in their commentary is that the training they received was very good, if not superior, in quality and that they were well prepared in their particular aircraft. Pilots were also trained in a 'Jungle Warfare School' or 'Survival School' to learn survival tactics, which included escape and evasion and how to deal with being captured and interrogated. Richard Hamilton, an Air Force F-4 pilot in the war, describes some of what he went through in Survival School:

> We learned knife fighting, all this kind of junk, which actually
> I think it gave you a lot of confidence in case you ever got
> in a spot; you knew where to stick the knife that wouldn't make
> a guy yell out loud and that kind of stuff. But the real sobering
> thing was our escape and evasion part of it, which [when]
> we literally got captured by Russians who were all dressed
> in Russian uniforms, spoke Russian, [and] had a couple of
> Orientals with them to make it [seem more authentic]. We
> were captured, stripped of our clothes totally. I mean we were
> naked jaybirds, threw a black sack over your head and threw
> you in these little, about five foot by five foot cells, and with

a wet can, as I call them, one of those big old cans that was
your latrine and that's all you had. And they'd call you out and
you'd hear all this noise going on and beating people and this
kind of stuff and you start conjuring up all this stuff that's
happening, and of course it wasn't but we thought it could have
been, and the longer it went, the more it went, the more you
started believing it. Then you were taken out to be interrogated
and you hear women's voices and stuff and here you are [naked]
. . . and you're all together with a black sack over your head
trying to seem like you're normal and these guys whacking you
on the arms and whacking you on the butt and whatever with
these little riding crops and they did smart, and asking you
questions and then they'd sit you down [on] a little milking
stool, which was a one-legger, and if you did anything you'd fall
over, if they pushed you, and they'd interrogate you and ask all
this stuff . . .

   Then they threw me in one of these little bitty boxes that,
obviously they're not big enough to get in, but they somehow get
you in there . . . But they do that stuff and finally you're getting
to the point of where you tell more lies and you just keep up the
lying and they keep catching you and you keep doing it again. But
it's actually kind of what really happened later in Hanoi. But we
also learned. [When] the whole thing was . . . over . . . we all went
down, had a big steak dinner at Harold's Club, a big prime rib I
guess it was, and everyone was all happy.

GOING TO WAR

How did the men and women feel about going to war in Vietnam and what
did they know of US policy in Southeast Asia before deployment there?
As with such an endeavor as preparing to leave for duty in a war zone,
there was a range of emotions and a variety of ideas about why they were
going to fight. Upon learning that they had orders to go to Vietnam, most
men took it in their stride, realizing that either it was inevitable, that it
was fate, that they were fulfilling their military duty, or a combination
of the three. The US military normally gave the men a brief period of leave
before they had to depart the country. It was during this time that they
had time to think about what they were about to do and discuss it with
their families and loved ones. Gary Smith, a US Army Military Police Sentry
Dog Handler, remembers that his family expressed apprehension before he
left in 1971:

Members of the 7th Motor Transport Battalion 'Roughriders' travel in convoy in armed trucks from Da Nang to An Hoa. American troops often traveled on the roads between cities in South Vietnam by motorized vehicle. Many times newly arrived soldiers made their way to their units in the back of 2.5-ton trucks, better known as 'Deuce and a Halfs', shown here.

[There was] a whole lot of being scared for me, apprehension, a lot of tears and a lot of not talking about it till the last day when I flew out. There wasn't a whole lot to talk about. The girlfriend probably should have been discussing marriage plans then; in hindsight now, that wasn't in order. Wasn't talking too much about future or anything.

It was just one day at a time, having fun; it was like being on vacation. I wasn't really trying to prepare on anything. I knew that on a certain day, it was a Sunday, I was going to jump on an airplane and head for California, and so we didn't talk about it. I'm sure with my girlfriend, I probably mentioned things, I don't know maybe, talked about what happens if I get hurt or killed, something like that. I don't think we dwelled on it.

Douglas Shivers, a two-tour veteran of the war, took the situation in his stride when he received his orders in 1969:

> It was kind of like, "Oh, well." I didn't really know what to think. I was just a kid. I was 19 then, I think. I took my leave, went home and talked to my parents. Of course my mother wasn't crazy about the idea, having lost her first husband in World War II. I was the only one of the two brothers, and I had one sister that went in the military actually. I'm sure she worried a lot. I heard later she was really upset while I was gone, especially at Christmas time.

Gary Blinn, a 1966 US Naval Academy graduate and a two-tour Swift Boat Captain in Vietnam, states that the mood at the Academy early in the war was very gung-ho:

> [At] the Naval Academy when the Tonkin Gulf Incident happened [1964], we were at flight school. We were just down in Pensacola [Florida] and so we cheered and felt that the US was almighty. I don't think any of us really thought about the battering that the French had already taken or any of the other historical aspects of the little country of Tonkin or how it related to China. During the course of Vietnam, there was some concern that maybe the war would be over before we graduated and so some of us asked if there would be a way for us to graduate early. We didn't really care about the Bachelor's degree. We just wanted to get a commission and get over to the war before it ended.

Mike Bradbury, a Marine who went to Vietnam in 1967, remembers his feelings about his duty and going to Vietnam:

> I wanted to go . . . When I joined the Marine Corps . . . I had something to prove and I said I wanted to go over there. There was certain time that you wanted to go over there and kill a Commie for Mommy and you thought this was for Mom's apple pie; you don't realize America wasn't being attacked . . . You know these are the bad guys and . . . you know and now you're going to go over there, your going to kick some butt like old John Wayne, and you know you get a whole different perception. You say, "We're going to go over there, we're going to do this, and we're going to slam these guys, and I am going to get as good as I can

with this Bazooka because I am going to kill as many of them as I can and I am going to come home with a chest full of medals and there are going to be big parades when I come back and it's going to be great." Well guess what . . . but you're under your own misconception there a little bit . . . I was anxious to go, I was anxious to go, man, I wanted to go over there.

Many men did not understand exactly why they were being sent to war in Vietnam. Some did not particularly care and simply wanted to get into the fight like Charles Hubbs, who went to Vietnam in 1966 as a C-123 pilot:

All I knew was I had a chance to get in combat. Got to go to combat, no way around it. That's what it's all about. I got my fill of that and I don't have that attitude any more . . . I was going to defend the United States. Help out those poor whoever; the South Vietnamese. Didn't even know who the hell they were at the time . . . [I] said [to myself], "Ok I've got to do this." This will enhance my career and I get to fly combat and test myself. Typical macho, young.

Stephen Katz, a C-130 transport pilot in Vietnam, did appreciate to some degree the political aspect of why he was going to war:

We [the US] were trying to support an ally, and we had made a commitment to a government that we were willing to support, and I was very supportive of what was going on. Again, it was a great adventure, which a lot of people may not understand my use of the term, but it was an exciting time . . .

The most common theme that resonated throughout those who went to Vietnam to fight was that, in the midst of the Cold War, they were sent to South Vietnam to stop the spread of Communism. Jim Calbreath, a US Army veteran who served in medical field hospitals in Vietnam, describes this:

What we were trying to do was stop Communism. At that particular time that was the Cold War era, that was good guys and bad guys. We were the good guys and they were the bad guys. They were the evil red horde. They were going to come over here and kill us and eat our babies. They wanted to bury us. One of the memories that I have of childhood is seeing Nikita Khrushchev on television and in newspapers, beating on a podium with his shoe saying, "We will bury you." That's what I grew up with and of course that's what we were being fed. That's what they wanted us to think. Our job, our goal, was to stop the evil red horde and that's what I knew . . . so that's what we were supposed to do. We were supposed to go over there and stop Communism in Vietnam.

In the end, going to war in Vietnam was wading into the same kind of milieu that people had experienced for a thousand generations. James Padgett, a driver with the US Marines in Vietnam in 1968 and 1969, saw his war in this larger context:

War is, you go kill folks. The guy punching that typewriter, maybe he's typing out a requisition for ammunition; in effect, he's contributing to somebody's death. Folks are going to die in wars; friendlies, unfriendlies, and everything in between. It's the worst thing man can do to himself is a war. But if you're going to do it, just do it right.

Marine helicopter pilot John Arick put it this way about going to war:

The good Lord has young people go to war because old people think too hard about the situation.

ARRIVAL IN VIETNAM

When the men and women of the US armed forces arrived in Vietnam thousands of miles away from home and worlds away in culture, they stepped into a world that was extremely foreign. The first impressions of Vietnam left indelible impressions on them. Some went to war in military aircraft, some by way of ship, some by commercial air, and some through another Southeast Asian country such as the Philippines or Thailand. When they stepped on to Vietnamese soil, the experience was usually memorable. Some could literally hear the war. Richard Schaffer, an Army Air Defense Radar repairman in Vietnam, remembers that he thought he heard just that:

It was hot. I remember thinking, wondering what kind of a strange place this was and hearing the sounds of war in the distance. [There were] rockets exploding in the distance, gunfire subdued in the distance. I mean it could have been miles away but we were hearing it. It could have been troops undergoing training exercises for all we knew, but you know you could hear the sounds of war. [I was] nervous, very nervous.

Almost every veteran who served in Southeast Asia remembers how hot it was. Many describe that first impression as a powerful wave of boiling heat and humidity hitting them as they stepped on to Vietnamese soil. Fred Marshall, an Army intelligence analyst and adviser to the ARVN in 1967 and 1968, describes both the heat and the war when he first arrived at Bien Hoa Air Base:

> God, it was hot. [It] felt like I was back in Fort Polk [Louisiana, in training]. We got there in the middle of the night. We walked across the tarmac into a Quonset hut terminal there. We knew we were in a combat zone because you could see flares in the sky and whatnot, a little bit of tracer fire going up in the air or coming down from helicopters up in the distance. Little muffled artillery and mortar rounds in the distance. So right off the bat we knew we weren't in Kansas any more. I just remembered how hot it was and how humid it was because we'd been on the air-conditioned plane for a long time. It just hits you in the face.

Once the personnel arrived in country, they were processed through and told which unit they were assigned to, if they did not already know, and where and when they would be joining their unit. Some of them knew exactly where they were going and what they would be doing. Others had to wait to find out, and the waiting could take a few days. For ground personnel, the main point of entry was Tan Son Nhut air base, just outside Saigon, from which they would eventually be ferried off to their units around South Vietnam. Many men remember landing there and being shuttled away on buses which were equipped with protected windows. Gary Cummings, who served with the US Army in Vietnam, remembers well his arrival at Tan Son Nhut in 1966:

> I certainly had the impression that we were going to be landing at Tan Son Nhut and might come under mortar fire or something. Instead we were met [on the tarmac] by someone in khakis. [He] marched us over to some terminal where we were eventually put on a bus . . . It was very organized [and] certainly

not the instant combat that we thought we were going to be coming into. I remember the pilot made very tight turns, [a] very tight descent into Tan Son Nhut. I imagine [they did this] because they didn't want to come under fire. I had never been on airplane, big or small, that made that type of descent into an airport. That got my attention. I didn't think that 707s were supposed to be doing that stuff. [Once we landed, we were put into] school buses with no windows [with] screens over where the windows were. It made sense. I think they said something about that the idea was that they couldn't throw a hand grenade in there. It made sense to me. We had the feeling that even at Tent City Alpha [at Tan Son Nhut AB] we're going to be attacked in our sleep. We had no idea what was going on in Vietnam at the time.

Tom Esslinger had a memorable and harrowing 'Welcome to the Vietnam War' experience during his first 24 hours in country:

[My impression was the] same as everybody else: hot, humid, smelly. That first night they put us in transient officers' quarters, which was a hardback tent with a plywood floor, which was about two meters from the wire fence that ran along one of the major runways of Da Nang airfield. So I got absolutely zero sleep all night because there were jets taking off and landing all night. Of course I was kind of apprehensive I guess. So the next day I was told I was going to the 3rd battalion 26th Marines and that . . . there was a truck convoy leaving [for Camp Evans] and I was to get on it, so I did. I sat in the back of a 6X6 truck and rode up Route One, which was quite an experience and quite an education. It was my first real look at Vietnam. We're going right up Route One, which is a major road. There's just all kinds of activity, small villages, commerce. The road itself was maybe a little wider than a king-sized bed. Traffic was amazing. The way to make your way along if you were a truck or a bus was to lean on your horn. So that all the walkers and bicyclers, and motor bikers would get out of your way. It was just like a mad house. I was just sort of amused and amazed by it. Then we got up there . . . just north of Hue, there was an ARVN truck coming. Just as it got almost abreast of us, it triggered a mine, which basically blew the cab over the top of our truck into the rice paddy on the other

side. Sort of deafened us for a while. These two guys were sitting
in this cab both got both their legs sheared off just above the
kneecap when they were blown up against the dashboard. That
was sort of my introduction to violence in Vietnam. It was kind
of scary. Then the rest of the ride I realized that I was sitting there
in the bed of this truck right over the top of the gas tank. [I was]
pretty nervous.

Douglas Shivers served two tours in Vietnam with the US Army. He recalls
that his arrival in country in 1969 was marked by an encounter with
soldiers who were leaving the war, both dead and alive:

Well, we got off the plane, and there were soldiers waiting to get
on the plane. Of course they had faded uniforms, and ours were
all brand new and you could tell we were new guys or Fucking
New Guys [FNGs] as they called us . . . Anyway, they were waiting
to get on the plane and they were cheering and they were happy,
and they were saying stuff like, "Look out for the claymores!"
They walked past us and got on. I think . . . that's the first time
I saw some of these big metal sardine cans that they sent human
remains on it [out of the RVN] . . . I didn't catch what it was at
first, but those were obviously human remains going back. They
were dead soldiers.

Those leaving Vietnam would watch the new arrivals de-plane and step into
the war. US Army veteran Alan VanDan, in Vietnam in 1968 and 1969, saw
the new guys coming in just as he was boarding his plane to leave:

I just nodded my head and got on that plane. I go, "Man, what a
bunch of suckers these bad boys will be."

Joining one's unit in the field provided for many different experiences.
Some individuals were flown in and dropped off with their unit, either at a
base camp or directly into the field, and some were driven from their point
of arrival to their new unit. Larry Burke, an Army infantry commander in
Vietnam in 1966 and 1967, recalls his drive to his unit's headquarters area:

After we [were] processed in we were put on a truck and we left
Tan Son Nhut to go to Di An, headquarters of the 'Big Red One'
[US Army, 1st Division]. I remember that we hadn't even been

issued weapons yet. We go up this road through this countryside, it's startling green countryside. Rice paddies and peasants working out there with the water buffalo and I didn't even have a weapon. Of course, I was in the truck with a guy, riding shotgun with an M-60 [machine gun]. I thought, "Man, this doesn't feel like security to me." . . . I remember that very clearly.

What was it like to join an existing unit in the field as the new guy? In general, the new men were accepted at a basic level by the unit, but they still had to prove their mettle to the others. The men who had been together wanted to know if they could trust the new arrival in a combat situation, whether he would crack under fire or whether he would do the right thing – fight with and protect his fellow soldiers. Sometimes the new guy was a replacement for an individual killed in action, a circumstance that made his acceptance into the unit that much more difficult. Allan Suydam was a rifleman with the Army 25th Infantry, in Vietnam in 1968 and 1969:

You're an FNG [Fucking New Guy]. You're 12,500 miles from home. You know absolutely no one and the elements are trying to kill you, along with all the insects and reptiles, not to mention the enemy, and you've got to put up with being an FNG, in that you have to prove yourself. The jury is out on you. These guys have been there for a while. They don't know if you're going to stay awake on guard duty. Can they trust you? What are you going to do the first time you get into a firefight? Are you going to react the way you should, or are you going to cower down where somebody has to carry you somewhere? There is a lot of emotion involved . . .

Frank Gutierrez, an Army infantryman in Vietnam from 1967 to 1970, describes the limited contact between the new guys and the old hands:

The guys coming in country were at the top of the hill. The guys coming home were at the bottom of the hill. So, it was a vast contrast because guys at the top of the hill, brand new fatigues, and the guys at the bottom of the hill, scruffy, long hair, bearded, tanned, boots that were almost suede-like because they'd been there for a year or two years, who knows how long they'd been there. There was quite a difference, and again, they didn't talk to you.

John Wear, a US Marine, distinctly remembers how he felt when he arrived to join his unit:

> . . . I remember seeing all the salty Marines coming back [from the field] and [I was] kind of looking down on the ground and keeping my eyes averted, being embarrassed because I was the new guy and they were the old guys and the salt. I remember being pretty afraid, like "Oh, shit, what did I get into?"

One issue that was unique to the Vietnam War and was, and is, a constant point of discussion amongst those who served was the fact that many men were sent over as individuals and not with a unit. For many this was a mistake that damaged the war effort. Marshall Paul served with the Army in Vietnam from January 1968 to April 1970 and recalls this issue:

> One of the big fuckups of the whole war was that they sent everybody over there as an individual instead of in units, and having the unit do a tour, and then bringing the unit back, and feeding replacements into the unit and maintaining unit integrity. What they did was they sent everybody over there by themselves. I went over there in a planeload of people in a 707, and you get there and then you're all dispersed, all different parts of the country. And so, most of us arrive at our units in twos and threes as strangers and sometimes you don't even see the guys you've been traveling with again. And then here you're the brand new guy, you're all by yourself, and nobody trusts you, and nobody knows you. And they have to take time to get used to you, to warm up to you, to teach you the routine. Why, hell, they wouldn't start teaching you for a while because they don't want to know you. And they figure, you know, you're probably going to get killed anyway, and they'd just as soon not know the new guy when he gets killed.

Philip Watson, who served with the US Navy in Vietnam from September 1968 to May 1969 as a radio operator, remembers how hard it was for him as the new guy:

> Us FNGs could get together and form our own little social group. Whereas on the riverboat, I was [on] my own, by myself

Returning from a patrol, American Marines traverse the marshes southwest of Da Nang near the massive US Da Nang Air Base. A frequent task of the US infantry unit was to patrol the varied terrain of South Vietnam to make contact with the enemy and to provide security for the local population and Allied bases.

. . . I never knew that [the ostracizing] was even happening . . . [W]hen that was done, it was just kind of a bizarre deal, and the old man, the chief that ran it [the riverboat], he looked grandfatherly [and] he was unfriendly. Everybody on the boat was unfriendly, and I think that was [because] I was a new guy, I wasn't a part of the team really. [It] was just kind of a "Hey, do this Watson, hey do that. You're relieved, get up, go do that." I wasn't a part of the camaraderie at that point. I was in [what] felt like a hostile group of people and I never made friends with them . . . I was the lowest ranking. I had no skills for the boat either. You know until you make a contribution, until you picked up the skills to make a contribution towards the whole thing you really [are on the outside] and I never even got to that point [before being wounded and evacuated].

Watson continues, describing that you could be an FNG even after you had been in country a while:

> Everybody was a FNG no matter where you went. When I went down to Sa Huynh, I was again an FNG, even though I'd been in country this time about . . . seven months. But I was still an FNG because I was new to those guys, but I had some skills at that point, radio skills and whatnot, so it didn't last very long. I wasn't FNG very long. [O]nce you worked there awhile and you made rank . . . you just naturally worked yourself into the organization that way. [But] in the beginning you were kind of ostracized and I think that's natural in . . . all the military groups.

Some men, like Chuck Carlock, a USAF helicopter pilot in Vietnam, did not hear the term 'FNG' very much.

> I really don't remember that term much. You know, that's always in all the books and stuff but I really don't remember them using that term. I think "asshole" was more appropriate. You know, "What's that guy doing living in our hooch over here?" They were really upset. But these guys became my friends shortly; it didn't take long and they figured out who'd hang with them and didn't freak out. They wanted somebody pretty cool in there in case they got hurt or got into the night. We flew at night a lot . . . and I can see their point of view. You didn't want some rookie up there . . . flying in those mountains in the dark that didn't have a clue what he was doing. That jeopardizes everybody's life and because sometimes you could get vertigo and you wanted somebody sitting where they knew what he was doing.

However, the isolation of the new arrivals was not always the experience. Some veterans describe how they were hesitant to befriend the replacements since they were usually the first to be killed in combat because of their lack of experience. In addition, the veterans who were already bonded by experience, again, had to find out if they could trust the new men, but they realized that in order to be effective in combat as a unit and to protect themselves in combat situations, they had to teach the new arrivals the ropes. Andy Roy, Army infantryman and helicopter doorgunner, describes this:

> I don't know how many times I've heard and read, new guys come

in, nobody wants to get to know them because they might die. That's a bunch of bullshit, that is absolute bullshit. You have to depend upon each other, I mean I've been in three different units; I've been with so many guys. You have to depend on each other and the first thing you do when somebody new comes in, usually the first question asked, "What state are you from?" And you know, your name, your rank and they can pretty well tell if it's your first tour or not. They might ask where you went to training at . . . stuff like that. A lot of units would assign the [new] person to a mentor for a few days . . . but generally everybody looked [out for them], and everybody was more than willing to offer advice . . . One thing we would always do is, "So you remember hearing [this about being in the field?"] and the guy would say, "Yes, I heard that all the time" and we'd tell them, "Forget it, that's one of those rumors" or you know, "No that don't happen. Don't worry about little kids coming up and offering you a soda to sell, no it's not going to have ground glass in it and no, it's not going to be an explosive. These people love their children just like everybody else and they're not going to blow their little kids up just to get an American," things like that. Then the person . . . wouldn't be put on point [out front on combat patrol] but they'd be put with experienced people. Everybody offered this person advice for two reasons: the first one was survival of the group. He makes a wrong mistake he could not only get himself killed, but somebody else killed too. Secondly, he's one of you now, he's one of the family and we look out for each other.

Once the men had arrived at their unit, the war really began for them. For many of the personnel who were in infantry units, or ready to fly a sortie over North Vietnam from an air base or from a carrier in the South China Sea, or preparing for a helicopter combat assault into an enemy-occupied area, or moving up a canal in the Mekong Delta on a patrol boat, the war was about to take on a new meaning. They were going to be tested, both professionally and personally, by what many veterans describe as the most intense experience of their lives: combat.

3
INTO COMBAT

In its attempt to defeat the Democratic Republic of Vietnam (DRV, or North Vietnam) and the Viet Cong (VC), protect sovereignty of the Republic of Vietnam (RVN, or South Vietnam) and win the Vietnam War, the United States used an attrition, or erosion, strategy. The objective was to break the will of North Vietnam to wage war against South Vietnam by killing as many of its soldiers and destroying as much of its *matériel* as possible. This would be accomplished by increasing the tempo of the combat through the use of high firepower (nearly the entire arsenal of weapons) and mobility (helicopter insertion and withdrawal of troops) which in turn would increase the DRV/VC's need for supplies. The resulting increased vulnerability of the DRV/VC infrastructure and supply routes (such as the Ho Chi Minh Trail Complex), the massive loss of life and denial of material resources, and a decreasing political will to continue the fight at such high cost, the US reasoned that North Vietnam and the Viet Cong would capitulate and cease its aggression against the government of South Vietnam. The result would be victory through erosion.

The DRV employed a strategy of enervation, or a policy of protracted conflict to break the US political will to continue the fight. This strategy would be accomplished by an effort to dictate the tempo of the ground war, to keep fighting despite the massive losses, and exploit US weakness through hit-and-run tactics and by allowing no set-piece battles. For example, when the tide of a battle or ambush began to turn against the North Vietnamese and/or VC troops, they would usually withdraw from the engagement. The DRV/VC would inflict casualties on the US and its allies over an undetermined length of time while simultaneously using the anti-war movement in America and its effects upon US policy to further its cause.

In the end, the attrition strategy failed and enervation succeeded. There were, however, multiple rules of engagement for the Americans that governed the battlefield and the skies throughout the war; many veterans cite these as a main reason for the American inability to stop the activities of the DRV and VC and to prevent the collapse of South Vietnam.

VARIETIES OF COMBAT

Fighting in Vietnam between the Americans and their allies and the North Vietnamese and Viet Cong took on a wide variety of forms. One's Military Occupation Specialty often determined the form of contact one would have with the enemy. In Vietnam, combat ranged from quick hit-and-run-style tactics, such as ambushes, to larger company and regimental-size encounters, such as the November 1965 battle in the Ia Drang Valley; from an air strike against Hanoi to close air support of troops in the field; from a naval bombardment from the South China Sea to Long Range Reconnaissance Patrols (LRRPs) in the RVN, North Vietnam and Laos; or from US support elements receiving rocket fire into a rear base area to American B-52 'Arc Light' air strikes on NVA and VC positions. Whatever the type of contact, it promised to have a lasting impact on those involved.

Many of the individuals who fought in Vietnam knew they would be tested by the fighting but did not know exactly how they would react once in combat. Randall Kunkelman was a US Army ordnance specialist in Vietnam. He reflects upon his performance in combat:

> Emotions really run . . . adrenaline really runs very, very strong and you don't know what you're going to do under any circumstances . . . I mean, you may totally freeze, you may think you're going to be John Wayne, and you may pee your pants. You might just stand there or you might just do your job the way you normally would do it in as good a manner as you possibly can. Under those circumstances, just things happen and you don't understand why. Most heroes, most people who do things, throw themselves on grenades, whatever, I don't believe that that is a conscious, thought-out process. I think it is a reaction that just happens and you don't know if it's going to happen with you or not. At the time, you find out.

There is no way to capture a personal description of every combat situation in the Vietnam War. What follows is a sample of different forms of combat, on the ground, on the water and in the air.

ON THE GROUND

Combat on the ground in the Vietnam War took on many different forms. For example, it might be a mortar attack on an American base, an event that happened on a regular basis during the war. It could be the Americans

Private First Class Milton Cook of the 5th Mechanized Infantry Regiment, US Army 25th Infantry Division, returns enemy fire with an M-60 machine gun during the 1967 Operation JUNCTION CITY. The unit had just received heavy sniper fire. In this engagement the US Army helped clear War Zone C, a major Viet Cong stronghold, of enemy forces.

and NVA (North Vietnamese Army) and/or VC ambushing each other along jungle paths or an American company-sized search-and-destroy mission. Ground combat could be a sniper shooting at a target of opportunity or tanks and other armor working in tandem with infantry to attack an enemy position. Unlike 'conventional' warfare, the Vietnam conflict was one in which enemy lines were blurred and territory was fought over but rarely held. Fighting on the ground was sometimes fierce at close range, within meters, or, in the case of an artillery barrage, a bombing mission or the like, remotely delivered from a distance.

In almost all instances, those soldiers, seamen and airmen who discuss their combat experiences describe various moments of sheer terror, excitement, high adrenaline, a reliance on training and an instinct for survival. Almost all of them describe combat as an experience that will stay with them for the rest of their lives. Andy DeBona commanded a Marine infantry company in 1967. He describes combat on the ground and the experience of being shot at by the enemy:

My anticipation of combat, I thought . . . that we would be
shooting at them, they would be shooting at us . . . I mean there
are different types of my definition of being shot at. You can be
shot at with mortars, artillery or their area fire weapons, and if
you get hit with them, it's bad luck. The other way to get shot
at is a personal shooting, the small arms fire. Now there are
different types of getting shot at with small arms fire, somebody
else could be getting shot at with small arms fire which you see
them getting hit over there. The other type, which is extremely
personal, is when they are shooting at you and they know they
are shooting at you because you got little things . . . digging up
around you – you can see, actually see the wink of the weapon,
you could hear the rounds going by.

Many American Army and Marine infantry units made contact with the
NVA/VC through an air combat assault via helicopter, a common experience
for the American infantryman in Vietnam. The troops would be flown to
an area and dropped off. They would then embark on a 'search and destroy'
mission. Jerry Benson, an Army infantryman in Vietnam in 1968 and 1969,
describes a combat assault into a landing zone (LZ) and subsequent action:

We were in what I now know as the Iron Triangle, which I
thought was called Hobo Woods. It was a four-day and three-
night operation. [This was] the only time that we ever went into
a landing zone that we were being hit on, a hot LZ is what we
called it, where the choppers could not come down and not touch
ground because of the land mines situation, booby traps. We had
to jump off the chopper about three or four feet with all of that
heavy combat gear. I lost my glasses and had to get to the brush
line as soon as possible. This was a three-company operation, 250
men on this operation, a lot of people . . . [T]here were a lot of
bunkers out there, and the other company lost a point man by
checking out a bunker. He got killed. So my squad was the last
four or five guys on the patrol. Their job was to go out and clear
brush for the choppers to come in to evacuate the dead, which
my squad leader did on that particular day. As they were going
back to clear an area, they got ambushed by another bunker.
There were bunkers everywhere out there in that environment.
So they got ambushed. My squad leader gets hit; he gets hit in
the leg. The next guy, which would have been me, gets hit and the

third guy gets hit. So I should have been the second guy in that environment. So I should have been hit that day, but because my radio was not working I was not back there with my squad. So here I am today, you know, a guy that's not wounded in Vietnam. They were not killed. My squad leader got a bullet in his leg . . . as soon as he got hit, his first reaction was to call "Mike 6," which is my platoon leader's code . . . So he's immediately coming back to the company area yelling "Mike 6!" The other guy gets hit somewhere, I can't remember where. The third guy got grazed, the bullet grazes his eye and he loses his eye eventually. But they all three get evacuated that day and I've never seen them again. My squad leader's a kid from Detroit, he'd only been in the country about two months, a month and a half maybe, and to this day he feels like he was not a part of our company because he was only in the company a short period of time, which is not the case. But I should have been in that group . . . I should have been hit that day. I may not be here today . . .

Infantry also made contact by going on day or night patrols out of their base camp in their area of operations. These patrols might last a few hours, a few days or a few weeks, depending on the unit and situation. Keith Erdman, a US Marine, describes how his unit patrolled in search of the enemy:

. . . Every four nights [we] went out on night patrol. You never really followed the same pattern or trail or whatever. Each time you went out you'd deviate so that if they were watching you they wouldn't be able to ambush you in any one specific place at any specific time. [Our] Captain was very astute about things like that. He dictated pretty much variance [*sic*], daily variances from your norm. One day they'd [the officers organizing the patrols] walk around the compound one way and the next day they'd walk around the area a different way, and the third day they'd walk even a different way, like going basically the same direction but they'd start at a different point . . . [I]f you took a clock and made a circle around your complex there . . . one day you'd leave at ten o'clock and go out, then you'd shift to the south and the next day you might go out and shift to the north and then swing around and shift back to the south part way through your patrol. The next night they'd go to the north and go all the way around [the search area]. Then they'd come in at a different point than they went out at. So, they were very good about that type of thing. It was amazing at night how much light there was over there because of the stars and the moon. During monsoon season, though, that was a totally different story. You could be out there in the monsoons and you couldn't see the guy a foot in front of you it rained so hard; it was just black.

Both the US and the NVA/VC forces set ambushes for each other. These ambushes were meant to catch by surprise the patrolling group (squad, platoon or company), usually along a footpath or trail, and inflict the maximum damage in a relatively short time. Andy Roy, a three-tour Army infantryman and helicopter door-gunner, describes setting up a typical ambush:

We learned very quickly that fighting fire with fire was an excellent way to deal with the situation, so usually . . . a company on the move would stop for the day and set up a defensive position, each platoon would send out during the day an 'Observation Post' plus a patrol to cover in front of their section. At night the observation post was replaced by what was known as a 'Listening Post' because you couldn't see at night so it was out there to listen, at the same time an ambush went out and during the day somebody would be taking notice, a platoon leader or someone, of possible ambush sites. So they'd look at the map and if there was trails around then an ambush was set up on those trails to try and catch somebody who maybe didn't know you were there, or if they were going to try and approach your position, you don't want to have to break brush and make a lot of noise so you may have approached by trails nearby.

Sometimes during the day when we weren't on any particular move anywhere, we'd just constantly send out ambushes, every night from static bases too, always ambushes going out. The enemy found it a little safer to travel at night than they did during the day, because they couldn't be . . . observed [from] the air or from a distance, from an observation post, so during the night most of the ambushes happened. I'd say every night Allied forces, South Vietnamese, American, Korean, Australian, Thai, Filipino, everybody all together, I'd say probably at least 3,000 ambushes a night went out and the vast, vast majority of

the . . . ambushes were conducted by Allied troops, and we killed
an awful lot of Vietnamese. You can't cover every possible trail
and still they were able to get through but we made it very, very
difficult for them.

Roy describes what made a good ambush site and what would happen once
set up:

Usually where trails come together, if it's obvious that the
trail is extremely well used, let's say up in the mountains
where there aren't any villages. If there's [sic] villages near
the mountains, [the] area between the village and the
mountains [are good sites] because the enemy's going to
come down out of the mountains to try and collect food and
intelligence information and the like. Certain bridges over
canals, these small bridges made out of bamboo and planks
and the like, I mean if you can only cross the canal every half a
mile or so, then those are good ambush spots right there. And
anything that looked . . . like it was near an enemy position
possibly . . . Sometimes you couldn't find any reason to ambush
a particular spot, but the standard operating procedure [was]
you will send out an ambush, so we'd just find a good place
and set up an ambush. A lot of times it was in a straight line,
near the trail, and we'd put out claymore mines – a claymore
mine is a hand-detonated mine with a hundred feet of wire.
It's a convex set up of explosives with, I don't know, I've heard,
six hundred, nine hundred, steel ball bearings; they were very
effective. We'd set up several of those and then a trip flare
usually in the center. If we didn't hear anybody going by then,
and the trip flare went off, then we'd just detonate the mines
immediately. Usually you could hear the padding of feet right
at the last second. Sometimes I used to get stunned, they'd
come walking down the trial talking like they were back on the
block someplace; I can't believe how many times I heard them
screw up like that, but usually we wouldn't get them all, but
we'd get a few and then we'd find blood trails, and actually
wounding a man is better than killing a man because . . . either
side has to use more resources to take care of a wounded man
than a dead man.
    Often times we captured a lot of our intelligence information

too, but like I said during the day sometimes if the company stopped, they'd set out ambushes on the nearest trails and the like and I can remember single couriers just walking suddenly right into the ambush, a lot of times being captured. Sometimes you don't have the luxury of being able to capture somebody because [you] come face to face and you don't know what he's going to do and he don't know what you're going to do and you can't take a chance . . . There were instances I do remember of units getting lost at night and walking into another Allied position's ambush and we losing some men to that . . . but those things happen.

Patrolling through the jungles of South Vietnam could be a harrowing experience. There was always the chance that your unit would make contact with the enemy, which was the purpose, but also the chance that someone in your unit would trip a VC or NVA booby trap. Frank Vavrek, commander of an Army infantry company during his second tour in South Vietnam in 1968 and 1969, describes just such an incident:

We were conducting [an] airmobile operation; flying the company into an LZ up in I Corps. We landed the whole company . . . Booby traps were really a real problem up there . . . [There] was a natural opening that we went into. We went in suspecting first wave in, look for booby traps, be very cautious, and we got on the ground . . . We received no rifle fire or anything like that, everybody moved very carefully and we spread out all around there . . . I remember calling a meeting of the platoon leaders then. It was early in the afternoon and I said, "Okay, we figured our order of movement." I gave . . . the direction, and everything that we were going to take and as I convened my meeting, the platoon leaders and the RTOs [Radio Telephone Operators] separated to go back to their platoons and one of them tripped the booby trap . . . Of course, I felt the blast; it hit me in the chest . . . it knocked me down, knocked the wind out of me, scattered the other guys, casualties just every which way . . . the shrapnel and the hot blast . . . I knew I'd been hit and as soon as I could, I ripped my shirt open because I knew something had hit me in the chest and there were frag [fragmentation] wounds. I had frag wounds there, frag wounds in my face, my arms, but none of them were critical . . . It was like a shotgun blast. I mean, I was peppered, my jacket was full of tiny holes and I had little flesh

wounds and marks and scars . . . My cigarette lighter was in my
shirt pocket. Keep it up high in case because of those stream
crossings and everything, keep it dry so it would always work and
a big chunk of shrapnel hit my cigarette lighter and just bent it
in. It was one of the old Zippos . . . [It] left a big imprint in that
Zippo right in my chest, so that's the part, I guess, that really
went up, said I felt something hit me, like knocked the wind
out of me, that's what did it. The cigarette lighter stopped that
shrapnel.

The intensity of combat was also a reality for the officers who led
the enlisted personnel. Charles 'Ty' Dodge, an Army infantry platoon
commander, remembers one moment in 1969 when he was faced with a
situation that tested his training as well as his emotional mettle. It was an
action for which he was awarded the Bronze Star:

We got into that [North Vietnamese] regimental base camp and
found a lot of very heavily defended bunkers and tunnels . . .
My dad had always taught me, in preparation I guess, he said,
"Never expect your men to do something you haven't already
done or wouldn't do yourself." So I took the first turn going
into a tunnel. I remember I had my .45 and a flashlight [torch].
I started crawling into this tunnel. I was scared to death. I had
never been in a tunnel before in my life. As I was going in I met
an NVA soldier coming out who had a grenade in his hand. We
were maybe four feet away from each other, three feet, really close.
I can remember it's amazing how much stuff you can think about
in an instant of time. I thought this guy's probably got a family at
home with kids and he's doing his job just like I'm doing my job.
Now it became a matter really of who could pull the trigger first
and that's it. The .45 blew him back into the tunnel and I never
saw him again. It really shook me up. That was the only close
time. So many times when you're in combat, certainly in Vietnam,
you didn't see the enemy. It was just all in jungle. You never saw
anybody. So to have a face-to-face confrontation like that made it
very personal. Brought a whole different kind of look to the war
for me.

The leaders of the infantry units had to direct their men in firefights,
control communication with the rear, request artillery and air support

and, importantly, watch out for their own safety. In fact, American officers in Vietnam were frequently the special targets of enemy gunmen. Michael Sweeney, a Marine company commander, remembers an operation as an infantry officer in which his company fought an NVA battalion:

> I tell you when there's a real fight going on, you're so busy as a leader that you don't really have much time to think about it. I mean I was just busy. We were calling in air. We were calling in medevacs. We were shifting people around, we're moving people around. I remember in the middle of it, we got in a fight and we were in an old graveyard. I was pointing to Barney Blank with my left hand, trying to get him to move and yelling at him. You've always got a radio in your hand, a handset and all that. I had a handset in one hand and was trying to get Barney to move one direction or another. I remember the flash and the snap and I knew that something had happened. I piled up behind a grave and Runk comes piling in behind me and says, "He shot your watch off." I looked down and sure enough my watch was gone. I haven't worn one since. I've never worn a watch since because of that. Runk says, "When you run to the next one I saw where the fire came from. When you run to the next one, I'll get him." I told him, "You give me the rifle and you run to the next one, Runk." Then I took off and Runk had an M-14 he'd picked up somewhere. He fired three or four times and piled up again behind me. He said, "I got him, let me go get him." I gave him two or three people [other Marines], he took off and went and got his [the dead NVA soldier's] weapon and helmet and ID card and left him there. He had a scoped rifle. There was no question he was trying to take me personally. I took great offense to that. That was a rare incident when you felt you personally had been designated as a target.

Sweeney led his Marines in a number of operations, one of which his company took on two NVA regiments in a major ground operation. He describes the action:

> That was just [a] running gunfight for six to eight days . . . The NVA poisoned all the wells. As they fell back they cut up water buffaloes and dropped the carcasses and the guts or whatever in the well, so we couldn't use the water. I remember drinking out

of a caribou footprint, wiping the green scum off of it and just hoping to hell it didn't kill me . . . we're down to, I don't know, close to 50 [Marines], I expect . . . We had a tank with us and I got a call from an OV-10 [Forward Air Controller] pilot overhead . . . saying that there were "hordes of gooks coming over the railroad tracks behind us." . . . I asked the classic question "What's a horde?" He said, "Many, many." So I called the battalion [chief] and told him what the observer had said. It was barely dark. [He said] "Circle the wagons and we'll do the same and we'll talk to you." I went around to every hole . . . and they're digging and getting ready and I tell them what the situation is: "Here's the deal. We're told we've got a lot of enemy over into this tree line off to our west." By then I was pounding the hell out of it with everything that would fly . . . I went around to each hole and about the second or third hole I heard "click". I turned around and looked and the two Marines in the hole were putting bayonets on . . . I said, "Oh God, this is not good." I told them if this is [General George] Custer's last stand we're going to make a hell of a deal out of it here. The kids all just dug a little deeper and put their grenades up and got ready. I had about as much concentrated firepower going into that tree line as I ever saw deployed in one spot. They never bothered us except they mortared the hell out of us in the middle of the night. I remember lying on my back in the hole I was in with my radio operator . . . We had a round, you could hear them coming toward us, walking towards you. "Boom, boom, boom." One hit on the front side of the hole. You could see the sparks and all that fly up. Then one hit on the back of our hole. That wasn't a real big hole. It was that close.

Riflemen under the command of these platoon and company commanders experienced the brunt of the combat in the ground war. These men relate many different experiences when recalling the firefights in which they were engaged, but one common thread is the sheer brutality and unforgiving nature of combat. Elmer Hale, an Army infantryman operating in the Central Highlands area, recounted an incident that occurred in 1967 as his unit assaulted a mountain position:

It [the mountain] was called Chu Moor . . . [W]e got up there, and we were standing beside this tree, and I told [the] Sergeant . . . we called him 'Pappy' because he was 38 years old [and] he was older than the rest of us . . . I told him "Pappy, something ain't right?" He said, "What do you mean?" I said, "There's some shit up here somewhere." I said, "We're going to hit some shit. I can just feel it. Did you notice the monkeys quit chirping and chattering and the birds quit singing? It's real quiet isn't it?" He said, "Yes." I said, "There's something around real close." So our Captain, he got like, I think it was five or six guys, and had them go up this mountain. You know, kind of seeing what was up there. They didn't go very far. They had movement off on the right hand side. The jungle in that area was so thick that this one kid threw a grenade and it bounced back on him and hit him in the back and it took a chunk out of his back the size of my hand. It was clear past his spine. You could see his spine. He lived and everything, but it had really done a number on him . . .

The next day we sent a patrol up there. They just made mincemeat out of them guys. Unbeknown to us, there was a regiment on that hill of NVA   there was four other companies besides us . . . We were all around that hill . . . We were trying to get up this hill and take this place. Of course, it was so well fortified. You couldn't move. It was impossible. They were dug in, they were camouflaged so well, that you could be ten feet in front of the bunker and never see it. In fact, the day that [the] Sergeant was killed, he was to my right, and we were going up this hill, and he turned around to bring the guys up behind him, bring them up on line. I turned to look at him and he was gone in an instant. Just phew! Well they ripped him with a machine gun is what they'd done. We left, we had to leave his body up there, and another boy from New York . . .

The day following [the] Sergeant's death we again tried to take this particular position and we failed again. By that time we were down to probably 18 to 20 guys at the most in this whole company out of 125 or 128 people. We lost a second lieutenant up there. That evening we were told that we were going to be pulled off of that mountain . . . I was either on the last chopper out or the next to the last chopper out . . . They ended up pulling everyone out of that area, off of the mountain there. Within a day or two, they brought the B-52s in. From what I understand, that after the B-52 strike . . . they sent . . . a crew in there to see what they could find or whatever. At this time they found [the] Sergeant and this other gentleman . . . that we left up there. I also heard . . . that [the] Sergeant . . . he had several tattoos on him. Supposedly the NVA carved him up pretty good. They took a knife and cut the tattoos off of him . . . and cut his genitals off and stuck them in his mouth.

Infantry relied on the support of artillery units which provided aerial bombardment of enemy positions from a distance. An individual could call on his radio back to the artillery and have them blast an individual enemy position or simply rain down artillery on a wide area in which there were suspected enemy positions. Many infantrymen credit accurately placed artillery as vital to their protection and to the destruction of the enemy and the enemy's position. Michael McGregor describes the 1st Cavalry Division artillery firing on VC positions on a ridge and the attitude his unit had:

We blew the hell out of that ridge that they were on, but by that time, they were long gone. I don't even think we got any fire back. Oh, I mean, we shot; we shot. If you fool with us, then you're going to have hell to pay and I think that was part of the lesson in the [1st] Cav[alry] that if you [infantry units] had any significant contact, that we had an expression: "We'll bring the world down on you." It was so . . . if you're [the enemy] going to do something, you better think about it quickly or just do it real quickly and run like hell because you may not want to be around for the consequence.

In addition to the enemy, another thing combatants in a war zone have to deal with is a phenomenon called the 'fog of war', the confusing effects of fighting and the tactical chaos that sometimes accompanies it, combined with the variables of terrain and weather and the physical and emotional intensity indigenous to combat. Don Cuneo, a Marine infantryman, remembers one instance when he experienced the direct result of the fog of war, when US Marines and the US Army exchanged fire with each other:

Probably the most exciting time was we had a firefight with the Cav[alry] right towards the end of it . . . They thought we were bad guys, and we thought they were bad guys and there was absolutely no communication. It's funny . . . But, it was just one of those things that young kids . . . out there and inexperienced, nighttime. Things moved. Bushes turned into monsters. You were scared to death, and you knew that these guys were going to sneak up with a knife between their teeth and do you in. So, somebody got excited and started shooting, and somebody got shot at and started shooting back, and then we found out it was each other and we were on the same side.

COMBAT ON THE WATER

When people think about combat in the Vietnam War, many picture the infantryman on the ground. There was, however, a large naval component to the war. US political and military leadership took full advantage of the fact that naval force was one of the major American military strengths. The US Navy and, to a minor degree the US Coast Guard, patrolled the waters off the coast of Vietnam and the many waterways – the rivers and canals – inland. The US controlled both the waters off the coast and much of the inland waterway network throughout the war.

The Americans had nearly every type of naval ocean-going ship in the waters of the South China Sea, from aircraft carriers to tugboats. All ships played a vital role in the overall war effort, and each had its share of incidents. Some men and women on board the ships saw combat, and some did not – it depended on the type of ship, its location and its primary mission in the war. Gary Blinn served two tours of duty on the water in Vietnam. During his first tour in 1967 he served as a gunnery and missile officer on board the destroyer USS *Benjamin Stoddert* (DDG-22). He remembers the combat in an operation in which he participated in 1967 and 1968:

> [Part of our mission involved] shooting up targets that were in the first five miles of the seacoast of Vietnam. And on the seacoast there were a number of fortified guns. Sometimes eight or nine of them would shoot at you at the same time. And they were bunkered and on the shore so you can imagine that they were camouflaged. And we were out there like a little sitting duck. But it was just grand fun. I mean, we'd fire and we'd see the explosions 30 or 40 seconds later on the ground and then we'd see muzzle flashes from the coast and know the time of flight, again, was 30 or 40 seconds before the flashes would start coming around us. I think we'd all been to movies as kids and in my day it was cowboy movies or war movies were the most popular so your first reaction in a firefight is, "Gee, this is just like the movies." And then you realize, "My gosh, this is real." But the adrenaline is pumping so high and I don't believe I have ever been afraid in a

firefight but I've always been busy. So you are so incredibly busy doing things but at the same time, so incredibly acutely aware of what's going on. And it was really kind of a boyish firefight in this kind of almost an artillery duel between our ships, which was moving and shooting, and theirs, which was stationary, hitting and shooting back.

The Patrol Boat/River (PBR), and the Swift Boat were the two vessels that were the principal weapons of the US Navy immediately offshore and in the Mekong Delta's vast canal network. They were designed to navigate the waterways of Vietnam where larger vessels could not go. The boats' main missions were to interdict the enemy's movement on and around the waterways as well as to ferry troops up the canals for inland operations.

David White served in the Mekong Delta area of operations on PBRs. White describes the PBR and its typical crew:

They basically took these motorboats, developed them on the east coast of the United States, the fiberglass type, and put them in the rivers there in the Mekong, and the basic take on this was that it was really ingenious to do this. These very shallow draft, fast moving, very versatile boats. They had two six-cylinder diesel engines on them. They run off pumps. The pumps blow the water out with water jets. You've got your propulsion and you're steering from the pumps. They were heavily armed. Most of the boats that we had, had two M-60s [machine guns] on them on each end. You had two forward .50s [machine guns]. You had an after .50 with a honey wheel mark .18 grenade-launcher right on top of it. Three M-16 rifles and two M-79s that shot the 40mm grenades. Actually, everybody was a gunner except the guy that was driving . . .

We had a four-man boat crew. We had a boat captain, and he could be either second-class, first-class, sometimes even third-class. We had a third-class gunner's mate or second-class and then the same way with an engineman, either third or second. Then a seaman to take care of the boat. An engineer, engineman, took care of the engineering part of it. The boat captain took care of all the charts, radios and he usually drove the boat. Gunner's mate took care of all the weapons, grenades. The seaman kept the boat cleaned. But anybody could flip-flop. All of us were taught to drive the boat. All of us taught to use the radios.

The US Navy developed special watercraft to operate on the multitude of inland waterways in South Vietnam, such as these PBRs, or Patrol Boats/River. The fiberglass PBR was very fast, highly maneuverable, laden with firepower, and performed superbly in the shallow waters of the Mekong Delta.

Navy veteran Larry Oswald describes the difference between the PBR and the Swift Boat:

> The PBRs . . . were smaller. They were only 31-feet long and their displacement was 7.5 tons for either model. There was no . . . cabin where you had a bunk or a sofa or a place to fix some food . . . Now the Swift Boat was 51 feet long. It was all aluminum. It had propellers down into the water. It had a much better radar because it worked offshore and needed to see these guys a lot further out. It wasn't as heavily gunned though. It had one 50-caliber machine gun operated from a perch up on top of where the boat was steered. On the stern they had an 81mm mortar that was mounted horizontally to be used like a cannon. It was pretty potent stuff. But inside the cabin on one of those, some of them had an air conditioner that was installed after they got in

country. Most of them would have a refrigerator, a real honest-to-God toilet, a couple of bunks, some good storage lockers. But the trade off was those guys [sometimes] operated offshore and the South China Sea was never calm. In a 51-foot boat that was brutal duty.

The vast, winding river and canal network of the Mekong Delta was a dangerous place. Oswald remembers the death of a PBR officer:

He was an officer who came up through the enlisted ranks. He was a mean son of a bitch . . . We all hated that son of a bitch. We got her [the PBR] up there, we were ready for our first night patrol, when the boats left; he was in the last boat . . . My most vivid memory of that night is he got on board the PBR, and halfway through the middle of the PBR is where the engines are. There were two flat covers that go over those engines. He was standing on those covered boards. He had a cup of coffee in his hands and he didn't have on a shirt or a flak jacket for shrapnel. He was just wearing olive drab pants [the color most commonly used to describe the American uniform in Vietnam] and some tennis shoes and holding the coffee cup. I lost sight of him just as his boat turned into the Vinh Te Canal. I went back down below and I was getting ready to get something to eat and get some sleep.
  All of a sudden up on the second deck . . . we could hear all kind[s] of chatter going on up there . . . Then I realized what it was. I could look to the Vinh Te Canal. It was pitch-black dark and there were green tracers and red tracers flying all over the place down there. Our radio room got a call that Literary Zulu actual is deceased. Literary Zulu was the radio call sign for those boats. It was made of letters that Vietnamese people have trouble pronouncing and listening to. When they say 'actual' that means the commanding officer. We got a quick radio message that Literary Zulu actual is dead. When they came back, what they had over the engine covers was basically [his] legs and boots . . . When [he] left my first thought was, "I hate that motherfucker. We all hate him, and if he gets killed I couldn't care less." And two hours later I had to supervise getting his personal effects and everything bagged and boxed so a chopper could come out and pick them up.

Charles Lloyd commanded a river patrol boat in the Mekong Delta in 1965 and 1966. He experienced first hand what a mine could do to a small river boat:

> They had rules of engagement that said you were supposed to stay X number of yards from the mainland or the riverbank . . . Sometimes I was taking chances by getting too close and that's what happened one day and I detonated a mine on the coast. Me and [my shipmates] saw this VC flag sticking up in the beach, it was real close to the little jungle area there . . . you couldn't see into it . . . but they could see us. So we got close to this thing and I started back out, all of a sudden [an enemy soldier] detonated a mine right . . . under us. Then everybody got blown over the side of the boat . . . when we came to, we were laying there on the water, I could see some of them [the VC] coming out from the shore trying to finish this up, and most of the men were dead or seriously wounded . . . I was so screwed up they couldn't get me to the [rescue] helicopter . . . Both my legs got mangled, my hips smashed . . . stuff in my stomach that they got out eventually, pieces of the boat or something . . . half a dozen broken bones and a lot sticking through the skin and completely blew away my knee.

COMBAT IN THE AIR

The massive amount of activity in the skies over North and South Vietnam, Laos, Cambodia, Thailand and the South China Sea in the Vietnam War took on many different forms: close air support of troops on the ground; B-52 bombing over North and South Vietnam, Laos and Cambodia; reconnaissance over the Ho Chi Minh Trail Complex in Laos; dogfighting between jets; helicopter combat assaults; Forward Air Controller reconnaissance and fire direction in small propeller and jet aircraft; helicopter 'dustoff' missions (medical evacuation); high altitude reconnaissance by U-2 aircraft; and much more. Unleashing its firepower through the air was one of the principal ways in which the US utilized its air supremacy. During the Vietnam War, the US dropped more tons of bombs on Laos, Cambodia and North and South Vietnam than all other American wars of the twentieth century combined.

The North Vietnamese attacked the breach of their air space by US aircraft with jet fighters (typically Soviet built and supplied MiG fighters), and constant, severe, and intense ground fire that ranged from small machine-gun fire to surface-to-air missiles (SA-2s or SAMs). The NVA and

VC troops on the ground also attacked American aircraft as they operated over South Vietnam and Laos.

Formal American air activity in the theater of operations began when the US responded to the Gulf of Tonkin Incidents in August 1964 with an air raid on strategic targets of opportunity in North Vietnam. Operation PIERCE ARROW marked the beginning of a formal air campaign against North Vietnam. Individual American air combat experiences ranged right across the board and took on a variety of forms. The combat was sometimes very benign. For example, an aircraft might land back at base or on a carrier, and the pilot notices that there were several small holes in his aircraft from ground fire to which he was oblivious while flying. At other times, the air combat was as intense as it gets. For example, pilots literally had to dodge SAMs flying at them as they stayed on a bombing run over and around Hanoi. Some pilots had the mission to hunt and kill SAM launch sites. Navy pilot Kenneth Craig completed more than 300 combat missions over North and South Vietnam. He describes attacking and taking out the SA-2 missile sites in the Hanoi area:

> I was one of the nominated SAM guys, so I was a designated 'Iron Hand' man, and . . . we carried Shrike missiles . . . a fairly new missile and it was [an] anti-radiation missile. It homed in on the [North Vietnamese] radar . . . which was directing the SA-2 missile. So they'd come up in their little consoles, turn on their radar and we'd receive it, zero in on it, and fire the Shrike at it; and the Shrike would go down and home on them and blow up the trailer, which included all the radar gear, and the [Shrike] missiles were ineffective, obviously, if it didn't have guidance. So, it was kind of cat and mouse after they found out we had those things . . . the North Vietnamese [were] very smart to adapt. They didn't turn on their radar . . . they'd use other means of identifying the aircraft and pinpointing where they were, and then they would almost have us in their sights, and then they turn on their [radar] just before they were ready to shoot. So, we got to this cat and mouse game where we would orbit up over long areas of SAM sites, and then wait for them to turn on the [radar] and just dive right [at them] and so they were firing at us while we were diving on them and firing these missiles and it was kind of like a game of chicken. You figure he'd turn off his radar before he got killed in his radar trailer and that's what they normally did. They were definitely afraid of it because it was accurate, very

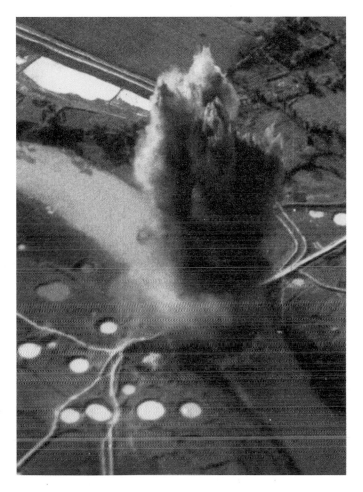

A highway bridge fifteen miles northwest of Vinh in North Vietnam is destroyed by a direct hit from a Navy A-6 Intruder's 500-pound bomb. The photo was taken by a rear facing camera mounted on the underside of the aircraft. The craters visible before and after the bridge mark the previous attempts to hit the structure.

accurate. And then once you saw where the Shrike went in, the explosion, you'd go down and . . . hit the SAM site itself with [small rockets] . . . We sort of dove in, fired the Shrike, rearmed, climbed and then dove in again on the smoke and the debris of the Shrike missile. It was pretty effective.

Craig goes on to describe what happens when a SAM is launched at your aircraft and how he and others would evade and defeat the missile:

Number one, when they fire them, there's a big, huge dust cloud on the ground because of the exhaust run . . . so you see this big plume and you'd see these things take off . . . when it got airborne, it was like a big strobe light, but it travelled really fast, it accelerated really fast to its MACH II or III . . . It had kind of like a rooster tail behind it. It was bright and you could see it . . . the controllers in the console [on the ground] were directing it to you for an impact kill. And when you saw them, then . . . you dove toward to meet it and then you started spiraling because it could not turn real fast at that speed [with] very small fins . . . you would want to get it to try and change its direction and . . . you would get it to change its direction and then it would usually pass you because it couldn't meet you in all the angle shifting that was occurring. And so that's how you ended up beating it.

The targets that the pilots went after in North Vietnam were ones pre-assigned before launch. If those primary targets were unavailable, then secondary targets were sometimes assigned. Pilots were also given the discretion to search for 'targets of opportunity'. Sam Johnson, an Air Force F-4 pilot operating out of Ubon, Thailand, who was later shot down and spent seven years as a prisoner of war, describes one such mission over the DRV in 1966:

We went into Dien Bien Phu one night and bombed a truck park in there. After we left there we still had some bombs so we recc'ed the road [flew reconnaissance] into Hanoi from there and found a convoy of about eight trucks and we got two of them, and they started unloading anti-aircraft pretty heavy at us so we broke off and started back and bombed a bridge on the way back; dropped the rest of the bombs on it.

The selection of targets came from higher up the chain of command. Richard Hamilton, an Air Force F-4 pilot flying out of Thailand, describes how this was done:

They [the targets] came out of Headquarters Air Force . . . They'd have what they called Joint Chiefs of Staff targets, JCS targets, and . . . the Air Force had a huge book and it's a bombing manual . . . and . . . for example, they'd say a double-span bridge, 182 feet long with three abutments, whatever, it will take 82 fighters dropping X amount of bombs on it. And so they'd say okay, divide 82 by four, come up with how many flights you're going to put out, put a couple of spare flights for anybody that dropped up, all the [refueling] tankers up, and they'd say hit JCS-1, which would be a bridge. And so you'd end up there within five minutes of each other, 80 airplanes in a row in a big stream coming from the same direction and all trying to bomb this bridge . . . Bridges weren't a fun target because one, they were really hard to hit with a visual bomb, and secondly, they're strong if you really hit them. I mean if you just hit the top or whatever, the bomb goes off, doesn't hurt the bridge, but you had to get the abutment where the bridge was held on . . . But things like that, those JCS targets were generally really crummy, people hated them because they were all done just academically, they had nothing to do with any kind of sensible targeting it seemed like.

Pilots who flew missions over North Vietnam had to concern themselves with a number of obstacles in flight: ground fire on the way to the target, SAMs, other friendly aircraft in the area, refueling during the mission, and enemy aircraft, just to name a few.

There were also multiple rules of engagement (ROEs) set by American political and military leaders that served as authorizations for all combat operations in the war. The ROEs were there to govern the battlefield, prevent geographic expansion of the war, and to limit civilian casualties, or collateral damage. However, these ROEs fluctuated throughout the war and, controversially, often restricted the US air forces from attacking certain targets in North Vietnam. For example, Soviet ships that ferried in supplies to the DRV sat safely in Haiphong Harbor. Chinese trucks, equipment and personnel making their way through northern North Vietnam were off limits. The American political leadership did not want to start a larger conflict with North Vietnam's more powerful Cold War allies. During certain periods of the air war against North Vietnam, American pilots could not attack targets of opportunity within given coordinates, marked by concentric circles, around Hanoi. These safe zones would expand and shrink and disappear for periods of time, depending on the political situation in Washington. These limitations were extremely frustrating to pilots who believed they were not able to attack the enemy with full capability as had been done in previous wars. Ken Craig comments on this:

All of us felt that we were carrying one hand behind our back because of the rules of engagement . . . some of them were humane and caring in aspect of trying to save innocent lives, etc, etc. But it just seemed to me where we lost the idea of what war is about. If we're going to commit and get our own guys killed, then we ought to extract an equal and greater cost to the enemy for that and I don't think we traded our lives very well at all. But we lost too many people on ineffective and worthless missions and didn't hurt the enemy enough. I think everybody from top down had this feeling that the military was not being appreciated by the [political] leadership and were doing a lot of things that inhibited us from even having a winning strategy. And Americans don't like to lose.

Richard Hamilton concurs with Craig:

We all thought it was idiocy . . . these rules of engagement . . . [W]e had this huge grease pencil board and it [contained] the rules of engagement, it was just full. You'd see these things and they'd change about once a week, so you had to make sure of what you could do or what you couldn't do. And every time they'd come out with another one, it seemed like it was stupider . . . But it was things like, if there's an anti-aircraft battery posted in the city, in the town square, you couldn't attack even if they shot at you because you might hit somebody else. And of course those days a good bomber could maybe get 50, 60 feet from the target, that's an average. So those things came up and that was frustrating, but most of us learned to live with it, but it was pretty crummy when you'd fly over [an] airport and see MiGs sitting on the ground and you couldn't attack them . . . There were a lot of restrictions that really made people mad.

Another one is we'd go out over these [rivers] and we'd see these sampans [small Vietnamese boats] and different stuff coming down the coast, and they'd be in groups of three and four and you knew they were carrying stuff . . . We'd go buzz them every once in a while if you had gas and you could see munitions on them, and we'd say, "Let us hit those." "No, they could be fisherman." And you'd see junks [small Vietnamese boats] and stuff and they're going down there and then they'd shoot at you but you couldn't shoot at them.

In the skies over South Vietnam, there were many American aircraft performing multiple duties in support of the war effort. For example, there were Forward Air Controllers (FACs) who, most of the time, piloted small, propeller-driven aircraft directing jet air strikes on an enemy position, B-52s flying at high altitude dropping thousands of pounds of bombs on enemy positions, Cobra helicopter gunships supporting helicopter combat assaults and jets providing close air support for troops on the ground.

FACs performed one of the more dangerous and underappreciated duties of the air war. The FAC flew at very low altitude, only hundreds of feet off the ground, usually in a slow moving propeller plane (sometimes in jets - a 'fast FAC'), looking for enemy troops or targets of opportunity. Once they spotted a target, they would call in air strikes. The pilot would mark the target usually by firing a rocket at the spot where he wanted the bombs or gunship fire to hit. Air Force pilot William Tilton describes a memorable FAC mission when he marked a road target near the all-important Mu Gia pass, one of the mountain passes through the Annam Cordillera mountain range bordering Laos and Vietnam. The pass served as one of the Ho Chi Minh Complex feeder routes from Laos into South Vietnam:

> We heard that there were some trucks burning along Route 23, the main road down from Mu Gia Pass towards Tchepone [Laos] . . . we saw a column of smoke and headed right for it . . . The first plane . . . [had] drop[ped] some bombs into the road area [and] got some fire started immediately . . . I think there were 16 trucks – looked like tank trucks – plus innumerous [*sic*] other vehicles . . . it was very dramatic. The guy in the backseat [of my plane] had me circle it and we stayed there and we put more air strikes in on it. We had some B-52s [also go in] . . . we were hearing a lot of secondary explosions so [I] got a grease pencil . . . and we started marking them on the side window, which is where we usually kept our strike information . . . I don't remember how many there were but there were hundreds and hundreds of secondary explosions . . . they were very loud. You could feel them, actually, and they were in towering flames . . . The next day is was still smoking. That was a pretty good strike.

Because they were so low to the ground, FACs often took significant enemy fire. Air Force pilot Frank Stone III served in 1968 and 1969 as an O-2 pilot and Night Forward Air Controller. He remembers taking ground fire after marking a target at night:

We are talking about machine gun or less . . . Many times I'd roll in [and] mark a target and they knew they had been discovered and just a wall of bullets would come at us. The O-2 was good in that respect since it had two engines, you could turn your lights out and put the props out of synch and they couldn't tell where you were. Then it would just roll off . . . and you'd see them firing in some other area but they couldn't pinpoint you by sound at that point.

The dense jungle foliage of southern and central Vietnam provided the NVA and Viet Cong soldiers places in which they could hide, eat, sleep and live relatively safe from enemy attack. More important, this ground cover also provided a base from which they could launch ambushes and general attacks upon American and Allied forces. In addition, NVA/VC soldiers and support personnel could forage the countryside for crops on which they could survive.

The United States military commanders on the ground in South Vietnam believed that one way to fight the enemy was to deny him this cover and subsistence. In the traditional sense, this usually meant seizing and occupying ground held by the enemy. In Vietnam, however, the US employed a different strategy that fitted well with the fluid nature of the battlefield. The policy was to kill the foliage, vegetation and crops outright, thereby denying the value of the land, rather than the land itself, to the enemy. To accomplish this, the US launched a massive effort to spray defoliants all over South Vietnam, in Laos and Cambodia, and along the Demilitarized Zone (DMZ), clearing hundreds of thousands of acres of land. Specially equipped C-123 aircraft, helicopters, river boats, towed vehicles and even personnel outfitted with backpacks, applied over 19 million gallons of herbicides between to the land 1961 and 1970.

The C-123 aircraft and its crews delivered over 90 percent of the total volume of herbicides used during the Vietnam War in an operation dubbed RANCH HAND. Spraying the jungle in such an aircraft took flying skills that were not normally taught in pilot training. The US began a special training program in which pilots designated for RANCH HAND could train to fly these very dangerous, low-level spray missions over hostile territory.

Once in country and on mission, pilots of the C-123s flew multiple missions that involved a number of individuals and aircraft working together. An important ingredient in the success of a mission was the type of defoliant used. Robert Turk flew 274 missions as an Air Force C-123 pilot between March 1969 and March 1970. He describes the different types

US C-123s spray defoliant on to the jungle below at treetop level in South Vietnam on an Operation RANCH HAND mission. These aircraft were specially modified with a herbicide delivery system that sprayed a thousand gallons of defoliant in a matter of minutes and could typically cover a wide area of territory.

of herbicides used in Vietnam and how they would be used on a particularly dense area:

> We had three different types of agents; we had agents White, Orange and Blue . . . Blue would burn in seven days, Orange would burn in 14 and White would burn in 21 days . . . We'd spray along the Cambodian border; I remember spraying there one mission out of Bien Hoa . . . and it had a triple canopy type thing and we were working on the top canopy and that would take the top canopy off and then we'd go in and go after the second canopy . . . and then the third canopy so that air FACs could see any [enemy] movement down there along the trails.

Flying at such low altitude presented the crews with another major problem: enemy fire. Often this consisted of small-arms fire from individual VC or NVA soldiers. Although some of the weapons employed were not the most sophisticated, the impact on the flight crews could be devastating. Air Force co-pilot Charles Hubbs remembers one such incident from a low-level mission during his 1966–67 tour:

> We only flew at 100 feet. Somebody before I got there came back with an arrow stuck in his airplane . . . I heard every round fired that ever went into my airplane . . . I'm flying with Ralph and he's a big guy. He was like an All-American at the University of Texas, football player. He's in the right seat and I'm in the left seat . . . we took one in the cockpit and I heard it hit . . . I never heard a bullet hit a person before but I knew that hit him. I thought he was dead . . . I said, "Ralph?" He said, "What?" "Are you all right?" "Yes, of course I'm all right. Hang in there and get your God damn stuff together." "Ok." So I look over at him and he's got a Bowie knife out, like Jim Bowie had, that big, and he's picking shrapnel and stuff out of his arm. I almost threw up. That bothered me more than bullets coming in the cockpit.

Enemy soldiers who fired at defoliation aircraft sometimes inadvertently revealed their own positions on the ground. In these cases, cover aircraft flying near the defoliation planes could respond from the air, often with lethal accuracy. Robert Turk recalled the details of one such mission:

> . . . we were coming, spraying down a hill and then making a turn at the bottom and we took a bullet right in over the pilot's head. I was co-pilot. We used to call him 'Magnet Ass,' because he always got shot. He flew a little bit high but the Plexiglas hit us all and I thought I'd been hit . . . I just remember the fact that the bullet came in and it kind of knocked us a little silly. We weren't really talking too much and the guy in the back threw out the smoke grenade, the [cover] fighter saw the person that shot us and killed [him]. Meanwhile, the other fighter came in and put down some suppression fire with 20 millimeters on the side, scaring the living daylights out of us. It looked like . . . you haven't lived until you're flying one hundred feet off the ground [and] you've got a 20mm [cannon] going off right next to you.

Another common type of combat in the air was close air support of ground units. Infantry on the ground could call in attack aircraft (fixed wing and helicopter) to shoot at or bomb enemy positions. This kind of support for ground troops was vital for the successful prosecution of the American war effort. Marine John Arick flew close-in fire support for infantry and other air components in the UH-1E helicopter and the Cobra AH-1G helicopter gunship in Vietnam. He describes how a typical insertion of troops would be covered:

> Four or five transport helicopters would be carrying a company of Marines and two or four Marine Hueys would be escorting. When we'd get over the zone, the Huey flight lead would talk to the ground if there was anybody on the ground already and say, "We've got your company coming in," and we'd put them on the ground. More likely, we would be putting this company in where nobody else had been or nobody else had been recently. So, the lead section of Hueys would make a pass over, identify the zone, do the navigating . . . fly around, see if there was anything, good, bad. Occasionally, but not normally, we would just expend some ammo, a few rockets, a few guns just to let the bad guys know that we were there, that we were ready to shoot and we softened up the [landing] zone. So the lead section would fly across the zone, low. The transports would come in and land. We'd come back around. The second section would come in if there were two sections . . . We'd come in while they were on the ground, fly over, look for bad guys. If they started taking fire, the second section would return the fire with their door gunners probably because they were down low. We'd be up high . . . and in a position once the target was identified to roll in with the external munitions, rockets and guns and shoot at the bad guys. Then as the transports were ready to come out, they'd call, "Coming out," and whatever section was in the rotation would come down on either side of them and just let the bad guys know you were there and they'd be lifting out.

When infantry units needed more firepower on the ground, either for protection from the enemy or to bolster their offensive maneuvers, close air support was a good answer. Door gunner Gregory Burch remembers his helicopter gunship coming in to rescue a besieged infantry unit:

> [The enemy troops] were kicking the shit out of this poor

Cav[alry] unit. They were blowing up their tanks, their armored personnel carriers, they were mortaring them. You could hear the guys screaming on the radios, "Come help me! Oh my god!" They were getting overrun and you could hear this going on. And we're like, "Where are they?" One particular lieutenant cracked, literally cracked. You'd hear him crack on the radio, [saying] "Get the fucking platoon sergeant over there!" "Well he's dead." "Well find me somebody!" The battalion commander is up there screaming and yelling, "Find me somebody to take over that platoon!" because the guy cracked and his platoon sergeant had been killed. Finally some private got on the radio, and [the commander] said, "Son, you're a sergeant! Get those men organized, get your asses organized!" And he was yelling at this poor private and the private's like, "I don't know what to do, sir." "Well, this is what you do, pop smoke, we'll send the gunships and they'll shoot the enemy." He popped smoke, and of course the enemy popped the same color smoke because they're listening in. Well, that didn't work and they tried, finally, I think what it was, the [enemy] . . . had blue, they had red, they had yellow, but they didn't have green and we finally got green smoke and we finally figured out where this poor platoon of armored personnel carriers was and we rolled in and we just sprayed everything around them. The guy said, "Bunch up! Get in the middle because the gunships are going to come in and kill everything that walks crawls or moves, within fifty!" We could get right down there on the deck and we went in and [I] remember . . . just shooting everything. We could see them running around. Once we rolled in the VC realized it was over, and they were trying to get away. We didn't let them get away.

Marine pilot Neil Whitehurst recalls flying his AH-1G Cobra helicopter gunship in support of besieged infantry and medical personnel during his 1970–71 tour of duty:

I think about an operation at a place called Phong Duc . . . which was a metropolitan area, a city with apartment complexes and high-rise buildings and which was south of Marble Mountain going down towards [the] Phu Bai area. And evidently an entire North Vietnamese regiment had come down a dry riverbed at night and attacked the United States Army Special Forces A Team or B Team . . . And we got a call that they were under siege and

that there were multiple medevacs and we launched everything
we had ... We flew out [to] Phong Duc ... around them was a
city and we encountered something that I'd never encountered
before. In fact, I didn't even [know] there were such a thing that
were called airburst mortars. I'd seen anti-aircraft fire in the old
World War II flak guns going off, but I'd never seen airburst
mortars in which the NVA would fire a mortar round and of
course as it peaked its trajectory and started down, at some point
in the air, 200, 300, 400 feet, it would explode. Of course, this was
specifically to take care of helicopters and that was really an eye-
opener because we were getting shot at almost from above as it
was dropping down instead of coming up.

There was an airfield nearby. They had these military
revetments where aircraft had normally been placed to try to keep
them from getting shrapnel in case they were to get bombarded
... I can remember flying over that particular area and seeing
many, many people huddled in these revetments and stretchers
... And we actually put, at one time, five CH-46s down at one
time [and] ... we were covering them and they were just loading
them up with medevacs just as fast as you can ... But the thing
that I remember about it was that and the old stupid rules of
engagement, while we're circling, 180 degrees out protecting
these birds on the ground, we're taking fire from an apartment
building, from an AK-47 or SKS. I went by, maybe the 8th or 10th
floor one time, and I was eyeball to eyeball and I looked in the
very end unit. There's this NVA soldier and he was a tall guy. He
was a nice looking fellow. He had a weapon. He was so disciplined
that he was taking careful aim and firing single shots at me, not
my airplane, but at me. And every time I went by, I'd kick my
rudder just so I would turn my tail to him a little bit which would
present a little less of a target. I was the pilot at the time flying
in the back seat and the rounds were landing like a foot behind
my head every time. In fact, he actually ended up shooting my
air conditioning unit out which just really teed me off. I kept
talking to my section leader ... and I'm saying, "I'm taking fire.
I'm taking fire from the 10th floor or 8th floor ... end unit,
permission to return fire." He [section leader] said, "No, we're in
a civilian area. We cannot return fire." I knew that the young boy
in front [in the front seat] was going to be nailed very shortly and
I knew that this was really not good.

So when the last of the five [evacuation] planes lifted off, I was fortunate enough to be the last bird that came around, that chased the planes out . . . And just as I got up to about to level with that floor, I said, I can't stand this any more. I selected ripple salvo on my 19-shot rocket pod and hit hard left paddle and turned my aircraft 90 degrees and I was not more than 300 yards away, 200 yards away and I just put about 38 rockets in that corner of that building. And I don't feel like I hurt anybody else. I mean, they [the rockets] all went in very small areas. I expected to hear something about it when I got back, but I didn't. It took out just kind of a corner of the building. I wasn't that proud . . . it was a mixed feeling, you know. It's one of those feelings you get when you're 23 years old that you probably wouldn't do again if you were 35.

High-altitude bombing was one of the many ways the US used its firepower to destroy the enemy. The B-52 unleashed massive amounts of ordnance upon the enemy and was one of the most frequently used American weapons in the air. Nguyen Phat Le was an NVA officer who fought in South Vietnam against the US and the South Vietnamese. He remembers experiencing a B-52 strike near Cu Chi in August 1965:

The first time in Ben Cat we were eating, when the B-52s came. They came in three at a time and dropped the bombs; the second group of three came five minutes after the first three left. The bombing was like an earthquake. Both big and small trees fell to the ground. We were living in underground shelters. My shelter collapsed, although it was not hit by the bombing. I felt like I was sitting in a metal case with someone outside hitting [it] repeatedly with a hammer. Through the gap we saw the area around us was covered with fire and smoke; [I] thought if one was attacked by B-52s it would be very hard to escape. My shelter collapsed and buried some of my friends. I felt like [I was] dead. We were terrified. I was close to the call [almost killed] many times. When we were moving out of 'R' region to go to local areas where we were to be stationed, the Americans were carrying out a military operation in the area, and the whole unit of a thousand men had to move from village to village by underground tunnels. Some parts of the tunnels collapsed due to the B-52s' bombing. We had to look for the way out. Sometimes we had to crawl through small holes just like a snake. The tunnels [around Cu Chi] were so crowded and lacked so much air that I fainted.

South Vietnamese Ambassador Nguyen Xuan Phong remembers what his uncles, who were NVA officers, told him about the B-52 bombing on the Ho Chi Minh Trail Complex in Laos:

My uncles said that they were many times on the Ho Chi Minh Trail and they had prepared themselves [for B-52 strikes]. They have big holes all along . . . You may use carpet bombing on those trails but carpet bombing would be effective only if they were not notified in advance . . . but as soon as your B-52s took off from Thailand or from anywhere else those Soviet 'fishing ships' out there [in the Gulf of Tonkin] informed them right away. Even in five minutes they were able to jump into their holes, put on the concrete cover and wait for the bombs to stop. You can throw any amount of bombs on them [but] that wouldn't destroy [the] trail.

The voices of combat experiences in Vietnam describe only one aspect of the war in Vietnam. Parallel to the memories of combat are the remembrances of those whom the Americans fought against and fought with – their enemies and allies.

4
THE ENEMY AND THE ALLIES

THE ENEMY

What did the American forces in Vietnam think of the enemy, whom they often could not even see? What did Americans and their allies see as the strengths and weaknesses of the North Vietnamese Army (NVA) and the Viet Cong? What was it like to face them in battle? The answers to these questions lie in the experiences of the men and women who faced the enemy, whether in the jungles or rice paddies, in the air or on the rivers. And they vary according to location, job specialty and personality. However, there are some notable consistencies when it comes to describing the enemy forces. Mike Cisco was a Marine sniper in the war. He remembers his feelings toward the enemy, feelings shared by many other American combat personnel:

> They were excellent . . . [W]hat you were there for was to make sure that you survived, and I don't think in general we hated [them]. In fact, if you look back at history, most . . . elite or professional soldiers or armies don't hate each other; it's a contest. It's a contest of gladiators. The best man wins. I think they had respect for us. We always heard they feared Marines more than others. I don't know that. The actions that they took against us made us think that was true. One thing we were always pretty well told was never to be captured as a Marine because of what they would do.

In the jungles of South Vietnam, contact with Communist forces usually was made by setting off a trip wire, a booby trap or simply walking into a well-laid ambush. James Wheeler, Jr, describes how he and his men could tell the enemy was close:

> There was something in the air. Their smell emanated in the air if they were in proximity. I'm not talking like it was something that you could just color in and see all the time.

Mastery and use of Vietnam's diverse terrains was one of the Viet Cong's principal battlefield advantages. VC fighters were especially adept at camouflage and concealment techniques that incorporated local features, both in the jungle and in open areas, as this captured photograph illustrates.

There were those instances where in proximity of the enemy either during a fight, after a fight or whatever it might have been, there was a smell. It was there. I guess you would say their body smell. Some people call it the smell of fear. I don't know if you've heard that term. I dare say if I smelled it at this moment I could probably say, "That's it" or "That isn't." It was just a dull, dank . . . nothing that I could really relate it to. I don't know that I could even say bad odor, bad body odor. I don't even know if you call it that. It was unique unto itself . . . It heightened your alertness.

Mike Bradbury, a Marine rifleman, remembers his general impressions of the NVA and VC. He faced combatants from both armies in the field in Vietnam, and respected them for their strengths:

The NVA is the only ones I really know about, I don't think I ever seen a VC. All I know about the VC, what I've heard about them, a lot of them are farmers by the daytime . . . I probably seen some Viet Congs, didn't know about it, but then [they laid] out on land booby traps for you. The NVA would pretty much fight you on your own ground, they would swap shots with you . . . and they would come charging up to the concertina wire [on a camp's perimeter]. And I had a certain amount of respect for them because they would kill us in formation and "Hey, alright guys, let's get it on," where the Viet Cong you hardly wouldn't see them. You would run into their booby traps and stuff laced with poison, the punji pit [a camouflaged hole in the ground with sharpened stakes implanted in it], and stuff like that. The NVA, well they were gutsier . . . [One of their strengths was] their persistence. We hammered them with B-52s; we hammered them and they wouldn't give up; you know they might retreat and they might regroup somewhere but they were not giving it up no matter what we hit them with. Their determination – we had them outgunned, we had an arsenal we never used . . . and they lived out there in the field, they lived off the land. I don't think their food supply was as good as ours but they're used to living in their back yard and you know when you're fighting on your home turf . . . it seems like you want to hold on to it more than the guy that is trying to move you out of there . . . The NVA, the strength of the enemy, was just determination to hang on no matter what we did to them . . .

Andy DeBona, the Marine Company Commander, gives his opinion of the VC and NVA:

The Viet Cong were not as well trained; in indoctrination, yes, all of them obviously had to be the same level of indoctrination just by virtue of the war that they were fighting way back in the mountains in the primitive conditions that they lived in. The support of the NVA, the logistical support was not really good. Their medics – we did find a couple of hospitals, one hospital in particular when we were in the Phu Bai area and nurses – they did have some female nurses and I am sure they had corpsmen with them, but we never got to see them because . . . when we would spring one of these ambushes, we would kill them all or wound them or take prisoners. So the VC were, in my opinion, not as professional simply because logistically, they were not able to be supported, they didn't have radios with them. The NVA battalion [that] was moving through did, but the VC, per se, were second-teamers. It's almost like [the NVA] read the same books as we did as far [as] infantry assaults.

One particular time in September, the battalion got hit with mortars, artillery, rockets, followed by a frontal assault; I mean it's just right out of the text book, across open ground, rice paddies and it's the first time that I have ever seen that, up to that point . . . Common tactics of the two groups, normally the VC, [in] my experience, would be [an] ambush type thing, picking on a soft target – when I say a soft target [I mean] either a probe or an outpost, somewhere that wasn't well defended. The NVA would have a much larger force involved while the biggest VC force we ever ran into was a platoon reinforced; the NVA we ran into were in regiments.

Marine Don Cuneo, who served in Vietnam in 1966, recalls that the NVA did have weaknesses. The most important, he thought, was their stubborn execution of battle plans, even when the plan was no good:

They weren't innovative. They weren't flexible if their original plan didn't go right. That was one of our strong points, that we could invent a battle in the middle of a battle. We could handle change and they couldn't. If they would attack you and the attack didn't go the way that it was supposed to and it got stalled in some way, they'd mill around and were easy pickings.

Marine aviator Neil Whitehurst, who flew helicopters in Vietnam in 1970, agrees:

The NVA – sometimes they were too disciplined. They didn't have the ability to . . . make a modification to [a] particular squad or fire team . . . or reconstitute, or fight a delaying action. The NVA, a lot of times, they blew the bugle, they would attack and they kept on attacking until someone blew the bugle to retreat. If the bugler got killed, they'd keep on attacking until they all died, just about. It was kind of like Pickett's Charge at Gettysburg.

Don Cuneo also remembers that it was sometimes important to be able to tell the difference between VC and NVA soldiers, especially when they were out of uniform. The Marines devised a method, as Cuneo explains:

> The haircut was the give away. If a guy had a real close-cropped haircut, he was [an NVA] soldier. If he just had the regular – I don't know how to explain it, not a military haircut – then you knew the guy was probably Viet Cong.

When Communist combatants surrendered or defected, South Vietnamese or American interrogators tried to elicit tactical and operational information from them, and occasionally were able to obtain their active assistance in the field. From these sources, the Americans learned about the hardships faced by the enemy they confronted, as Mike Bradbury recalls:

> We had a *Chieu Hoi* [a defector] down there, he was like a Kit Carson scout [defectors who go in the field with the American troops], and . . . he is just a little peasant soldier. They [Hanoi] had him carry two rockets all the way down the Ho Chi Minh Trail, way down almost in the Delta. He hand-packed them, and he evaded air raids that he happened to get caught in . . . and he got down there and got the two rockets [delivered, and] inside of a day they fired both of them at one of our installations. Then [the Communist commanders] told [him] to go back up north and get two more. He went crazy, took his pistol out, shot the guy that ordered him to do it and then came over and defected [to] our side.

In the Mekong Delta the labyrinth of rivers and canals greatly complicated the Americans' efforts to interdict Communist supply lines and isolate the Viet Cong from noncombatant villagers. The US Navy deployed newly designed boats and specially trained men, but the Viet Cong had mastered the riverine battlefield environment, as Michael Harris remembers:

> They always invariably shot for the engines [on our boats], and [they] disabled engines, and when they could do that they would create a chaos in the middle of the river, especially in a tight river, and then we would have to work our way out of it while they continued to shoot us up. Then they also, when we had troops on board, they would shoot those rockets up at a trajectory where they would hit underneath the flight deck, on the inside

preferably, and all the shrapnel would come down on the troops. That was extremely successful. So, they weren't dumb. They knew what they were doing.

US Navy forces deployed on the rivers and canals of the Mekong Delta region faced different weapons. Michael Harris also remembers the enemy weapons that were most feared during his tour in the Delta in 1968–69:

They had a B-40 and a B-50 rocket launcher . . . The rockets had stages; they would burn through metal and explode and keep going and explode a second and third time. Our boats actually had half-inch rebar around the outsides everywhere possible . . . to try to set off that first stage of the rocket, but invariably it would burn on inside and explode and the shrapnel would go off of all the steel and end up wounding many guys . . . I recall the damage done by these rockets. It would look just like you had a cutting torch and you would cut a piece of one-inch metal. It would just burn. One incident we had [came when we had] just offloaded troops in a very small river and I was sitting up on top on the radio and kind of turned to my left and a Viet Cong stood up – I very seldom saw the Viet Cong, only on three occasions – stood up with one of these B-40 rocket launchers, took his time to aim at my boat, and released the rocket in a big puff of black smoke and it was the typical slow motion thing. The rocket came, missed me by about six feet, missed our boat by about six inches, and he was aiming in the place that would do the most damage, and it hit a tree on the other side of us and the tree fell over . . . The officer jumped on the radio and wanted to know if anybody saw it, and I told him right where it was, so they moved a napalm Zippo in there and flamed the area and there was two dead Viet Cong in a hole there. So, that was the most feared weapon. Of course the mines were always a great fear because they could take an entire boat out. We had one boat, Tango 151-5, run right over a 500 pounder. They estimated it just collapsed the boat like a sandwich and killed two Americans and some ARVN and the boat immediately sunk. So there was always that threat of the water-borne mines [too].

US Marine Mike Bradbury remembers the enemy weapons he and his men feared most:

[We feared] the mortars because they were so good with them. They didn't even have high-tech sights on them. They had a little traverse shroud and the two peg poles, two steel pegs in the ground with a little aiming stake hanging from a stick and they'd just run it back and forth, "Yeah, that looks good," and drop one in. The gooks, they could land a 61mm mortar in your back pocket, they were that good. They had higher explosive weapons, the RPGs [rocket-propelled grenades] were feared . . . but they weren't all that accurate. If an RPG hit you, now that's what we call the "Gook Bazooka", that was very destructive, but the ending sights were crude on them and they weren't all that good with them. The 122 [mm] rocket, we didn't fear too much [from] those because they saved those for the main bases, not the smaller bases, but the mortars! They were, well they weren't the most powerful weapon they had, but they were deadly accurate with those things.

Frank Gutierrez was an Army rifleman operating in the field in the Cu Chi sector. In this area northwest of Saigon, Communist forces had developed a vast underground tunnel complex that provided shelter for both men and supplies. The complex included hospitals, training areas, billets and caverns for weapons, ammunition and food storage. The tunnels also provided access to American camps for Viet Cong combatants and spies, as Gutierrez recalls:

We got to the point where . . . we had a lot of attacks during the day. At any time you could get mortared and you would have to run to the bunkers and hope you didn't get hit. There were a lot of guys that got killed during the day because of mortars . . . And we'd get a lot of probes into the bunker when the Viet Cong would come and try to get into the wire. We were right on top of them, so [the VC] wasn't necessarily [actually] com[ing] through the wire because they would come up in holes because of the tunnel system. That's what made it particularly dangerous because we never knew where they were going to pop up. We often wondered how things happened in the night and we never saw what was going on, guys getting their throats cut. Nobody ever knew where [the Viet Cong] were going to come from. [This happened on base] quite often. They were in there, so they knew exactly what we were doing. We knew that there was a tunnel system, but we didn't know how extensive it was. My understanding is . . . that one of the high level commanding officers killed some Viet Cong popping up out of a hole right into division headquarters . . . As a matter of fact, I found out later that the Viet Cong were calling in direct fire into the base camp, inside the base camp. So, they were inside the wire – so they knew exactly what was going on.

The Communists' electronic communications and intelligence gathering systems were also surprisingly sophisticated. As Ray French, a US analyst during the war, recalls, the enemy's electronic intelligence operations made them even more formidable opponent:

North Vietnam communications were very crude compared to ours, but it was also very effective for guerilla-type warfare . . . From [the] strategic viewpoint of the North Vietnamese, it allowed them to get the proper information to their field commanders and also [to] maximize the Viet Cong effort in support of the North Vietnamese . . . They knew who the enemy was, they knew what the terrain was, and the field of battle, and they also had collected from the Russians and the Chinese some technology whereby they were able to, through the use of signal intelligence, collect our [operational] orders for our aircraft. They were able to collect air order of battle information in respect to where our [air] forces were going to be, as well as our ground forces, and this made them very attuned to what was going to happen from our planning sources. Our communications were doing a lot of things 'in the clear,' meaning that the bulk of our communications when we entered Vietnam was non-secure. The use of secure communications was practically nil during the Vietnam War. They used collection devices to collect an awful lot of information.

The Viet Cong and NVA, meanwhile, had their own appraisals of American forces during the war. Nguyen Phat Le, an NVA officer, describes his opinion of the Americans during the war:

You cannot fight well without hatred. However, I think the Americans fought better than the ARVN. The Chinese said, "In order to destroy one US battalion the VC needs one division," but Nguyen Chi Thanh [People's Army of Vietnam/NVA general,

Viet Cong combatants were highly mobile, and could relocate quickly to take advantage of changing tactical situations. In this captured Viet Cong photograph, guerrilla fighters are shown moving through dense underbrush with their automatic weapons.

commander of operations in South Vietnam, 1965–67] did not think so. He argued that if we needed one division to fight against one US battalion we should quit fighting Americans because we did not have enough men for that. He believed that the VC could fight the Americans one on one; one VC division could fight one US division. But in order to fight the Americans, one must get close to them, not fight from a distance. The best way to fight the Americans was to fight them when they were moving or at night when they [were] stationed together. The VC fighting tactics were different from those of the Americans. They would surround enemy with ground forces and destroy them with artillery and rockets rather than attacking directly with ground forces. One time after being attacked the Americans used helicopters to drop their men to surround us with the intention to destroy us but they did not succeed because we knew very well the geographic set up of the region; we withdrew fast and the next day we returned with tanks to pick up the dead bodies. The area was flattened after the battle. Three villages in Suoi Cut were destroyed but the inhabitants were not so sad because they collected a lot of money and personal possessions left behind by us and by the Americans. We had a different view about killing. We killed the enemies, the aggressors, to regain independence for our country and to save our people. We did not feel guilty about the killing, therefore we had no nightmares; not like the Americans – when they killed they thought they killed a Vietnamese as a human being.

THE ALLIES – SOUTH VIETNAM
As for the Americans' view of the South Vietnamese forces, experiences and opinions varied. Ron Ballweg, an Army helicopter pilot, remembers very distinctly how he saw the ARVN:

[They were] worthless. We would take them out in the morning on a search and destroy mission and drop them. We'd pick them up at 5:00 that evening. They'd all have dead chickens hanging over their shoulders. It was a big game to them. I remember one time we had an insertion [a helicopter lift of troops into a battlefield] and this [ARVN] guy wouldn't get out [of the helicopter]. Now that scared us. He ran back and forth from side to side in that aircraft . . . He didn't speak English but I made sure that he knew that he was getting out the next time, one way or the other . . . He could have had a [bomb] satchel on him. We don't know. Because during the day they were your friends, at night they were the VC. That was not a comfortable ride . . .

Charles Lloyd served in the US Navy on river patrol boats in the Mekong Delta. He remembers how he felt about his counterparts in the South Vietnamese Navy:

The [South Vietnam] Navy . . . where we were, was an irregular thing. It was like, I don't want to say the Navy Reserve; the 'junk force' they called it. They just had those old wooden junks and they had primitive weapons, old World War II stuff . . . We'd find them sleeping at night and we were out there patrolling. Sometimes you didn't know whose side they were on. These Popular Forces weren't worth a hoot when they attacked the base camp. They went and sat off [like] a bunch of monkeys or something. I didn't trust them at all . . . The Navy was just some Junior Lieutenants and they were okay. They used to invite us to parties and have a few drinks and stuff. One day they brought a ship down there, a small one, smaller than those destroyer escorts . . . It was just like an overgrown gunboat and we had given it to them, so it was run by the Vietnamese Navy, what little navy they had, and that thing was so screwed up. I mean, nothing worked on it. It couldn't hit the broad side of a barn.

There was one really fat guy, one of the Navy Junior Officers there . . . they called him "the tiger" or something like that. He was just so gung ho. He didn't last very long. There weren't too many like him but . . . I guess they had some good ones. They had very poor leadership, a lot of corruption, and they just weren't as motivated as the VC or the others. The North Vietnamese were [motivated] because of the ideology behind [their war].

American forces worked with the 'Ruff Puffs,' or the 'RF/PFs,' South Vietnam's Regional Forces and the Popular Forces. The RF/PFs were a local militia/police force created in 1953 by the French who hoped to use them in their effort to pacify the countryside and hold on to their colonial empire in Southeast Asia. After the French defeat, President Ngo Dinh Diem transformed the RF/PFs into the Civil Guard (CG). The CG was then divided in half to create, first, the People's Self-Defense Force (PSDF), which later became known as the Popular Forces. The remaining CG units were known as the Regional Forces. The RF/PFs totaled 304,494 in 1968 (152,549 RFs and 151,945 PFs). Members served near their villages, working with the ARVN and the American military forces in the local countryside. US Navy veteran Charles Lloyd remembers a unique experience with a PF soldier's wife:

We had humanitarian duties . . . Some of these Popular Force soldiers that were assigned to the Green Berets, [and] one of those [PF's] wives was having a baby, [which] was coming out the wrong way. There was something wrong with the birth. We had to pick her up from that same camp, get out [of] that shallow [water] and go all the way back up to where the ship was anchored to take her to the doctor on the support ship. It was the seaward side of the island [and] it gets kind of rough sometimes, so we were flying off there, bouncing around as usual. My boatswain's mate sticks his head up and he says, "Mr. Lloyd, you better slow down, I think she's having a baby." I said, "Oh shit." He says, "What do you do?" I said, "What *do* I do?" . . . I said, "Put some hot water on her." We had one burner stove bolted next to the navigation lead to make coffee with. So he comes on, sticks his head back up there, "Well I got the hot water, now what do I do with it?" [I said] "I don't know! God damn if I know! Make her some tea or something. I don't know what the hell you're supposed to do with it." . . . So I just put [it] as fast as this thing would go, got her to the ship and the baby was supposed to come out as they were carrying her up the ladder to the ship, [to] sick bay. A couple guys going behind her would have to catch it when it fell out. That was, if she had it out on [our] . . . boat . . . [the baby] probably would have died or something.

The US forces also worked with Montagnard tribes in the mountains of Vietnam, using them as local self-defense units. Originally formed in 1961, the US Army Special Forces reorganized the local tribesmen into Civilian Irregular Defense Groups (CDIGs) in 1963. The CDIG mission was to conduct border surveillance in the Central Highlands area on the South Vietnam–Laos border. These groups operated out of remote mountain camps, stopping VC and NVA infiltration and working as mobile strike, or 'Mike Force', battalions supporting each other. There were about 40,000 tribesmen in the CDIG force, all of whom received salaries, development aid for their tribes and medical care. James McLeroy served with the US Army in Vietnam as an Infantry Officer with the 5th Special Forces Group and patrolled with the CDIGs:

The US team Sergeant would plan the patrol routes and we would patrol in a fan shape [pattern] – basically loop patrols in various directions around the camp . . . Of course the one and only tactic was, you stomp around until you bump into somebody and then they all go to ground and then I get on the radio and try to get some air strikes in there. And that's it! It was like Forward Air Control with a bunch of jerks running around, but . . . they [the CDIG] didn't believe in fire and maneuver [tactics] . . . They felt that the Americans were going to do the fighting and they were just going to be there to go along and that's how they earned their pay . . . and if they could kill one VC then they felt that patrol was a success and now it's

'Combat taxis' of the US Army's 145th Combat Aviation Battalion maneuver into position to extract soldiers of the ARVN 25th Infantry Division following a combat operation in 1966. Air mobility tactics, which relied upon helicopter-borne troops and supplies, were central to American planning for battlefield cooperation with South Vietnam's forces.

time to go home . . . They had a kind of an unwritten contract: "Okay. We understand we have to go on these little patrols and we've got to try to kill a VC, but once we do that now, we've earned our [night's] ration, let's go back to the camp now." They would just refuse to go on certain [patrols]. I saw one of them get killed just because of sheer laziness. He wouldn't take proper cover and concealment and he got his blanket wet and he wanted to dry it and he was smoking a cigarette and stood up to hang his blanket out to dry and a VC shot him dead . . . You think about losing your life over something like that. When you know that all you've got to do is stay down and stay wet and don't dry your blanket out and don't smoke a cigarette . . . and you can live. But they're that kind of people. I just didn't have any respect for them . . . It was just bullshit.

THE KOREANS

From 1965, the Republic of Korea (South Korea) deployed tens of thousands of ground troops to Vietnam. The Korean force level in Vietnam reached a high of 50,000 men in 1968, and the Koreans remained in Vietnam until the final US withdrawal in 1973. The Korean troops were respected for their tenacity, and US servicemen nicknamed them 'the RoKs.' As Army medical technician James Calbreath remembers, the Korean troops were believed to be ready to take on any military task, and to do so with enthusiasm:

> . . . during Tet [1968] the VC had gotten into town, like they did into all towns, and had taken over the radio station and the TV station. And so they were broadcasting from the TV station and the ARVNs went in and they tried to get them out but they couldn't get them out. The US troops I don't think really ever tried to get them out. So they called in the Koreans, and the Koreans just drove a tank up in front of the building and just started firing and just literally blew the building to smithereens, went in, drug out the dead VC and hung them from a telephone pole. These were the people who were protecting us, [so I thought,] "It sounds good to me." The Koreans were tough and crazy.

The Koreans had a reputation for brutality that battle-hardened forces on all sides of the Vietnam conflict respected. Marine Don Cuneo recalls one action involving Korea's Marines in 1965:

> I remember going into a village right after the Korean Marines had been in there . . . We were told not to drink water out of the well because they had just fished some people out of there. Most villages had their own well or two. But, I know [the Koreans] had gone in there and they had taken some fire, and their edict was that "if we take fire, everybody pays for it".

AUSTRALIA AND NEW ZEALAND

One of the United States' strongest allies in Southeast Asia was Australia. Australia was a member of SEATO and supported the American policy of maintaining a sovereign, democratic and viable South Vietnam. Australia's military involvement in the Vietnam war began in 1962 with the arrival of military advisers, and it deployed its first combat troops in 1965. The peak commitment of Australian forces came in 1969 when 7,672 served in the South. Australia left South Vietnam for good in 1973 when American ground troops departed. A total of 386 Australians were killed in action in the Vietnam War and 2,193 were wounded. Australia coordinated its military efforts in South Vietnam with New Zealand. Together, the Australian and New Zealand forces numbered just under 9,000 troops at their peak. New Zealand also backed American policy in Southeast Asia and did so with military, medical and economic aid. It first dispatched personnel to the RVN in 1964 and sent combat troops in 1965. New Zealand lost 83 killed in action during the war. All New Zealand combat forces were withdrawn from South Vietnam by 1971.

The Australians and New Zealanders brought special skills to Vietnam. As Richard Brockett, a member of the Australian Army Training Team in Vietnam in 1964–65, remembers, his comrades-in-arms already had extensive experience in anti-guerrilla warfare before arriving in Vietnam:

> [Colonel] Ted [Serong] was the commander of [the Australian Army's] Training Team . . . in November 1964 when I arrived . . . His strengths were his firm conviction on the need for a coordinated pacification strategy as part of counterinsurgency and also a firm commitment to irregular warfare with civilian and police predominance plus good intelligence. That probably dates from his experiences in Burma. In my case, I would draw on my experiences in Malaya, to say, in both cases, good examples of the way it should be . . .

The Australian advisers were specifically selected for assignment to Vietnam because of their language and organization skills, and other qualifications. Richard Brockett explains:

> We were the professional soldiers and we were expected to be able to do anything the Army asked us to do, and there was no quibble about it. The selection process for the team in '64, '65, up to then was extremely rigid. You had to have psychological tests as well as various other aptitude tests to determine your suitability to such employment, one of which would be your ability to live and work largely on your own . . . I wasn't American, I wasn't Vietnamese, although I tried to be as much Vietnamese as I possibly could, so I didn't find it at all odd or at variance with my expectations in the slightest. In fact, I thoroughly enjoyed the job. It was probably the best posting I had in 22 years in the [Australian] Army, without doubt.

Allen Cameron served with the New Zealand Artillery in Vietnam from 1967 to 1968. Cameron was assigned to the 161st Field Battery and worked with Australian infantry units. He remembers how Australia and New Zealand became involved in the war and the specific ways in which their forces were suited to the task:

> The early part of 1965, as part of our SEATO commitments, I think we were invited to join [the US] party [in Vietnam]. Basically, they said, "Well we got this little scrap going in Vietnam and we'd quite appreciate a little bit of help from you, New Zealand and Australia." So the Australians decided to send an infantry battalion and New Zealand decided to send artillery battery. Now you must remember, in 1965 New Zealand had a standing army of about 5,000 soldiers, of which about 1,200 – probably somewhere between 20 or 25 percent of them – were serving in Malaya and Singapore and Borneo, so it didn't really leave an awful lot of options for the government when it came to sending troops to Vietnam. So they decided to send an artillery battery; when they did send a battery, it was a short battery. It only had four guns instead of a normal six guns that were sent over there . . . "We'll send you these guys but please don't get too many of them killed because we can't afford to lose too many."
> . . . I think it is the fact that [if] the United States Army was to lose a battalion of men, it would be a tragedy. An utter tragedy. If Australians were to lose a battalion of men or New Zealand was to lose an artillery battery, it would be a total disaster, remembering the size of the country, just over three million people . . . I think it probably frustrated the guys who went in the initial . . . group in July 1965 because they weren't supposed to be out there hunting up the Viet Cong or the North Vietnamese, although we did manage to sort of get to where we wanted to be towards the end. But that was the situation. We didn't have a huge army and we didn't have a lot of people who we could send – that tended to come later. As then in the United States there [were] those who didn't want us to send troops to Vietnam; we had the, what you call, the protest and all that sort of thing. Basically, the same as what [the Americans] had, just on a smaller scale . . .
> Then in '66 the Australians sent another battalion, plus an artillery battery. New Zealand increased its commitment to the full battery and then the Australians–New Zealanders became

Beginning in 1962 Australian military advisers, like the one shown here fording a stream in Phuoc Tuy Province north of Vung Tau, brought their experience from Malaya and Borneo to Vietnam, training South Vietnamese troops in counter-insurgency warfare. Australian forces remained in Vietnam until December 1972.

the first Australian task force which was then sent down to the Phuoc Tuy Province and based in a place called Nui Dat, Nui Dat meaning 'small hill'. It was just a dot in the map and we built this . . . base camp around it, which eventually swelled to have something about 5,500 troops . . . The one thing that I probably feel most disappointment about is that although we went there, we did the best we could with what we had [but] I don't think that we really shouldered our share of the burden, I'm talking our share of the shit . . . Yeah, we did the best we could with what we had. Now we are from experience . . . probably better at the guerilla warfare, jungle-type warfare that we did, than we are standing there in a large group and [going] toe to toe with 2,000 screaming Vietnamese and [cutting] them down. We're probably better at sneaking through the jungles and picking off one or two or three at a time, which is what we did and what we did very, very effectively because, by the time the Tet offensive came along, we had basically cleaned out

Phuoc Tuy Province, and it [had] very little guerilla warfare
going on. So at the end, I suppose the powers that be, they
passed to us to do what we're best at. It was called 'search and
destroy' . . . We went into the Viet Cong, into the areas, and we
went looking for them . . . Most of the . . . skirmishes might
have lasted an hour or more. That was about it.

Cameron also remembers how prepared the New Zealand troops were for
the type of guerilla combat that existed on the ground in Vietnam:

The call went out to the [New Zealand] Army in general: if
you want to serve in Vietnam . . . you've got to join the Royal
NZ Artillery . . . Now what served us well was the fact that . . .
most of [the soldiers] . . . had served in Malaya. Some of them
had been there twice. But they were hard regular soldiers, they
were good soldiers. They are the guys that probably taught us
more about the jungle craft, than the instructors themselves
'cause these guys . . . had served in places like Malaya and
Borneo and some of them go back as far as Korea. That's
where we got our professionalism from. Because I think it
was acknowledged – don't mean to pat myself or my fellow
soldiers on the back – [but] I think it was generally
acknowledged that the average New Zealand soldier was
probably one of the best in Vietnam, leaving aside the specialist
units . . . I had spent a reasonable amount of time in the
countryside and the bush, so the type of living in the bush was
not a problem. As I say we were a fairly small population. The
country [New Zealand] is fairly heavily forested . . . and we lived
quite easily in our bush because there was nothing in our bush
that ordinarily we don't really have. We don't have snakes, we
don't have any kind of predators. The only thing that [might]
slightly do you any harm in New Zealand's bush is a spider and
you would [have a] hell of a job finding one of them, so the
bush is quite easy to live in . . . You've got to carry your food
with you because we don't have the berries and fruits and things
that other countries do . . . Jungle craft, the military jungle craft,
well, that was taught to us as part of our training. Patrolling,
that was taught to us as part of our training. Infantry tactics,
once again, part of our training. Even as an artillery unit, we
still did infantry training.

The Australians and New Zealanders made an indelible impression on the Americans that they encountered. Joseph Pizzo worked as an Air Force mechanic. He remembers an encounter with an Australian at Phan Rang Air Base:

> I had a lot of free time. I used to go to the craft shop and work on leather wallets and things and we were actually stationed with the Australian Second Bomb Squadron at Phan Rang and I saw some of the Australians at the craft shop where they were working on wallets. I said, "Oh, this is great, how do you like Vietnam?" [The] Australian turned around and looked at me and said, "How do *you* like fucking Vietnam?" I said "Oh, excuse me, I didn't mean to ruffle your feathers there, bud." I just thought Vietnam was a beautiful place. It's really too bad there's a war going here.

Helicopter pilot Ron Ballweg only had contact with the Australian forces from a distance:

> I talked to them on the radio because we would fly through their area. Their area was "kangaroo controlled". When we were leaving our base camp to go down to Vung Tau to take a re-supply run we would have to go through their area . . . Ran into them a couple times in the clubs. They're pretty decent guys.

VIETNAMESE CIVILIANS

The civilian population of North and South Vietnam was caught in the middle of much of the fighting. Many American men and women on the ground had substantial contact with the civilian population and remember their experiences well. Michael Sweeny, a Marine Corps company commander, recalls watching the South Vietnamese population go through their daily lives in the middle of a war:

> . . . I thought it was interesting to watch them. They were just going about life. You could see artillery going off, airplanes flying and bombs dropping off in the distance and here they are out in their paddies planting their rice or whatever and going up and down the roads on their bikes. Just kind of going on with their lives. I don't know that [this] particularly surprised me, I just thought it was interesting.

David Crawley, a Marine rifleman in 1968 and 1969 in Vietnam, remembers
the civilian population he saw while he was on infantry maneuvers:

> Until I reached my first firefight it was just sweeping through
> villages and seeing what they meant about the people – very quiet
> and to themselves. Because with [the war] going on, they were of
> course scared to death because they were going to be killed by us
> or [by] the North Vietnamese and all these people were farmers
> and wanted to be left alone.

Many times civilians were the Americans' only likely source of information
about Viet Cong movements. Platoon commander Frank Vavrek recalls
how frustrating it could be to try to obtain information from them:

> We'd ask for information, you know, where booby traps are: "Do
> you know where VC are?" They wouldn't tell you nothing and
> then we'd walk and we'd trip booby traps and we'd get people
> hurt and killed and we'd get angry at the civilians: "Why didn't
> you tell us?" But now I look back and hey, we're asking these guys
> to tell us [about] their brothers, their husbands: "Where are all
> your men? We want to go kill them." And the VC were their sons,
> they were their husbands, these villagers.

Many other Americans who served in Vietnam have fond memories of the
civilian population, particularly the Vietnamese children. Army helicopter
pilot Ron Ballweg remembers his observations of civilians:

> At times [I felt like a guest in their country]. At times, I felt like
> all they wanted to do was take my money. Very rarely did I ever go
> into town. I mean there was nothing there for me anyway. At times
> I really felt sorry for the kids . . . They were rag tag. My God, we'd
> be somewhere and they'd come running up. We all just gave them
> – if we had candy – we'd give them candy and stuff. If you threw
> it they were just like a pack of dogs going after it. I found that the
> Vietnamese women were very, very pretty when they were young.
> They aged extremely fast . . . You would see a girl at 18 or 20 years
> old – she could be on a magazine cover. Ten years later she looked
> like she was 60 . . . I remember seeing their homes built out of beer
> cans. They would flatten the beer cans, open them up and that
> would be the siding and the roof of their home. Things like their

culture was totally foreign. You'd see them going down the road
– if they had to go relieve themselves, it was right there on the side
of the road . . . They would use a rock to clean theirselves with
. . . So it could be some of that. The hygiene was non-existent. The
rivers over there – I never did see a clear river. They're all mud.
I'm sure it was all from sewage. It had to have been. Even when
we were in the dry season it was still brown water. It could have
been [because] war had been going on there for hundreds of years,
always. This was nothing new to them. It wasn't where we were
going to stop it all. They probably thought, "[The Americans] are
here for a while; then they'll go, and it'll be back to normal again."

John McNown, Jr, US Army platoon commander, remembers what he saw
and thought about the Vietnamese civilians:

They were small and they didn't speak English . . . They were
mostly farmers where we were. We were in an area that was
primarily rural. We never operated in any big villages. We're going
through hamlets all the time. All you saw was farmers. I felt sorry
for them. We were going through in the daytime [and] the NVA
were coming through at night. I thought what a terrible way.
It's a hard life. It's a hard life being a farmer in rice paddies . . .
You'd see young women that were beautiful young girls out there.
They'd be 18 or 17 and then you'd see women that were probably
26 or 27 and they already looked old . . . You very seldom saw a
young man. Anybody above 15 got drafted by somebody. So if
you saw one you picked him up as a suspect. So you saw old men
and women and a lot of children . . . You'd go into their little
homes, their 'hooches' as we'd call them. They had mud walls and
thatched roofs. Things were always pretty neat in there. They had
little brooms. They had dirt floors but they would kind of keep
them swept. I just thought they were industrious. Probably would
have been good people under other circumstances.
    Of course they resented us. If we had armed people coming
through our homes we'd resent them I'm sure. I guess if I had
an overall feeling [it was that]I didn't trust any of them . . . We
[found] booby traps outside every village. We'd get sniped at.
There wasn't any question that these people did not want us
there . . . Certainly where we were [it was hard to tell enemy from
friend]. They all looked alike. The Viet Cong – they all dressed

like the normal people and not necessarily black pajamas, shorts
or whatever. They were just somebody that was out there in
the fields someplace. Sometimes they were farmers by day and
soldiers by night. Sometimes they were just soldiers all the time.
Certainly the population there hid those people. They truly
were fish swimming in the seas . . . I don't think there was ever a
question when we went through a village whether it was really a
friendly village. They'd tell us stuff and the kids would be nice,
trying to make money or something . . . You didn't see fear and
resentment in people's eyes. [But you could tell by] just their body
language. Just the way they stood and the way they watched you.
Just like any place where you walk in [and] all of a sudden, you
think that you don't belong. It was that feeling.

Some Americans made little effort to understand the Vietnamese, at least at
first. Don Cuneo remembers his first impressions of Vietnamese civilians,
formed when he arrived in Vietnam with the US Marines in 1965:

I thought [Vietnam] was backwards and I thought [the
Vietnamese] should learn the American way of life. It never
occurred to me that maybe they didn't want to.

It was American policy to do everything possible to limit civilian casualties
in the war. That order had to be carried out on the ground by junior officers
who directed the infantry units on a daily basis. Most of the time orders
were followed. Occasionally they were not. Vietnamese civilians did become
targets from time to time, and they paid for it with their lives or loved ones'
lives or the loss of their possessions. Mike Morea, a Forward Air Controller
in 1966 and 1967, remembers the necessity of calling in fire on villages in
South Vietnam:

We bombed villages all the time. We tried to. By that I mean
villages that were collections of buildings usually with some trees
around them. That was the typical configuration, surrounded by
open fields. We would bomb villages [and] we made a considerable
effort to determine that they were empty and . . . at least the intent
was [that] we were destroying infrastructure. We were destroying
places where the VC did live on occasion, had lived, had fortified.
But at least in my case and I think in most cases, if I saw what
looked like ordinary people walking around, and you could tell,

children certainly, even women and probably they were VC. But in any case if you saw that kind of people just moving around in what looked like routine habit patterns for a small village, I wouldn't [call in planes to] bomb it and I don't think most people would have. The ones that we did bomb were empty, lots of obvious entrenchments and gun emplacements inside the village and under the trees and that sort of thing, and those are the kinds of things that we did attack pretty regularly. Unfortunately, of course, in the process of doing that we were decimating the countryside and driving what loyal ordinary people there were out there completely crazy, I'm sure, but that had been going on since forever.

On occasion, there were incidents in which American soldiers confronted civilians directly under hostile circumstances, as Marine Don Cuneo remembers from his tour in 1965:

I was involved in a couple of instances where we burned a village down . . . We took fire from it, and the people had been told that if something like this happened, you're going to lose your village. This was, I want to say, pretty early on in my tour. I can remember us being outside, and all of the villagers that were there were all huddled together and they wailed all night long as the village burned. It was pretty sad now that I think of it. At the time I didn't . . . I just wished they'd shut up.

The civilian population was not always passive while things around them, things that they had known all their lives, were being destroyed, whether by American, ARVN, or allied forces, by the Communist forces, or by the random circumstances of war. Michael Sweeney remembers one incident that illustrates the defiant spirit of Vietnamese civilians caught up in the conflict:

I remember we stood in a sunken roadway there and watched the old women dismantle hooches that had been built out of bamboo poles and palm fronds and stuff like that, that obviously had been a hospital or shelter of some kind for the NVA. We ended up rounding up about 70 or 80 people and I remember hearing two or three times, "Let's waste them." I got the Gunny [gunnery sergeant] . . . I told him to get out there and get the word to those people, "That's not what we do." So that put a stop to that right away. I sent the [Veitnamese] people back toward Liberty Bridge. I'll never forget there was one old patriarch who had about one tooth and looked like he had to be 1,000 [years old]. [My men were] all strung out together and I passed the word to all our fire support people and all that, to make sure the aircraft and nobody hits them because they're just civilians coming out. Even though we'd dug up all kinds of weapons and all kinds of stuff, we don't make war on those kind of people. The old man was the last one in the line and as they stepped out of sight through a bamboo wall . . . he turned around and flipped me off . . . I'll never forget it. It was one little gesture of defiance. They went on their way and we went on our way.

5
THE REAR

What occurred on the frontlines of the Vietnam War was only a portion of what went on during the conflict. When not on patrol in the jungle, in rice paddies or in the mountains, when not in the skies above North and South Vietnam, when not patrolling the Mekong Delta in a PBR, when not bombarding the enemy from a destroyer in the South China Sea, American personnel were 'in the rear'. Being 'in the rear with the gear' meant not being on the frontlines, or not in the action. The rear could be an air base, an infantry headquarters, Military Assistance Command, Vietnam (MACV) in Saigon, Udorn or Ubon air base in Thailand, on Rest and Recuperation leave (R&R) out of Vietnam, or on-board a ship not engaged in action. One could also be in the rear while at base camp located out and away from a major base, say in the middle of the Central Highlands or on a naval base at the mouth of a canal in the Delta. At times, the personnel 'in the field' resented the support personnel in the rear because they were not out 'fighting' the war; they were subject to less danger and had a significantly better chance of surviving their tour of duty and returning to 'the world', or back to the US. Army platoon leader John McNown, Jr, remembers this issue well:

> There was a lot of tension there. We did not like the people in the rear. Actually we may have disliked them more than the NVA. At least you respected the NVA. They were all out there suffering and doing stuff . . . We called them all REMFs [Rear Echelon Mother Fuckers] . . . There was just a lot of resentment . . . Partially it was because they in a lot of cases looked down on the field troops. They would be giving the guys a hard time that their hair wasn't cut or they didn't have their uniform all up to snuff exactly or something. Sometimes if your hair was down way over your collar, that's a problem with the company. You just really resented these people that were back there getting their three squares [three meals] a day and sleeping on a bed and stuff, giving you a hard time. I think that was the case probably

Downtime spent away from the intensity of the front lines was vital to the sanity of those who fought the war, and card games were a popular diversion. Often, veterans recall that some of their best memories of their time 'in country' was spent just hanging out with their buddies away from the front.

in every war. Maybe a little bit more in Vietnam than other places . . .

They didn't resent us, we resented them. They sort of looked down on the people. They thought all the dummies are out there in the field. You would have people that would say, "They should have attacked harder. Why didn't you guys do this? Why didn't you guys do that?" It was sort of a game with them. You'd get back there and they'd say, well, these guys aren't very well motivated. They're a bunch of slackers and stuff. We had a company clerk in our company that had to take off to Chu Lai every time he heard that some people were coming in because there was supposedly a contract out [to kill him]. People he didn't like, he'd tear up their in-country R&R orders. Said they didn't deserve to do that. I had to send people back one time. They were sending guys in the monsoon when I was CO out to the field with wool blankets. I knew for a fact that back in the rear area they were using poncho liners for curtains and bedspreads, because they looked nice. I had to put some people on a helicopter, a resupply helicopter, send them back in and literally go through the battalion rear with their rifles pulling down first sergeants' and armories' curtains and bedspreads. They were saying, "You can't do that. That's our stuff." I had people out there that had wool blankets and when they get wet . . . So there was just stuff like that that happened all the time. We had somebody that was taking all the beer and soda and selling it to the villagers. We couldn't get any. We were supposed to get one beer and one soda in the field every day. We were having to buy them from the villagers because there wasn't any in the rear, because this guy was selling them to the villagers. So we were paying a dollar for something we were supposed to be getting free.

Some veterans whose tour was spent entirely in the rear describe their experience in Vietnam as a 'holiday' or a 'vacation' simply because they were never exposed to the enemy or experienced any enemy attacks. Many describe their experience in the rear as one that was at times tolerable, at times harrowing and at other times boring. They found meaning in their work, in their relationships formed with other support personnel and in doing their duty for their country. Whether 'in the rear' on assignment or there temporarily, individuals found solace from the war in a variety of forms of entertainment including card games, movies, music, alcohol, prostitutes, letters from home, bouts of humor and having pets.

QUARTERS

Where one lived in Vietnam depended on one's individual specialty, location, branch of service and rank. Gerard Otten, an enlisted Air Force English Language Instructor for the South Vietnamese Air Force, describes his compound at Tan Son Nhut Air Base:

[Our quarters were] barracks style. They were two-story tropical barracks that were built just for that purpose. We had probably 25 guys on each floor. They had screens. There were no windows that closed. There were just screens. They were pretty nice. We had a locker and we had a foot locker and we had tropical ceiling fans . . . Compared to most people's situations, it was pretty plush actually. We had access to a gymnasium. There was a library. There were movies. There was an outdoor theatre. Actually there was an indoor theatre at MACV headquarters, which is where [Generals] Creighton Abrams and Westmoreland stayed, which was only a short walk away.

Richard Hamilton, an Air Force F-4C pilot who flew missions over Laos and North and South Vietnam, describes his quarters and surrounding amenities at Ubon Royal Thai Air Base, at Ubon, Thailand:

> [W]e moved into hooches, which is an experience. Hooches are basically open buildings with two roofs on them and the sides are primarily screen and fans in there, and there's no air conditioner whatever, and basic light bulbs running down the ceiling . . . I guess the rooms were about 15 by 15 [feet], and we had two racks [beds] which would be double bunks, metal, kind of narrow maybe three-and-a-half-feet ones . . . And [we had] these . . . gray metal Air Force lockers which we had almost everywhere, all the places had them, and then a foot locker, and that was our home, and we went in and dumped our stuff, what we could, and stuck it in the locker and everyone kind of got acclimated [*sic*] and started looking around and "Where's the john?" And it was still an open shed privy basically, but just larger, I think it was a six-holer or something like that. There weren't any paved streets. It was just all red dirt, and the sidewalks and stuff were basically these – they looked liked ladders . . . I worked as a bartender for a while, and behind the bars you have these slats that you walk around [on] so if you break glasses or anything, it's underneath, it's not on the thing, but that was our sidewalks.

Bryan Grigsby was a DASPO (Department of the Army Special Photographic Office) photographer who was based out of Saigon in 1968 and 1969:

> [I]t seems like every veteran you ever see seems to be this haunted-looking heavy combat veteran of the worst of it, when in fact out of all the troops that were there, only one in seven was actually involved in direct combat; the other six were in the rear with the gear, or some form of rear, whatever the rear was there . . . [W]e lived a lot better than those guys . . . we had air conditioners in our room and we had maid service of a sort. . . at 'The Villa' . . . [When] we were out in the field,

you know we lived different degrees of experience; I mean everything from sleeping on the ground, to in tents, on cots . . . The Villa was three storys high, it . . . didn't really stand out much . . . just typical for that neighborhood. We were, I guess, a couple of miles from Tan Son Nhut Air Base and that was why we were where we were at because it was close to our transportation for getting around the country, and it was our office and home. Downstairs was a dining room and a kitchen and a front reception area which served as the NCOIC's [Non-Commissioned Officer in Charge] office and then a little enclosed room that was the OIC's [Officer in Charge] room. Then the next floor was sleeping quarters that were sort of ringed around a large room that was used for all kinds of packaging stuff, you know working on gear and at night showing our movies – we could get movies from the exchange system there at Tan Son Nhut. And then the next floor up was all sleeping quarters, and then above that was a rooftop area where we'd go drink beer and at night, watch flares dropping around the perimeter of the city and stuff like that.

Mike Bradbury was a Marine in the field. His 'rear' area was Camp Evans in the northern part of South Vietnam. He describes a typical base camp rear quarters:

We lived in tents and I was just lying on a cot . . . during our [watch], whenever we were out on the perimeter, we all had our own bunker so we stayed in the bunker . . . all sandbags under. We were always filling sandbags, we were forever filling sandbags, building bunkers wherever we go, and for the most time in Evans we spent in the camp. When we were out on individual operations and stuff where we would just sleep on the ground, usually under bushes . . . with our ponchos.

William Holmes, Jr, was a Marine Officer stationed at Da Nang as an Air Control Officer. He lived in a tent that was very basic:

We had strong back tents and they were probably . . . 12- to 14-man tents, very large tents that were thrown over a framing of 2X4s . . . [T]he tops were secured down with tent lashes and tent pegs and so forth. We had a flooring in the bottom of our strong back tents, so it was pretty nice, I mean, particularly compared to what the combat troops had. So, we had it pretty good. We had water outside, and we'd go outside and get water. It seems like to me there were showers somewhere, and . . . just pretty normal stuff.

Gary Smith was part of the Army's 981st Military Police Company as a Sentry Dog handler. His quarters at Tuy Hoa were better than the typical tents reserved for enlisted personnel in Vietnam:

They were old Air Force barracks, which was a whole lot better than anything I had seen in Vietnam up to that point. They were on concrete slabs. The sides of the building were metal . . . The bathroom, the latrines, were enclosed in metal too, flushing toilets, showers that drained, just like stateside combinations . . . The buildings were wide open; there was no privacy. We did have wall lockers, and if you asked the Hooch Maids [local Vietnamese women who worked on American bases] to go buy you some curtains, they would go buy you silk curtains and you would hang them up and that would divide off your little area.

Naval personnel in the rear experienced time away from the frontline differently from the infantry and aircrews. Those naval support personnel on board a ship in the South China Sea worked, slept, and ate all in the same location – they did not leave the ship except for liberty call, free personal time ashore, or for R&R leave. The naval personnel in the Mekong Delta area of operations might have a rear area that was a ship at the mouth of a river, out on board a vessel in the South China Sea, a base on a river or on an island near the area of operations. Charles Lloyd served in the US Navy in Vietnam in 1965 and 1966 on river patrol boats. His 'rear' area was a small base camp on an island just off the South Vietnamese coast:

If we weren't on our boats out on patrol we just stayed in this little base camp with barbed wire around it. There was a little Vietnamese village just outside of there. It was on the southern end of the island, a little harbor there and around the other side of the island was the Green Beret unit or team and they had a couple [of] companies of Popular Forces [local South Vietnamese militia] . . . The only time we ever left the base camp was to go out on the boat, patrol the island and go over to the mainland

and patrol the coast, sometimes go a little bit into the bay or the river. We never left the camp on foot, didn't go anywhere outside the gate except into the little village sometimes, get our haircut or something.

SUPPORT PERSONNEL

There was a variety of support jobs in the rear that kept the men on the frontline going. These positions may not have been the most glamorous, but they were absolutely essential for the overall war effort. For example, there were airplane mechanics, clerks in headquarters offices, mail couriers, drivers, truck and jeep mechanics, airport runway personnel, communications operators, radar operators and repairmen, to name a few. The men and women who worked these jobs took great pride in what they did and in their contribution to the overall war effort. Joseph Donald was an Air Force mechanic on the all-important workhorse C-130 transport airplanes, the principal supply aircraft of the war. He recalls his duties and the teamwork involved in keeping the aircraft ready to fly:

> We had the whole aircraft. I was aircraft general, which meant you service the whole aircraft: fuel system, hydraulics, any of the fluid systems. You maintained the aircraft, the airframe, everything. If you broke a landing gear you repaired that landing gear. If you broke a nose gear, you repaired it. If they damaged a wing they fixed it. If a fuel cell went bad, generally on each base they would have a fuel specialist because that was a critical path item. You would assist that fuel specialist or the sheet metal people. I came out of high school as a sheet metal repairman. When it came to repairing the sheet metal on my aircraft, I probably had more knowledge than the guy who was coming out to fix the patch on my aircraft. I already knew how to use tensions. I knew how to drill holes and how to rivet. Those things helped the whole operation, I mean tremendously. Everybody would just come over. A lot of times the sergeant would come over and he would tell me, "Hey this guy's having problems. Can you take a minute and go over there?" Sometimes that minute would end up [being] hours trying to help somebody else resolve an issue on their aircraft. But I never refused because I always felt my airplane was in good shape. I did things basically by the book. You had a schedule. Everything

was scheduled to be changed, get it changed. Don't wait until it falls apart. I did it virtually as they recommended unless we couldn't get the part. Now there were times being in combat you couldn't get the parts. As soon as the part came, then we took care of it.

Gary Smith, the Sentry dog handler, had a duty to walk the base perimeter at night with his big German Shepherd, Rolf.

Rolf was supposed to be doing all the work. All I'm supposed to be doing is reading the signs. Dogs have a better sense of smell, hearing and seeing. Your post would be, I can't even remember the length of the post, but they weren't that long, probably 100 meters long, maybe a football field, maybe a little bit longer. You used the dog to watch for any intruders coming in. We were usually way behind the tower line . . . The tower line was in back of the perimeter fence, which was all lit up, and the perimeter fence was concertina wire strung together, probably about six feet high . . . The perimeter was always lit and we would be walking behind that in total darkness. You had no light; you didn't use a flashlight. We did have a two-way radio. We had hand-held radios, basically a walkie-talkie, a commercial type, for the military, [so] that we can converse with other handlers and the SOG [Special Operations Group, a Special Forces unit] . . . [I]f we were walking, that would be something that we would never do was shout at each other. [We] didn't want anybody to know where you were at. I wouldn't want the tower guards to know where I was at because I would be afraid that they would probably shoot us . . .

   If you were on the beach, you were right on the tower line . . . You had to walk right next to the towers when you were walking your post because several times I remember . . . the tower guards wanting to come down and pet the dog because they hadn't see a dog for so long . . . Out on the other side of the perimeter we were . . . maybe 200 yards away from the tower line. We were way off the beaten path . . . [The beach patrol] was relaxing because . . . you could see . . . the perimeter lights were lightened up [*sic*] out in front of you . . . I mean I don't care how much trust you put in your dog, it still is more comforting when you know you're seeing out there . . . [O]bviously, my sight was not as good as Rolf's sight and his hearing and everything but you had a little bit more degree of comfort there . . .

When you're walking in the grass on the other perimeters, you had no idea what you were walking into. You had no idea if some kind of trap or snare was set for you. You had no idea what kind of snakes were at there, you know we always kept hearing about the two-stepper [snake] or . . . punji sticks . . . Those types of things didn't dwell on your mind all the time but at the same time it kept you wondering what you were getting into . . . There were only a couple of times we had alerts while I was there and I trusted him [Rolf] to lead me into whatever it was, never did find out what they were. We call it alert when he senses something, he'll either start pulling . . . he wanted to go find whatever it is he smelled, heard or saw. Some dogs would just perk up their ears and tilt their heads up like they were trying to get a better smell, but that was called alert. Then you had to follow it and find out what it was that he was sensing.

Richard Schaffer was an Air Defense Radar repairman stationed at Quan Loi, Phouc Vinh, and Camp Evans. He describes his typical duties and the lengths to which he would go to make sure he could repair the radar for which he was responsible:

As a radar repairmen you didn't have a shift. If the equipment was down you were working, that's basically the way it worked. I mean if you worked around the clock because a piece of equipment was down, you did it, and if you had three days off because everything was running fine, you had three days off. Probably on a weekly basis there were things that [malfunctioned] . . . if it wasn't the radar set itself, a piece burning out in it or whatnot, then it was the radio equipment or something. We'd go out and . . . you'd spend time working on that. So usually we [were] working on something several times a week, you'd be putting in a full, four, five, six hours straight of doing something, and then there were those occasions when . . . if your transmitter went down on the radio then you would have to sometimes go other places to get the equipment, to get the parts you needed to replace it if you didn't have parts on hand and you were supposed to.

We had a parts trailer [where] we kept an inventory of parts, but sometimes those parts were in short supply, so where you were supposed to have a couple of magnetrons on hand, which were part of the transmitting system, those tended to burn out after so many hours of usage . . . you might have two on hand and one working in the unit, the one in the unit burns out, you change it and get it up and running and now you've got to make sure you order more parts. Well, maybe before the magnetron would come in, you'd burn the other one out and now you wouldn't have any spares . . . the equipment was down, now you've got to go get the equipment back up again . . . you might call . . . the radar rep in Saigon and say, "Hey we need this equipment. Our radar set is down and here's the parts we need" and he would try to get a line on where they had some in country, and then we would fly to wherever that was to pick them up and bring them back and get them installed and that might take you several days . . .

I saw most of the country . . . I'd say probably at least once a month I was on the road trying to scrounge up some parts. The drives were . . . more harrowing because you ran into convoys, you ran into delays . . . you might hear, "Well, why is everything stopped, why aren't we going forward?" "Well, there was an ambush up ahead you know and so they're cleaning up" and later on you'd go through and you'd see the results of it, kind of . . . thing. The flying wasn't too bad, although you flew over areas where you could see the bomb craters, where you know the B-52s had come in and you know dropped their load on an area . . .

Eliseo Perez-Montalvo was an Air Force aviation mechanic and debriefed pilots on aircraft maintenance issues. He was stationed at Da Nang Air Base in 1967 and 1968. His job demanded communication skills, technical knowledge of the aircraft and a rapport with the pilots:

The aircraft would taxi right up to the building, the little shack that we had right on the flight line, and the pilots would come in, and we had six or seven of us that were knowledgeable of the different systems, hydraulics, fire control they called it, that's the weapons delivery systems, inertial and radar – that was me, the airframe . . . [W]e had all these people that were knowledgeable and we would talk to the pilots about how the systems worked.

Then we would call the shop and we would tell them, "653 came in with this and that," . . . and the history of it. We kept cards on each aircraft, critical data. And we would diagnose what the problem was and tell the dispatcher at our shop what we felt was wrong with the aircraft. And we knew when they were coming in, especially during the night. There were not as many sorties flown [at night]. And we knew within five minutes which way, when they would arrive.

Well, we sat around all this time. Some of us would play cards. Some of the guys would take a nap in between debriefings. I would cook tacos. We had a refrigerator and I would hustle ground beef from the Navy people and I would hustle tomatoes and lettuce and onions. My mother would send me salsas and peppers, tortillas, but they were often spoiled. We found we could buy canned tortillas made by Old El Paso and we would make tacos in the office there in between debriefings. Well, it just happens that just about every pilot that's ever been trained in the US has spent time in the southwest where the weather is favorable for flying, where we do most of our training. And they all have been exposed to Mexican food. And they would come in, and the odors – we put our food away when they came in. But they would look and they would say, "Sarge, it's got to be you." Well, I was invited to their quarters to make tacos for them . . . [on] more than one occasion.

Joseph Pizzo worked at Phan Rang Air Base as an Army Fire-Control System Mechanic.

I . . . repair[ed] the fire-control system on the C-119 K Flying Boxcar gunship. This gunship had four mini-guns, four 308-caliber, or 7.62 mini-guns and two 20-millimeter cannons on it. They fired out of the left side of the aircraft. I worked on the fire-control system, which was the airborne infrared television system, the side-looking radar system and the starlight scope, which were the targeting devices for those guns. The pilot had an optical sight that any one of those . . . could be inputted to his optical sight to show him where the enemy was and where the good guys were . . .

When the guns got to where the good guys were, they would stop firing automatically, it could pass over the good guys and automatically resume firing when they got to the other side of the good guys. It was all built into the fire-control system, which was really handy. The pilot didn't have to know he was going to hit the good guys to let off the trigger; the pilot fired it from the steering wheel, the trigger on the control yoke in the aircraft.

All the ground troops loved it. As a matter of fact, when I was in Officer Candidate School in the Army, one of my classmates, I was talking to him one day, he said that he was in Vietnam at the same time I was, and his platoon of 30-odd guys was being tracked by a uniformed NVA battalion of two to five hundred guys and they'd surrounded them . . . one night and they thought we're going to die and they called one of our gunships that was supposed to be in the area. And the gunship said, "Don't move," and they said, "Right. We can't move, we're surrounded by two to five hundred guys. We're not going anywhere." He said, you saw the whole jungle lift up in the air and come down flat and there was nobody alive out there. The gunships made one pass firing about ten to 15 seconds and just leveled the whole jungle. Turned it to nothing. It was incredible. So it was interesting [to meet] someone while I was in OCS who had actually been saved by one of my gunships.

Larry Wasserman was a mechanic on C-123s, the airplanes that sprayed defoliants in Vietnam. He remembers doing a variety of things while he was at Bien Hoa Air Base in 1967 and 1968:

[We] repaired everything, whatever needed to be done. We were all general aircraft people that took care of general maintenance needs of the aircraft – batteries, hydraulic fluid and mechanical things, rigging flap cables, things like that. There were limited numbers of personnel in some cases, certainly a limited number of specialists. If two planes came down with severe engine trouble, that would be the entire personnel section of the engine facility. You worked on anything, not only your particular aircraft. If your aircraft was flying or out on a mission and an emergency came up on another aircraft that they needed to get ready, whoever is there, gets picked. It didn't matter, you couldn't say, "Well that's not my airplane. I'm not going over there." Most of the time, if the aircraft was in good shape and there was really nothing wrong with it, your main job was seeing that the spray tank got filled properly and that everything was working. You'd do your pre-flight checks before the pilots came out and did theirs. That was about it. We were the flight line crew so we had to learn the aircraft hand signals for ushering the planes out and bringing them back in. The most interesting part was learning how to back up the planes. The last row or the first row depending on how you want to look at it, where the planes were closest to the herbicide tanks, they would have to be parked backwards. They would have to be backed into the slot. We'd have to learn how to judge the distances of where to turn the plane and back them up so they were on the right spot at the right time . . . We'd get to get in the cockpit. Sometimes we'd have to move the aircraft ourselves. They couldn't be bothered with bringing pilots out just to move the aircraft on the ground.

In addition to military personnel, there were other Americans in the rear. Jennifer Young was a Red Cross 'Donut Dollie', a volunteer for Vietnam who operated in the rear to assist and entertain the troops while they were away from the frontlines. Her job duties ranged from organizing games to serving coffee to talking to wounded soldiers in the hospital. She describes some of what she did in 1968 and 1969:

Generally [we] had scheduled stops [at bases] and you tried to get there the same time, on the same day of the week so that the officers knew as they were planning their men's schedules, "Oh, the Red Cross girls are here" so that will allow this group of men to have free time to play the girls' [games]. We would have a schedule so that they could, in turn, schedule their men. Some officers thought that it was important enough that they deliberately scheduled our visit in; it wasn't like we would arrive at a place and say, "Yoo-hoo, we're here, doesn't anybody want to come over?" It was like, "Okay good, you're here, the men are waiting for you, let's go over here to this mess hall and you can set up there," or this flight line or whatever. Some officers felt, I think, that it was good for their men to do this, but then some of the men would say . . . "You know, when you girls come every week our Captain makes us come here and play your games, but what's the game going to be next week?" They didn't want to admit that they enjoyed it, like this week it might have been Concentration, maybe next week its going to be some kind of word game, you know whatever . . .

[The men] were fantastic. They tried to watch their language, once they got into the games, the competitive ones just really got enthusiastic because a lot of times it would be Team A against Team B in Concentration, you wouldn't have individual against individual. They just really enjoyed it and some of them enjoyed visiting with us before and after . . .

[I]n addition to the games we would look for any kind of means by which to interact with the guys that was okay with the military. In other words, sometimes the helicopter that we were in would fly in with a hot meal, maybe it was an LZ or a firebase that had no mess tent or mess hall or anything, and the chow would be on the helicopter. Well, we would serve the chow, because number one, it was time to eat. Why do you want to play a game when there's hot chow and people are hungry? So it's like okay, we'll serve the chow . . . [A]t Tuy Hoa [Air Base] . . . at night we were driven around the perimeter in a truck. We would get to the bottom and they, the driver and the guy up in the tower, would do the interchange, the password . . . and then we would actually climb up the ladder carrying a cup of coffee to the guy and then look through their starlight scopes and kind of chit chat with them for a little while. So that was like a means by which to see more people, maybe even go to people who otherwise maybe wouldn't seek us out, wouldn't go to our games. At the flight line at Cam Ranh Air Base we would go around in the back of a pickup truck with a huge vat of Kool-Aid during the day, and the guys pulling maintenance on the airplanes would [come over], we'd stop and serve them Kool-Aid and talk with them briefly.

Another type of support role was transporting personnel and transferring various cargo around South Vietnam. Supplies moved around the country by a variety of means, much of it by transport aircraft. These missions were routine but also dangerous. Such crews flew in a war zone, received enemy fire from time to time, flew day and night in all types of weather, and experienced occasional equipment failure. Equally, the men who supplied the American war effort were critical to the continued prosecution of the war. Gary Jackson was one of these men. Based out of Taiwan, Jackson

*One of the vital duties of support personnel was to move supplies from one base to another.
This long column of 'Deuce-and-a-Halfs' is transporting ammunition along Route 4 from
Saigon to the Area Logistics Command at Can Tho in the Mekong Delta.*

piloted a C-130E transport plane in 1967, 1968 and 1969. He describes
what his supply missions were like:

> We would get into, let's say Tuy Hoa, and we would land there,
> after we['d] bring in the airplane – this would be a fresh airplane
> that had had major maintenance done on it and it was ready to
> go . . . [M]ost often we would go to Okinawa [Japan] and pick up
> cargo there, and bring it in country [into the RVN] because that
> was an intermediate shipping point . . . So we'd bring that in,
> bring the new airplane in, and go into crew rest. At Tuy Hoa that
> usually meant you go into a tent for a few nights . . . And you'd
> stay there for a day or two until a hooch became available. Then
> you would move over to one of the hooches . . .
>
> Your crew duty day was ten hours. That meant from the time
> you reported to pre-flight, which was three hours before takeoff,
> until you finished for the day, was supposed to be no more
> than ten hours. In that seven hours of flying time, you would
> probably make five or six flights, and you would leave out of

Tuy Hoa with a cargo for someplace, or you would fly someplace
to pick up cargo. Sometimes we'd pick up cargo in Qui Nhon,
that was a port, and Cam Ranh Bay . . . Within a typical day you
would land on a long concrete runway two or three times and
you would land out in the jungle, two or three or four times.
[We would carry] just about anything you can imagine, from
shower clogs [shoes to wear while in the toilet areas] to potato
chips to beer, to artillery shells to artillery barrels – I think
they were 170-millimeter artillery pieces that we could carry
– halftracks, jeeps, troops, passengers. We'd evacuate wounded;
we'd evacuate refugees. We'd evacuate troops and haul troops in.
Produce. The town of Da Lat was about 50, 60 miles due west of
Cam Ranh Bay, and it was in the mountains, about 5,000-foot
elevation. A lot of produce was grown around there, pineapples,
lettuce the whole thing. We'd fly in there and load the airplane
up completely with produce and then haul it around to the
different bases.

The C-130 pilots also carried the dead and wounded. Jackson remembers
doing this.

That was not pleasant. The first time that I did it . . . at some
point in the flight I needed to . . . use the urinal, so I started
to go to the back and they were laid out in the floor on litters
in body bags, and the body bags were kind of extended
[distended] from gas, and every little bump they'd quiver, and
the odor was – oh, it was atrocious . . . and I smell it every once
in a while [now] . . . canned Lysol smells that way, and it still
brings up these images. I was kind of horrified . . . When you're
flying you're insulated from all that . . . you can fly a whole Air
Force career and then never get close, and that's the closest it
got for me, that and the hauling [of] wounded. It was just 14
[bodies]. That doesn't sound like very many, but when you see
them laid out on the floor like that, that's a lot of bodies, that's
a lot of dead guys.

The first time I [carried wounded] we had flown into Da
Nang and we were stopped to have cargo unloaded or we were
waiting for cargo to be loaded. The navigator and I went over
to the snack bar to get us a sandwich and as we were walking
back, there was a lot of activity going around the airplane, and

he recognized that they were getting us rigged for emergency medical evacuation. So they rigged the airplane up so that litters could be brought in and stacked on stanchions, as many as we needed. And so we got in the airplane and jumped in the seat and called for clearance and we took off. We flew up to Dong Ha, which was a Marine base just south of the demilitarized zone and it was after dark when we got there, and we stopped and we left the engines running because they were under threat of attack, and they loaded – brought the litters on . . . since the engines were running I was in the seat the whole time, so I didn't observe this. Then one of the nurses came up and told the pilot that they had some head wounds. When they had head wounds you had to be real careful with the pressurization because that could make the problem a lot worse, and we had been having pressurization problems with that airplane all day, so we decided that we would just stay at low level, not getting higher than 3,000 feet all the way back. So we took off in the dark and flew low level to the beach. It was just a few miles and then turned and flew down the coast into Da Nang.

After we'd landed at Da Nang, shut down the engines and I got out and watched them. As soon as we landed there were these big ambulance buses that pulled up to the back of the airplane at the same level as the ramp of the airplane, and they just carried people directly into the buses . . . [I] stood there and watched them unload for a while. The one that got me was, he was going feet first . . . There was this muddy boot, muddy fatigue pant leg and then a bright white bandage around the stump. It was very quiet; nobody was saying anything. You didn't hear any moans or anything. It was just very orderly, and there was this contrast between mud and jungle fatigues and bandages, bright white antiseptic bandages . . . I have no idea, of course you never heard any more, never knew what happened afterwards. That was part of flying those missions. You'd be in the middle of something and you never knew how it ended.

Personnel in the rear also faced the enemy, but usually from a distance. Very often the VC or NVA would randomly fire mortars or rockets at an American base. The attacks usually came in the middle of the night in order to have a more profound psychological effect. South Vietnamese who worked on base sometimes turned out to be VC spies. Infiltrators were sometimes caught as they tried to pass intelligence through the main gate of the base as they exited after a day's work. Sometimes, base workers were found shot dead in the concertina wire that surrounded the base after they had been part of a coordinated VC night attack. Some workers were caught walking off distances by foot inside the American compound so they could give the exact distances between buildings to the VC/NVA soldiers who gauged and set the firing distances for the mortars.

Many men and women in the rear recall these scary and sometimes very deadly night rocket and mortar attacks. Richard Schaffer describes remembers what he experienced at Quan Loi, Phuoc Vinh and Camp Evans:

> We would come under attack every so often. At one time I had
> a little logbook . . . I was logging in the attacks and things and
> that got destroyed . . . Probably . . . about 15 times or so I think
> we came under attacks in all three bases . . . Most of the time
> it was rocket attacks. Quite often not more than three rounds
> would come in which would mean somebody was just setting up
> out on the perimeter someplace, by the time they set them off
> they were probably long gone from the area. I know one night
> at Camp Evans . . . we were kind of sitting out, and there was a
> firefight around the perimeter and there were several helicopters
> out and gunships and they were shooting rockets in and you
> could see the tracers going in and they were like sitting on top
> of the bunker watching the war like you'd watch a movie, and
> everybody's out there you know in their skivvies [underwear]
> and just sitting around, laughing and joking about it. All of a
> sudden the three aircraft that were out there on the perimeter
> came in all at the same time to refuel and they came in and shut
> their lights off and sat down and almost immediately we began
> to get shelled and here we all are, we're sitting out there and
> we're scrambling to get under cover . . . because we're alongside
> the airstrip and what are they doing, they're lobbing the stuff
> down the airstrip . . .
>
> I think the worst night was, we were at Phuoc Vinh and . . . the
> major military units supporting the base had left and the next
> one had come in and we got shelled . . . probably continuously
> for over an hour, and when I say continuously I mean like
> shells going off every ten seconds and just screaming overhead
> and you know bright flashes of light and noise, it was just

horrendous. We were literally shaking in our boots, I mean it was horrendous. And that particular night we never received any instructions to go to our defensive positions, so basically we hunkered down in a long trench that had like steel culvert over the top of it and then sandbags on the top of that and sandbags around the end. So you could see the flash of light and everything . . . I think that was probably the worst night because . . . for over an hour it was non-stop just explosions and . . . ground shaking and everything. That was a scary time . . . [I] shook like a leaf [and] prayed a lot.

Pete Perez-Montalvo remembers a particularly bad incident when the enemy reached into the base at Da Nang:

There were snipers; there were attempts to penetrate the air base. The closest I came to dying in Vietnam was that day. It was probably about 10:00 [am] or so and I was going back to my barracks and I was in front of the mess hall, this metal building. My barracks was across the street and in between the barracks, you could see Vietnam. There was a field with serpentine wire. There was a fence. There were Marines [assigned there] that had had two injuries [in the field]. Rather than take a chance on having to rotate them back [to the US] if they were injured a third time, they would assign them to very boring duty maintaining surveillance on the perimeter of the air base and they lived in these dirt towers and they had these . . . one-man revetments where they could hide and fire back. Well, on the other side of that, maybe a couple of hundred yards, maybe more, there was a tree line and there were huts and shacks and Vietnamese people living there and it was from that area that a sniper shot at me.

I was about to walk across the street to my barracks and he had me by . . . the azimuth, but he didn't have me on elevation. There were two shots that hit up above my head on the wall, maybe about 16, 14 inches above me. I hit the ground. I was trembling. I was breathing very heavy. I crawled to a bunker nearby. It didn't take long to dawn on me what it was. But I went back and I looked at the bullet holes . . . it was my lucky day – he missed me. I eventually made it out to the barracks and I changed my

[soiled] clothes. I started drinking. I had beer in my refrigerator
. . . And I drank a few beers and calmed myself down . . . it was
just something that happened.

Many of the men who were 'out in the bush' doing the fighting tease that
those in the rear had it easy, that they were the lucky ones. The men and
women in the rear, however, were as much a part of the American war effort
as the personnel on the front lines. The war machine could not run without
them. They were instrumental in the success the US experienced during the
war. They also tasted the war in a way no one else did.

6
THE MEDICAL CORPS

THE AMERICAN MEDICAL ORGANIZATION IN VIETNAM

The war in Vietnam, like all those before and after it, produced illnesses, wounds and deaths in large numbers. All participants made provisions for treating their wounded and disposing of their dead, and the Vietnam conflict produced innovative approaches to both problems, not least of which were the Communists' underground hospital complexes and the Americans' battlefield helicopter ambulances.

Most of those Americans who received medical attention during the Vietnam War were treated for illnesses rather than battle wounds. Some of these illnesses were endemic to battle and to living conditions in the field, but others were caused by the insect and animal life that characterized Vietnam. Frank Vavrek, a platoon leader in the Army's First Cavalry Division, described the special problems encountered by infantrymen who were attacked by biting ants:

> They had these ants over there in those jungle areas that just
> clustered like on ends of the tree branches or leaves right
> about shoulder height, and if you're moving through the
> jungle, if you're not watching real careful, a soldier would walk
> underneath one of those branches, shake the branch, and I
> guess about a million ants would drop on him. Are you familiar
> with fire ants? . . . So that's what we're talking about. You know,
> when they bit, they hurt . . . So, these things would fall out
> of this tree on to a soldier [and] start biting him. It would be
> around his neck and his face because that's where they'd land
> originally so one guy – you'd think one guy's going crazy – he
> starts slapping himself and . . . you'd have to rip his clothes off
> of him and just smack him and try to get them off of him and
> then he would all be infected and festered up so we'd have to
> evacuate him. He'd be an actual casualty because all that venom
> that was in you would be reacting . . . So, we'd have to evacuate

him, let him go back to the medical aid station and get hydrated
and everything else; keep him calm until he could come back
out and join us again [in the field].

Illnesses, heat exhaustion, allergies, poor hygiene and a diet of dehydrated and
canned foods took a heavy toll on operational readiness amongst American
forces throughout the conflict. Impure or inadequate water supplies,
particularly for the forces deployed in America's mobile warfare units early in
the conflict, were a constant source of concern to commanders like Vavrek,
because of the potential for their men to contract debilitating illnesses:

You're in ninety- to one hundred-degree [heat], high humidity.
Guys were beating the bush, climbing up these steep mountains
and they'd get hot and . . . we would be thirsty. You'd be out
there in the middle of the jungle and you couldn't get any water
until you either reached the top, opened up an LZ, got them to
fly water in to you, or we'd take water from the streams, natural
flowing streams that we could find. Sometimes you're so thirsty,
we had those Halazone [sterilization] tablets to put in there, but
you had to wait 20 minutes: put [it] in there, shake it up real
good, wait 20 minutes before you drank your water. Well, they'd
be drinking [the] water right away.

Margarethe Cammermeyer, a senior nurse at one of the largest US hospital
complexes in Vietnam located at Long Binh, noted that cases of illness were
far more numerous than those of battle injuries:

The first thing you think is, in a combat zone you're going to
have combat wounds, [but] the majority of problems are medical
problems. I think it's something like 10 or 15 percent of the
actual patients end up with combat wounds. So the majority of
[the work involves identifying] fevers of undetermined origin
and ruling out malaria and dengue fever . . . [as well as treating]
trench foot and pneumonia and gastrointestinal stuff.

However, the extensive US in-country facilities for medical treatment were
focused on the needs of those who would be wounded in action against the
enemy. The system included field medics on the scene of battle, helicopter
ambulances, battalion aid stations and more sophisticated 'evac' hospitals
that treated the seriously wounded. There were also fully staffed regular

hospitals at major bases both in Vietnam and beyond, for more difficult cases including surgery, recovery and rehabilitation. The basis of the system was professional medical workers, and all US military branches provided specialized training for their doctors, nurses, technicians and medics. For battlefield surgeons, that training emphasized traumatic injury assessment and care, as Jim Evans, a physician with emergency room experience who was drafted by the US Army, recalls:

> Well, they did like a demonstration where they had like, a two- or three-gallon can that was filled with very, very thick gelatin . . . They had put yellow dye on one side and then they shot an M-16 through it and it just demonstrated how the wounds have been contaminated because the yellow dye went all the way through this block of gelatin . . . Well, the point was that with the wounds we would be seeing, they were going to be contaminated. So tissues had to be removed that had been severely damaged by the concussion of the projectile, plus you had dead tissue that had to be removed, plus the projectiles had introduced bacteria and junk . . . It was just impressive about the amount of damage that an M-16 or an AK-47 would do. I'd seen a fair number of patients with severe trauma when I was at Parkland [Hospital in Dallas] . . . It was no preparation for what I eventually saw [in Vietnam].

The Army's training of its frontline medical personnel was not always as comprehensive as those who served might have liked. Mastery of military protocol, for example, sometimes took precedence over medical work, according to Cammermeyer:

> The basic training that I had was ten weeks long . . . We saw mock war attacks. We were involved in litter bearing courses, triage, and we had to impregnate our fatigues because they were the old green fatigues. We had to soak them in a type of disinfectant so that the mosquitoes wouldn't attack . . . We learned to polish our boots, how you get in and out of a vehicle depending on your rank, and who walks to the right or the left of whom. All of the protocol was part of our training there. How to work in a hospital and fill out a chart and take care of patients. We had some clinical time, but most of it was classroom.

Jim Evans, who served as a battalion surgeon in Vietnam, recalls that the doctors in his draftee class who were sent to Vietnam were given no specific training for conditions there, or for the range of battle wounds they were likely to encounter:

> There were some [draftee doctors] who were going to be staying stateside. There were some people going to Europe. My feeling is what we got was sufficient [instruction] for stateside or European assignments. Those of us who were going to Vietnam, we were really not well oriented I don't think, about what our situation was apt to be like . . . Those of us who were going to be sent to an active combat situation should have had more information . . . I was not prepared [for] the destruction on human bodies . . . there were guys who had hit mines or booby traps with multiple amputations. There were burns from white phosphorus. People would come in and the white phosphorus would be in their skin and it was still burning. You had to neutralize it with like potassium permanganate. [One weapon] the US used, I guess artillery, was called fleschettes, basically little arrowheads. [If a casualty] came in [with fleschette wounds], they would look [at first] like they had minor wounds, and then you would turn them over and you would see . . . part of the body was gone. Artillery, shrapnel, it was incredible . . . it was the horror of war.

TREATMENT IN THE FIELD

Servicemen who sustained major wounds were usually treated first by a field medic, an enlisted man who had been given basic training to stabilize patients, stop blood loss and prepare the patient for transport to a hospital facility. In the field, these medics often had only seconds to reach a severely wounded comrade and initiate the procedures that could save his life. In some situations, several men might simultaneously be injured, and medics had to make split-second decisions prioritizing the treatment of wounded patients. The US Marines' field medics were known as 'corpsmen,' and one of them, Robert 'Dev' Slingluff, recalled such an incident that occurred on his second patrol in Vietnam:

> We're coming in from patrol and the person in front of me steps on a booby trap, blows off his foot and hits the person behind me as well. So I go up and I treat the guy and we call in for a medevac helicopter . . . The first thing I did was try to run to him, not knowing what the heck I was going to do. I mean this is a

different experience. So I get there and I start to tie a tourniquet around the leg, and the guy behind me is saying, "Forget about him, he's dead, I need help!" I'm going, "Wait a minute!" So I said, "I'll get to you." I tied the tourniquet off and put a battle dressing on the leg and then went back to the guy behind me who had been hit by shrapnel in the lower part of his body . . . By that time [another] corpsman was out there and he was applying battle dressing, pressure dressings on that guy. Time just went berserk . . . I know the three major things for the corpsman [are] to stop bleeding, maintain airway and prevent shock . . . These are the things that you have to do. So at this point there was no question about airway – the guy had an airway – so it was basically bleeding and shock and the first thing you have to do is stop the bleeding . . . It may seem like it takes an hour, but it doesn't, when you start to work on it. The tourniquets are fairly easy to take care of. The guy obviously had other wounds around him. Part of the booby trap had lodged between his radio and his flak jacket, which wasn't doing a whole lot of damage to him, but it was burning, so you had to get the radio off the guy and the flak jacket off and things like that and check him for other wounds.

Pressure-sensitive booby traps could cause particularly grievous wounds, and in an instant field medics and corpsmen could be called upon not only to stabilize the wounded but also to perform field amputations. As Dev Slingluff explained, all other members of the unit were also affected by his actions in one such emergency:

One of the guys, a guy named Bob, walked into the tree line and stepped on a booby trap which exploded and took off one of his legs, and when I got to him the full booby trap hadn't exploded and his other leg was caught in the trap. It was, in my opinion, obvious that he was going to lose that [leg] as well . . . Well, there was a guy who was right next to me who was kind of holding Bob down and he saw that the booby trap wasn't exploded all the way and he knew that not only was Bob's life in jeopardy but both his and potentially mine were in jeopardy if we screwed up with the remainder of the booby trap. So I was kind of jumping around from side to side trying to get the best angle to perform the operation that I had to perform and he's going nuts because he's saying, "You're going to knock that thing, you're going to

knock that thing," and I'm just telling him to shut up. "This is
bad enough, don't bother my mind with this! We're going to get
through this!" . . . So I had to cut off the other leg and call in the
helicopters and put him on board. So he was a double amputee
and when I was treating him [I] hit this moral dilemma. I mean in
my opinion, Bob was as good as dead. I didn't see how he could
survive anything like this. So the dilemma is, do you try to save
a life that you feel is gone anyway, and the response is yes, you
have to. If not only for the possibility that the person can live but
because the people around you are seeing what you're doing and
if you don't do something they lose confidence in your ability to
do something. So it was as much for kind of future events as it
was for trying to save Bob.

Not all medics, despite their training, could function in the field when
a crisis developed. Whether through battle fatigue, a failure of training,
or outright fear, there were occasions when field medics froze. One such
instance, involving a corpsman newly arrived in Vietnam, was recalled by
Marine Don Cuneo:

I did see a corpsman one time . . . who – when we called
"Corpsman up!" – he looked and he looked again and he said,
"Oh, shit! They're shooting people down there," and immediately
went into almost like a seizure . . . I remember that this was his
first operation, his first time out in the field, and I think it was
more nerves than anything else, because I never saw that guy again.

Corpsmen and medics also had to rely upon other members of their units
to help in a medical emergency in the field. In a firefight, several servicemen
might be wounded simultaneously, or during a village sweep, a lone sniper
could attack an entire unit. Riflemen, machine-gunners, and others in the
unit pitched in to help, sometimes finding themselves literally keeping
one of their buddies alive. Radioman Don Cuneo remembers just such
a situation which, despite his best efforts, a wounded comrade did not
survive:

We would go down this path and into the village looking for the
bad guys . . . Later on when we're out around this well area, a
shot rang out. It was a sniper, and right over by the well we hear,
"Corpsman up!" And this kid was down, and [a] corpsman was

over there and working on him and Dave and I ran up, and this kid had been shot in the thigh . . . He'd been shot in the upper, inner thigh area and the bullet had severed his femoral artery. We must have spent, it seemed forever. The corpsman was trying to get this artery and tie it off. I ended up trying to get the artery, I mean, literally, [I] had my fingers inside this guy's wound. We must have worked on him for an hour. In reality, you couldn't put a tourniquet on it because of its location. We'd get the thing, the corpsman would get ready to clamp it off and it would slip out again. We kept telling this kid, "You're going to be okay. You're going to be okay." Eventually, the corpsman got the thing tied off and we called in a medevac chopper there. The landing zone was about a quarter of a mile away. A couple of guys put him in a poncho and took him over to the LZ. Apparently something happened along the way. Either they dropped him or something happened. It re-opened the wound. We got a call from the helicopter as it was flying over that the kid had died. About that point, I started to shut down . . . This haunts me to this day because I don't know this guy's name. He deserves more than just to be remembered as somebody that got killed.

Sometimes, particularly when extraction by air ambulance was impossible or when NVA forces would attack an American camp or compound, the wounded were hand carried to a nearby aid station, often located within the camp's perimeter. There, a trained doctor would have access to more equipment and medicines, and complex injuries could receive more sophisticated treatment than was possible in the field. When a sustained attack was under way, the lone physician could find himself almost overwhelmed with seriously injured patients, as Jim Evans remembers from his experience in 1970:

I was sent to Kham Duc for two weeks from the 91st Evac [Hospital unit]. We were ordered to go there. Snipers got inside the perimeter. It was a mass casualty [situation]. I was the only physician there. I was with some medics and you evaluate the casualties and take care of what needs to be done. If they are clearly dying and nothing can be done then you make that immediate assessment that there is someone that you *can* save, someone else that you can stabilize. Say, someone with a very

severe head wound, they are clearly dying and that was the
assessment: they are dying. You cannot prevent it . . . It was like,
you take care of those who will survive. I know this sounds very
cold and calculating but, you know, you salvage the people that
can be salvaged; if they couldn't be saved then you had to make
that decision and not get distracted. From this [vantage] point
it's very hard to say that, but when you're in the middle of that
situation it was like, "yes or no".

In most situations, however, those wounded in the field could be placed on
a 'dustoff', a US Army ambulance helicopter flown by pilots and crewmen
dedicated to extracting the wounded from the battlefield and racing them
to the nearest medical facilities that could treat their wounds. The dustoff
crews relied, in the first instance, upon dispatchers who took the calls
for help from field units and translated them into flight orders. Dustoff
crews had an on-call schedule during which they had to be prepared to be
dispatched at a moment's notice. The helicopters were kept stocked with
fuel and basic medical supplies, and were also ready for immediate liftoff to
the site of an 'evac' request. The calls were treated as medical emergencies,
and each crew member had a job to do in preparing the aircraft for the
mission, as Army pilot Steve Vermillion remembers:

If the call went out to launch the helicopter . . . we grabbed our
weapons and three of us ran to the helicopter and the three
that ran out there obviously were the crew chief, medic and the
co-pilot. It was the co-pilot's job to get the helicopter started
and brought up to operating speed. The aircraft commander
found out where we are going, a general situation and how many
patients we had . . . Your briefing would be, "Here's a quadrant
you are going to. This is the unit that you are going to support.
This is their call sign and frequency. They've got X number of
wounded," [and] whether they are litter or ambulatory and maybe
what kind of wounds, fragmentations or gun shot wounds and
whether the LZ is 'hot' [under enemy fire] . . . That was handed to
[the pilot] on a piece of paper. That was no more than a minute
or two.

The flight to the makeshift landing zone for the evacuation of the
wounded was in many cases made while enemy combatants were not only
still in the area, but often still engaged in an exchange of fire with American

American medevac helicopters, which the US Army termed 'dustoffs', flew rescue and aid missions in all weathers and all terrains. Helicopter crew members shared in the often dangerous work of carrying the wounded to improvised landing zones for evacuation.

forces on the ground. The pilots had to account for the danger to their aircraft, their crew and themselves, in making their approach to land. As Ernie Sylvester, an Army dustoff pilot who flew more than 1,300 hours in Vietnam, recalls:

> We had two approaches. We could either fly in from a distance out as much as a mile at a very high speed, low level, in between the trees and whatever terrain we could find to protect us and we would again, theoretically, try and go over the area that was somewhat secure. We could do that another way by coming in and doing a spiral and trying to stay over the immediate area and basically dive into the area in a spiral turn, keeping the aircraft down to a reasonable exposure above the friendlies [American or allied troops]. Both of them, though, were very fast approaches, almost a screaming approach, and a new pilot could probably never maneuver an aircraft and be able to stop it in the short distance that we had going at 100 miles an hour to

a dead stop without ballooning up and sitting down right next to the wounded or casualties. When it was a hot LZ in a zigzag pattern, we'd probably be in excess of 100 miles an hour. We were told on some occasions not to go in, but we typically were able to find a way to get in.

I would rather go into an LZ when they least expected us instead of them building up or setting up their position whereby they could shoot us out of the sky. Now at night, you could go into an area with a normal approach, blacked out, and they'd have a very hard time seeing you. Therefore, that is one of the reasons I, quite frankly, liked to fly at night because I felt my aircraft and crew were safer. Now, in both cases, both going into an LZ hot or at night, our crew in the back was hanging out the side, clearing us left and right, forward and rear, of obstacles that we would be coming on to in approach in the last few hundred feet or so. That could be a matter of five to ten seconds where they were having to be extremely alert and if they were taking fire, to try and put out some form of suppressive fire and tell us where we were receiving fire, so we could either continue the approach or do a go-around and come in from a different area . . . I very seldom aborted a landing because of the enemy fire or under unusual circumstances because . . . they only had one chance to shoot at me.

The dustoff pilots had received essentially the same training as other military helicopter pilots before coming the Vietnam, and only on the job could they pick up the particular skills of medical evacuation flying. Steve Vermillion, a decorated US Army helicopter pilot, highlights the difference between his pilot training and his flying in Vietnam:

[In training] everything was smooth and it was coordinated . . . They taught you a certain procedure to fly a confined area. You know, you flew the high orbit, couple of orbits around and then you would descend down and you would do your lower reconnaissance and then you would set up for a nice smooth approach and a nice touch down in the confined area. Combat flying just took that and threw it out the door. We flew in a manner to be deceptive to enemy observation. We changed our flight attitudes, our angles and banks, the whole nine yards. In other words we went from Driver's Ed[ucation] to the Daytona 500.

Nighttime helicopter flying in Vietnam was especially dangerous, because the dark obscured potential hazards such as trees and rocky landing sites. More dangerous, however, was the propensity of the enemy to use the cover of night to mount attacks. Not only did this mean that dustoff pilots had to exercise extreme caution in flying through nighttime enemy fire, but they also were called out more often to do so. Steve Vermillion recalls one such nighttime medevac mission that he flew northeast of Saigon early in his tour in 1969:

We got a call to go out there and extract US wounded. I had only had one or two night missions thus far so this is a new experience for me. They called us and said, "The fire support base essentially is being overrun." . . . It was a ten-minute flight or so. So once we lifted off you could see the flares and the tracers and everything start to fly. So we got closer – lots of activity. They had gunships that were trying to suppress anti-aircraft weapon systems. You could see the tracers going into and out of the fire support base. You could see the mortar rounds impacting inside the compound from the enemy fire. They were lobbing mortar rounds in and rocket-propelled grenades. Our first lift, well, we orbited out to the east a little bit. Here again I'm the 'newbie' [recently arrived personnel] so I get to fly going out to the site because Steve [the other pilot] is looking at his map. He's talking on the radio and planning and he points and I drive the direction he wants to go. Kind of like the donkey and the stick; you know, you slap the donkey on the head and you steer him to go one direction or another. He had me set up an orbit to the northeast [and] it seemed like the more I orbited out there the higher and the further away I got. You know, it was like this desire to avoid that area where everything was happening . . . [The men on the ground] finally called and said they are ready. They had six or seven wounded that they needed to 'evac' at that time.

So Steve took the controls and there was a lot of illumination from parachute flares that were hanging in the air. Obviously the parachute flyers are either artillery or mortar fired. They go up and around, detonate, and then this high intensity flare hangs from a small parachute that ultimately drifts down. So the objective is to keep the area illuminated. That gives them visibility on the ground for seeing the enemy coming through the wire or where they are at. It also gave us kind of an eerie look at what

Wounded combatants were not always safe, even after medical help arrived. As a wounded infantryman and a field corpsman look on, enemy machine-gun fire rakes the medevac helicopter in which they are riding, following an ambush of American troops near Da Nang in September 1967.

this landing zone or this fire support base looked like. We were supposed to land to a flashing strobe light. There was so much activity going on inside that fire support base that it was real hard to pick up this strobe light. He would ask me if I could see it and I would say, "Well I see a lot of flashes there but nothing is jumping out as being different." He said, "Well we'll just continue on in." What we ultimately landed to was the strobe light but they were intermixed with the mortar flashes that were coming in. So it was kind of an anonymous flash. There would be a mortar round impact, then we would see the strobe light. [The mortar rounds] were all kind of landing about where we were supposed to land as well. As we made our approach in and coming over the wire you could see the Vietnamese, North Vietnamese coming through the wire. They were shooting at us. Obviously the ground unit was shooting at them. So it was a lot of chaos. We took a few hits throughout the night coming in [on additional evac missions]. Once we got on the ground folks there in the bunker weren't really anxious to come out and bring the wounded to us, nor could I blame them. They were getting their butt kicked pretty hard and they had taken a lot of incoming [enemy fire] and a lot of wounded. So our medic crew chief went out and helped them carry the wounded back in to the helicopter. Then we exited . . . We made probably three or four lifts that night back into that landing zone or into that fire support base . . . Well, we made one pickup outside the fire support base too. There was a recon element that got ambushed so we went out there. Probably [we evacuated] about 20 [wounded men] altogether.

HOSPITAL FACILITIES

Once the wounded were loaded into the helicopter and the pilot had flown the aircraft from the area, the crew tried to keep patients as stable as possible, covering them with blankets and sometimes administering fluids. The pilots, meanwhile, would communicate with the medical facility to which the patients were being flown. At the hospital, physicians, nurses and operating room personnel who were also on call gathered to await the arrival of the wounded. US Army medical technician James Calbreath described the tensions felt by medical personnel on the ground:

> . . . this is where you first learned to live by the helicopters. You hear the helicopters coming in. We would be working in the lab and the NCO would say "Okay, it's your turn to go up to the ER," so we would send somebody up there to wait for the helicopter's arrival . . . They would pull [patients] off of the helicopter on stretchers and [take them] right into the ER and then we would basically just stand there and somebody would hand us a tube of blood and say, "Go do your stuff." . . .

Nurses and technicians often saw the patients first. If there were multiple cases, triage would be performed, and technicians would open pathways for intravenous (or IV) fluids and, in the most severe cases, blood transfusions. Calbreath describes his work in such situations:

> My specialty was "cut downs". When a person is severely injured, they're in shock, they've lost a lot of blood, the vein will get very small and it's difficult to get a decent sized needle into a vein

that could support blood, because when you are delivering blood you want to use as big a needle as possible, get it in there as fast as possible. So what had happened was, you couldn't get into a vein. I had been drawing blood for years and years and I was quite effective at it. Somebody who was severely injured like that, you can't find the veins, so . . . I would do cut downs and I would surgically go into the inside of the arm and – you know, where the veins and arteries are supposed to be – so you just kind of start cutting until you come across one and you open that vein up, insert a needle, stitch it in place, throw a couple of stitches in to hold everything in place, open it up, start throwing blood into it.

Meanwhile, other personnel would be reporting the nature of the wounds to the operating physicians, and preparing the operating theater. Susan O'Neill, an Army Nurse Corps operating room (OR) nurse who served in Quang Tri, Chu Lai, and Cu Chi during her tour in Vietnam in 1969–70, described the fast-paced preparations that accompanied the arrival of wounded from the dustoffs' helipad:

[The wounded] would show up at the side of the OR on a gurney with a chart under the head. We'd go, we'd take a look at the chart, see what's going on, push them through the doors, get them into a suite . . . Somehow, I only remember like three or four, but I tend to think maybe three suites that had kind of eye-level walls between them and you kind of clean [the wounded] up and do whatever you need to with them in a little receiving area if there was a line, and then take them into the suite proper and make sure that they were ready for surgery. It would mean shaving the area if you could, if it wasn't just massive to the point where there really wasn't much you could do preparation-wise. Draping it, one person scrubbing in – either the tech or the nurse – and another person, usually a nurse, circulating, being the one who made sure all the stuff was ready and [who] uncovered the instruments, got them ready to go and that. At the time, the anesthetist would be there working at their head and one of us would have to put in, usually, some kind of IV to make sure that they had saline running so that we could attach blood if they needed it throughout the surgery. Also, usually the anesthetist would have a line of his own running because he'd be starting them, though we'd be working on the other hand.

One of the defining characteristics of the Vietnam conflict was the use on both sides of fiendishly dangerous weapons that caused horrific injuries. Susan O'Neill describes the physical impact that landmines, which were used by all sides in the conflict, could have on the human body:

> Mines were usually what brought us our amputations or potential amputations. Those were really, really nasty things. There was a species of mine, they called it a "bouncing betty", that actually, I guess if you stepped on it, it triggered something that would bring the thing out of the ground and it would hit at kind of mid-level . . . the idea being to debilitate people rather than kill them. What it would do is, it would hit you so you'd get abdominal fragments, you'd get leg damage, you might get some major artery damage that someone would have to tend to immediately in order to keep you from bleeding out. The genitals were generally part of the target area, so some of these guys that we got in were just a mess. They'd be double amputees, they'd have genitals problems where pieces of them would be missing, and they'd have abdominal fragments . . . It really, really tied up the space and tied up the [medical] personnel, which once again was the object of it all. These guys, I often wondered how they adapted when they got back [home] because they're . . . in so many cases there was so much missing, and it was just so freaking painful. I mean, these guys would be screaming – when they were conscious – they would be screaming for morphine, plus add to that the shock, the pain, the shock of looking and seeing that the bed where the covers are over you are flat beyond your knees or even higher. It just had to be awful.

Medical workers not only had to treat these wounds but they also were often personally affected by the enormous suffering of their patients. Medical technician James Calbreath especially remembers,

> . . . the traumatic amputations, because you're walking along and you step on a landmine, it takes your right foot, runs it about halfway up what used to be your shin and then the frag [exploding fragments] comes across and removes your left foot, so what you have is . . . a compression and a traumatic amputation. That I remember as being the most, that was the toughest one. Those were ugly. You knew that this person . . .

yesterday they were thinking, "Gee, I remember when I was in high school and I was the safety on the football team and maybe I'm going to do something like that when I get back," and today they're going to be in a wheelchair the rest of their lives. You think of that in the brief second that you see them. You look and you think, "Well, yes we're going to lose this much of this leg and that much of that leg is gone. How many units of blood is this?" You start looking at the things, you look at the color and decide whether [they have] got enough blood in their system to establish an IV in their arm or hand, or are you going to have to cut down. Can you do this one and still save the other two who are in [the] back?

The most popular category of weapons in the Vietnam conflict, used by all sides, was fragmentation devices, including not only land mines but also grenades, mortars and bombs of all sizes. These weapons were designed to explode, propelling balls or shards of metal or, in more sophisticated bombs, small arrow-shaped metal blades intended to inflict maximum physical damage on human beings. Nurse Susan O'Neill describes the 'frag' injuries she saw in her operating rooms in South Vietnam:

We got . . . an awful lot of just fragment wounds which could be grenade, could be mine, could be rocket-propelled grenade. It could be almost anything and [those] was the ones that would break up and they'd send the little fragments through and you'd be picking up metal fragments, but you'd also be picking up bone fragments because the object was to shatter the bone and make it its own missile, so that you increased the damage in the wound and it was just nasty stuff. That was a lot of debris . . . Often times, the nurses would be doing stuff that nurses would not do stateside. We would actually be wielding tissue scissors, what they call Mayos . . . often with the curved blades, and we would be cutting out tissue. You'd cut out anything . . . you'd cut down to whatever would twitch because everything else was dead . . . More times than I've even cared to think of, someone would come in with a really nasty wound, say in their thigh, and it would involve – though things looked like the leg was intact – it would involve, say the femoral artery. There was no way to save it, so the leg would have to go below that point. And these were the guys who, they'd come in with a leg and they'd leave without one . . .

The thing that stands out in my mind . . . was the amount of the red clay that was so prevalent all over Vietnam. It would gum up . . . it had a grind to it. It was granular, granular but clingy, and that would be in the wounds. So, you had to wash them out and then, once you got all the crap out of them, from just the clay and the junk and the bits of vegetation or whatever they happened to be among . . . then you got right down to the other pieces of armature that were in [the wound].

The Vietnam War also included the deployment of napalm bombs, explosive devices that spread and ignited the jellied petroleum product that had been notoriously used by French during the Franco-Viet Minh War in the late 1940s and 1950s. During that earlier conflict, the US had supplied much of the napalm used by French forces. In the period of direct American military involvement in Vietnam, it continued to be the weapon of choice in certain tactical situations, particularly if large numbers of enemy were concentrated in a small area susceptible to tactical bombing. Although American medical personnel rarely saw the effects of napalm in their operating rooms, as O'Neill recalls, it did happen:

The problem with napalm is that when you drop it, if the wind shifts, there's really no telling where it's going to go. It was more than once, we would get in members of [an American] platoon who had run afoul [sic] of napalm that was dropped and suffered a wind shift or something of that sort, and [it] ended up getting our people instead of their people or their forest or whatever the hell we were aiming for. It was very nasty because it would stick to you, being the gel sort of thing it was. You could actually find sometimes, if you were to strip off a burned shirt or something, you could see where the buttons were and you could see where the cuffs were . . . because where the lines were, it would burn into them; where the seams were, it would burn into them. It was just awful, awful stuff. The real pity about this, I think in some ways, is that a lot of these guys would come in – and civilians too because when napalm [is] dropped, it's not a precision instrument – but the people would come in often quite sensate. I mean, they'd be talking to you and they would be alert. They would be in pain or maybe not in as much [pain] as they should've been, because the burning . . . [had] gone past the nerve endings, which was really awful because of the ramifications of that . . . The object was to get them as stabilized as possible. We would take them in; we would debride the wounds as much as possible. In some cases and some relatively minor cases, I think we had done a little very rudimentary grafting of skin to kind of try to cover areas before we sent somebody out [to hospitals in Japan] . . .

For their part, while VC and NVA soldiers had a less elaborate medical treatment and support system than did the Americans, it was nonetheless impressive on its own terms. Camouflage, mobility, dispersal of buildings, and underground locations made the Communists' facilities less vulnerable to attack. Le Cao Dai, an NVA physician, remembers the hidden field hospital he ran:

> [It would] be very dangerous if you put a [medical] mark [on the hospital buildings]. [It] would be more dangerous than hiding yourself . . . [Our hospital was] not exactly underground . . . [but was] split . . . [because of American] bombing . . . Each house must [hold] up to six people and each house must be far away from the center, at least 50 meters, so my hospital . . . was dispersed in this very large area. If I wanted to go from one part, [from] the beginning and to the end of it, would take me maybe three days to walk. Total it had 450 [beds] but later we have to diminish to 350, because of the shortage of food . . . In principle the supply of rice is only for the patients. Staff had to plant [rice] to provide [for themselves], so . . . [for] every three people we have to plant two hectares of rice.

Devastating injuries were suffered by combatants on all sides, and the fact that hospital facilities were sometimes the targets of enemy attacks made the work of medical personnel even more difficult. At Communist facilities, the greatest threat was posed by American bombing. As Le Cao Dai recalls:

> The most horrible was the B-52. [It happened] many, many times . . . They mostly bomb[ed] at night . . . and they always came regularly. We were only surprised for the first and second raids. Then after that I look at my watch . . . It was so exactly, so it becomes familiar . . . You hear the bombers far away approaching . . . The most important thing is not the direct bombing but the indirect, because the soil covered us and people died because

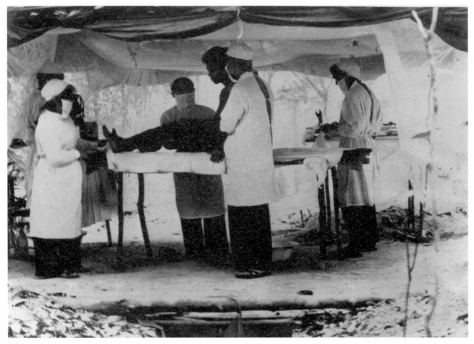

VC and NVA medical personnel often worked in highly mobile, well-concealed field hospital units, where equipment and recovery facilities were limited, while underground complexes in base areas housed more sophisticated semi-permanent medical facilities.

> some bomb explodes and goes through you and the soil came and covered your tunnel. So after each bombing we have to get out of [there] and . . . you have to call, "Are you still alive?"

During an operation he performed in 1969, Le Cao Dai's operating room was suddenly filled with smoke from a smoke grenade, which American spotter aircraft used to mark target locations for bomber aircraft:

> At the time I'm operating [in] the operation room . . . A few minutes later [came the] bomb. We are operating! It was an operation, his belly was open. I cannot run away. I have to put a piece of, how you call it? . . . inside the bellybut[ton] . . . [Anyway], the next time when I saw outside, I saw [bombs] real close to us, so I decide we have to go. I had to put my hand with my glove inside [the patient] to keep the skin and all, to keep [it] all [on] the table. [We got] the operation table and the patient to [the] underground [area].

In the late 1960s, as the conflict expanded and more and more American personnel became involved, the number of US and Allied wounded grew. More elaborate and extensive facilities were introduced, and the management of long-term rehabilitation cases became more refined. The network of American military medical facilities extended far beyond Vietnam, to American bases in Japan and in the United States. Burn cases were a special concern, because of the vulnerability of patients to infection and to secondary illnesses such as pneumonia. These and similar high-risk cases would be flown to American military hospitals in Japan, often accompanied by a physician, as Jim Evans remembers:

> [For the] severely wounded requiring continued medical care . . .
> physicians would fly with them by helicopter to Da Nang and
> then we were on military jets like [the] military equivalent [of]
> a 707. If they needed pain medication, if they needed additional
> IVs during the trip, we monitored the vital signs, sort of whatever
> their needs were. Once we got them to Yokota [Air Base in Japan],
> then I think there were like helicopter flights to Tachikawa or
> wherever, whichever military facility [the wounded] were going to.
> Once we delivered them we would have their chart with them and
> then we would transfer them and turn over the medical care to
> people in the hospital.

The Americans' advanced medical technologies and the rapid evacuation of the severely injured from the battlefield by helicopter saved numerous lives. Even many of those who had sustained devastating neurological damage in combat lived long enough to reach the specialized physicians at major hospitals like the 24th Evac Hospital at Long Binh. There, such patients could be stabilized and undergo surgery, although for many the prognosis was not good. Long Binh had one of the first neurosurgical nursing wards for battlefield casualties, but as its head nurse Margarethe Cammermeyer explained, some of the patients treated there had suffered what were, in effect, terminal injuries:

> The head injury patients we were usually able to evacuate [to
> Japan]. But those who had high spinal cord injuries would
> not be able to be evacuated. I don't know whether or not that
> changed over time. But if someone was essentially bound to a
> respirator then there really wasn't a mechanism to keep them
> on the respirator and to enable an evacuation to take place. This

is, I think, one of the many conflicts of having an extraordinary medical team out in the field that gets to a patient so quickly that those who would normally die survive because they may be ambooed [evacuated by helicopter ambulance] . . . into the hospital where they end up on a respirator and then we can't do anything for them. So in some cases we had to assist the individual in becoming unconscious, if you will, by slowing down the number of respirations per minute that the machine would sort of force them to take, so they would slowly lose consciousness before we would turn off the machine.

Death was an inescapable part of everyday life at the American military's medical facilities in Vietnam. A special detachment, known as Graves Registration, was responsible for the handling of bodies and the deceased's personal effects until they were shipped back to the United States. When a death occurred on her ward, Cammermeyer was relieved to have the enlisted men of Graves Registration take charge:

I could never bring myself to cover [the deceased's] face. So we would just have everything in place so that when they came from Graves Registration – which is an extraordinary group of people who deal with the remains of people who have died – so they would come over and we would move the body onto their gurney from the bed . . . It wasn't until they left the ward that the face was covered. Just wanting to make sure that we hadn't made a mistake. I think also out of respect . . . [for the Graves Registration personnel] – all [they] see is death and mangled bodies. Having to deal with only the dead and dying. These are young people doing it, and they were young people that they were taking care of. I know that field medics don't understand how hospital medical personnel can survive and do the work that they do on a continuous basis, because all they see every day is people that are sick and wounded and maimed and dying. I guess I would say the same for those in Graves Registration, of the extraordinary tenacity they had to have to every day deal with the remains of the dead. Sometimes [bodies] would come in, in pieces. They had to make sure they were identified and that their belongings were there and that they were in a body bag and ready to be sent off. We certainly were grateful that they were there, but also in awe of their experience.

TREATING THE ENEMY

American forces did occasionally bring wounded enemy combatants to American medical facilities for treatment. As US Army artilleryman Mike McGregor recalls, wounded enemy personnel found by his unit sometimes received medical help as they were taken into custody as prisoners of war. Others were so seriously hurt that to 'hump' them to an aid station made little sense to some men in the field:

> Oh, they brought [enemy wounded] there because the field medic worked on them and then the other medics did some more stuff with them and there was a couple of guys there that could talk some Vietnamese, so they talked to them until they could get a medevac [helicopter] and take them back to LZ Betty, which was a main airport at Phan Thiet, and get them to [a] better medical situation. We didn't kill them or anything . . . We've done [that] a couple of times, but it was when you find somebody who's cut in half or something. I never did it personally, but I saw a couple of guys shoot some [enemy] guys that way, just to put them out of their misery.

When injured enemy combatants were brought to American medical facilities, most medical personnel willingly treated them on a humanitarian basis. Even US military personnel working in South Vietnam's civilian facilities, as they sometimes did for training or good will purposes, had occasion to treat wounded VC or NVA soldiers. Clint Chambers, a US Air Force flight surgeon who worked for several months in a South Vietnamese provincial hospital in the Mekong Delta, recalled his attitude toward wounded enemy soldiers:

> You can't make a distinction on something like [enemy status].
> I imagine [that] where they were, out in the field, why, they might make a distinction, but when they got to us, we made no distinction as far as whether they were Viet Cong . . . They were just people who needed help, as far as we were concerned.

On occasion, Communist forces were known to look for opportunities to gain access to American medical facilities. Helicopter pilot Ernie Sylvester recalls an incident in which VC forces, which regularly monitored dustoffs' radio frequencies, called for American medical evacuation for their forces by posing as South Vietnamese troops:

I've had Viet Cong call a medevac in and we have picked up their wounded. They called it in as if they were ARVN soldiers, real close to the Cambodian border in an area called the Plain of Reeds, late in the day. But when we got over there . . . we talked to them. We learned how to say "throw your smoke" and say "toi la bac si" [which means] "I am a doctor." Then they threw the smoke and we fluttered right in there and when we got there, there were a lot of people in black pajamas and they were not Vietnamese soldiers, South Vietnamese soldiers. They were Viet Cong and we took those people and told the hospital that we felt that they were Viet Cong when we dropped them off . . . We were concerned. But if we took off [without them], we would have gotten shot down. We were literally in their nest. So obviously the best thing to do was pick up their wounded and leave . . . To me, it did not truly matter. Some people would probably argue this point. I had an obligation to try and save a life. So to me, it didn't matter if they were Viet Cong or [South] Vietnamese or civilian. We probably picked up three that day. We probably only picked up three because we realized the situation we were in. They didn't necessarily know [how many we could carry in the helicopter] other than they'd probably seen on many occasions a load of three litters.

They were seriously wounded and we loaded them on litters and evacuated them . . . The danger that we had was that they could have brought us in and gotten patients on board and they could have pulled a hand grenade in the aircraft. It would have eliminated us all and they could have done that just to get the aircraft down. We thought about that. All of those kinds of things, all the alternatives, all the bad thoughts rushed through your mind at nanosecond time warp. But we did what we thought was appropriate at the time and it worked. We tried to treat them [but] our crew chiefs and medics were prepared to try and eliminate them if they did something funny.

According to US Army infantryman Elmer Hale, who served his tour in the Central Highlands in 1967–68, the Communist forces' medical needs could provoke other kinds of confrontations. Enemy units operating in his sector kidnapped an American civilian aid worker and demanded that she treat their wounded:

Up the road not very far from us, probably less than a quarter mile, there was a big white building up there. We had kind of moseyed down there, and I heard these kids in this building. I thought what in the world is this? I walked in there and I mean this place was full of orphans. I mean full of them. I talked to this lady. She was a nun, and she was out of Seattle . . . Her first name might have been Patricia, but I'm not real sure about that. She was an older lady at the time. She was in her fifties I'm sure at this time. She came up there to me. She was with a Catholic relief organization of some kind . . . She said, "I run this orphanage." I said, "Where do you get your funds?" She said, "From Catholic Relief. Sometimes I can get some help through the military, but not very often." I talked to her for probably 30 minutes. She was a very unique lady. She was a registered nurse, and she said periodically the NVA would come in there at night . . . and capture her and take her up in the mountains and would make her treat their people. She'd done this on more than one occasion. How long she was over [in Vietnam] I have no idea. I walked out and I thought, "Boy, that's quite a woman."

HUMANITARIAN MEDICAL MISSIONS

Several countries, though they declined to become militarily involved in the conflict in Vietnam, nonetheless contributed medical personnel and equipment on a humanitarian basis. Japan, West Germany and New Zealand (before it committed combat troops in the late 1960s) all sent medical teams. Wounded Communist fighters were among those who sought medical services from neutral third parties. As Army medical specialist John Buesseler, who served in Vietnam in 1969-70, remembers:

[There was] a German hospital ship. They had no combat forces in Vietnam. They only provided this hospital ship as humanitarian aid. It was docked at Da Nang. It would go right in and dock on the port. We wouldn't do that because the VC might come running up with a satchel charge and blow a hole in the boat. But, whenever the German hospital ship was in the harbor at dock, it was told to me, that the town was very happy, because they weren't shelled. When the German hospital ship was not at the dock, then the VC would periodically throw some mortar shells in just as part of the harassment that goes on in warfare. They wouldn't shell them while the hospital ship was in because the VC used it. They'd dress up in civilian garb and infiltrate the

city and go down to the dock and go aboard the ship and they'd
get taken care of. The Germans made it their policy, they didn't
ask any questions. It didn't matter who, if they were ill they would
take care of them, civilians or Viet Cong. Now, the ARVNs and all
the other forces had their own health service support hospitals.
So, really the hospital ship there took care of local civilians and
Viet Cong [and] NVA. Very strange. We knew it and there was
nothing we deemed appropriate to do. You couldn't go down and
stand at the gangway and ask for ID. It was their ship and they
were doing what they wanted to do. But again, it's one of those
funny things that happened in the war.

Communist soldiers sometimes received care from Americans during
MEDCAP operations, which were designed to provide basic medical care
to Vietnamese civilians. These programs were part of America's 'heart
and minds' campaign, to develop an affinity amongst Vietnam's civilian
population for Americans and American aid to South Vietnam. According
to nurse Margarethe Cammermeyer, MEDCAP initiatives also served
another purpose:

> People in the health care industry would go out into villages,
> usually with some medics who had been in certain areas and
> identified that there were villages in need. So doing outreach was
> part of what [American medical] people wanted to do for sanity
> and for something positive . . . particularly for children.

As dustoff crew member Robert Smithee recounted, however, the
Communists could exploit Americans' inability to recognize them as Viet
Cong combatants in order to secure medical attention from MEDCAP
teams:

> It seemed like a couple of days a month you had to go out to
> one of the local villages and you'd treat the sick. You'd have an
> interpreter, somebody would go with you, a base representative,
> and treat the people. My personal opinion was it was an absolute
> waste of time. It was [supposed to be] about winning hearts and
> minds and stuff like that. It was pretty much throwing medical
> supplies down the drain because if you gave the supplies away,
> they get in the hands of the VC . . . It kind of left a bad taste in
> your mouth to [go] back out to this village [because] you were

probably treating some of the people who were shooting at you the week before or the night before . . . A reasonable percentage of the time that you'd go in and treat people who obviously had combat wounds; anywhere from 14- to 15-year-old kids to other people and some older guys that you knew were VC, but there was nothing you could do about it. They were there and they need to be treated, and you knew it was either shrapnel or something like that, because otherwise they're too healthy . . . But, this was one thing that came down [from higher up]: "We're winning the hearts and minds so you're going to have to go do it anyway."

For some American medical personnel, the MEDCAP operations were valuable opportunities to share their skills with civilians who rarely, if ever, saw a trained physician. US Navy physician Mike Rankin remembers:

That was to me R&R when we could do [a MEDCAP mission]. That was great because first of all I may have been foolish about it but I wasn't scared when we were doing that. I don't think there was a time when we were out on patrols when I wasn't scared. But I wasn't when we were doing [MEDCAPs]. That just seemed like, you know, something we could relax and do together. I even talked to the Marines and even some of the Force Recon [Special Forces] people [learned] how to give shots and all of that and they were loving it too . . . [The Vietnamese civilians] seemed to be nice people and they would bring their kids in and all of that . . . I had originally planned to go into pediatrics so that was an interest of mine anyway. So [we did] all the basic immunization stuff. I mean we had lots of stuff. We had clubbed feet and we had, you know, we certainly had mine injuries and all of that. There was very little I could do about [that]. A lot of war injuries. The kids had stepped on punji sticks and all this kind of thing, which you certainly wouldn't see in an average pediatric ward, but you did what you could . . . I think the parents and the kids and all of them just kind of understood that. That you couldn't fix their clubbed foot, you couldn't undo all the damage they had gotten, but you could at least do something.

However, a sense of futility crept into many Americans' views of MEDCAP missions. Their efforts, however well intentioned, could not address all the basic hygiene and dietary deficiencies that lay behind most health problems in the villages of South Vietnam. There were also times when MEDCAP personnel were placed at risk from 'unfriendlies', some of whom were supposed to be America's allies. Jim Evans recalls such an incident in the Quang Tri area in 1969-70:

> . . . One of the first [MEDCAPs] I went to was near Wonder Beach . . . We were out there in a Jeep; there were several medics . . . We took care of the people and then the local [South Vietnamese] militia wanted all the medicine. It was in a metal chest . . . So they pulled weapons, locked and loaded, and the medics pulled their weapons out and lock and loaded, like M-16s. So it was just a stand off. No shots were fired. We loaded up. We were, I think, in the ambulance, which would carry several of us plus the equipment, and drove off, back to the Quang Tri combat base . . . with the medicine, yeah. I thought we were going to get killed . . . I was terrified. I realized that we could have been shot. Hey, it was a VC area and it was just damn scary. We got back to the battalion and they were just saying, "Why are you worried? Why are you upset?" [Our commanders] would not provide security. So I quit going.

Those who volunteered their time to work at ARVN or civilian Vietnamese clinics sometimes felt defeated by their outdated medical techniques and poor conditions. Margarethe Cammermeyer recalls what she observed at a civilian hospital in Cholon, a suburb of Saigon:

> The hospital was huge. There were two, sometimes three people in one bed that was the size of a twin bed. You realize that not only are the people small, but when you have amputations or when they're used to sleeping on the floor without anything, that this was still an accommodation for them. The caregivers were their families. They sat around the bed and cooked for them or slept underneath the bed on a concrete floor. The medications were ones that the doctor would write a prescription [for]; the family would go out to a local pharmacy, buy the medication, bring it back to give to the nurses who then distributed back to the family with a whole day's dose being given at one time, for the family to distribute as they were able to. It was like something that we would think of as occurring during the Crimean War.

American medical personnel of all ranks suffered along with those they treated. Their work was never easy, and for many, there were few outlets for the emotional burdens they carried. Susan O'Neill, the operating room nurse, describes her very private method of coping with the stresses of treating the sick and wounded in Vietnam:

> At least once a week, things would build up to the point where I would just want to cry and then I'd go out to the helipad, once again, find a corner of it and just cry my eyes out. It might not be any specific thing that was bothering me, it was just like things would build up . . . People will tell you, "Well, it's great. It gets it all out." But it doesn't, it just makes you tired and makes you weary and stuff, but I think in the long run, it was helpful. I am . . . one of those people who will stand back and intellectualize, but it's going to hit you sooner or later. When it does, it will be an oddball time when you actually have the time to think about things or you have the time to let the emotion . . . just kind of overwhelm you. So, that was an out for me . . . Both [my] planned yelling – the singing at the top of my lungs – and the unplanned – giving in to crying . . . I think helped keep me on a keel somehow. Plus I was just so angry. I was just so angry at what was happening all the way around and I think that might be a healthy thing to do in war, to be angry about such things.

On balance, most medical personnel on both sides of the conflict were glad that they had been on hand, in whatever situation, when someone needed medical help. As physician Mike Rankin of the US Navy recalls:

> [We would] try to be good guys out there.

7
EVERYDAY LIFE

The men and women who served in Vietnam experienced and participated in an event – a war – that had a dramatic personal impact on them and changed their lives forever. The range of experiences, the emotion that went along with them, the hardships, the laughs, the camaraderie, the death, the fear – all of the lasting memories became a part of who they were as individuals. Sometimes it was the mundane, the routine, that stuck with the participants as much as anything else that happened to them in Vietnam, including the combat. What were those routines and what was everyday life like in the Vietnam War? The majority of time for the typical veteran was not occupied by constant fighting. In between those intense moments of combat, and in their typical days, what happened?

For the average soldier, pilot and seaman in the Vietnam War a typical day varied from person to person, from branch to branch, from location to location, and from specialty to specialty.

THE US MARINE ON THE GROUND

Bill Hancock was a rifleman and radioman in Vietnam in 1967 and 1968. He describes what his unit's activities were like on a day to day basis:

> I would say a typical day was . . . we'd be out on ambush
> somewhere and we'd get up in the morning [and] you'd be
> on a hundred percent alert starting at six o'clock in the
> morning and get up, maybe make some C-rations, eat them,
> get rid of anything that accumulated during the night, you
> know paper or any kind of stuff around there, bury everything,
> get ready; you'd go on patrol during the day, almost all day
> long you'd patrol. They'd send us out in squads and we just
> walked through the area and walked through villages and
> other things looking for any sign . . . we were searching for
> the VC and, we were an infantry unit so our job was to find the
> VC or NVA and fight them, so that's what we did. We patrolled
> all day looking for them and I guess we were trying to get in a

fight . . . We found them on numerous occasions. I would
say, during my time over there . . . I was in 40 or 50 firefights.
And then . . . we'd patrol and we'd stop, take ten-minute breaks.
As soon as you got a ten-minute break everybody (except for
whoever was on watch) passed out because you didn't get any
sleep over there.

We'd set up a perimeter when it came during the evening
hours . . . we'd wait till dusk and then we'd . . . send out our
ambushes . . . or go out on ambush. Two out of every three
nights you went out on ambush . . . We would go out at dusk
and we would . . . have a designated place that we were going
to set up. The officers would find them [the ambush spots]
and they'd just assign us a place along a trail . . . where they
thought there might be some VC activity or some NVA
activity and we'd walk out, and then before we got to the
spot we'd bust back into the brush, walk along the trail, you
know so we didn't give away our position and then we'd lay
alongside the trail in two-man positions about every eight
to ten yards or something, and wait for somebody to walk
through to shoot at.

THE AVIATION GROUND CREW
Timothy Lockley served in Vietnam on different 'temporary duty' tours
between 1966 and 1972 as a Crew Chief and Maintenance Supervisor for
airplanes. He worked out of Udorn, Thailand, one of the major air bases
from which the US launched aircraft against all targets in the war zone.
Lockley describes his typical day:

Well, it was 12- to 16-hour days when we were working, and of
course I was on the . . . ground crew, but we were what we called
[a] dedicated ground crew, which meant we generally flew with
the airplane, and of course I was the low man on the totem pole
[on the airplane] so I got all the dirty stuff to do . . . the real dirty,
gunky stuff, but it was hard work all the time and of course it
was hot no matter where you were, it was always hot, very humid,
but being from Mississippi that wasn't that big of a problem,
but it was very, very hard, very, very difficult work under those
conditions . . .

At the time [1966] Tan Son Nhut [Air Base] wasn't nearly as
built up as it was a couple years later so there were . . . a few

problems with supplies here and there, occasionally we'd have
a breakdown and we'd have to wait for them to send a part in,
but it was just hard, physical labor. There were three aircraft
with us and we would sort of alternate, but even when you
weren't flying missions, you still had aircraft maintenance and
they were our airplanes and we didn't have any other support
so basically you do all the work yourself . . . [B]ack then most
of the most common things [repairs] were like changing tires,
it was preventive maintenance as much as anything. You would
do a pre-flight check before the aircrew came out and then they
would do their pre-flight, and pre-flight meant you walked all
around the airplane looking for leaks, you walked across the
wings looking here and there, you went in the inside of the
aircraft looking for leaks, you do pressure checks, engine run-
ups, different kind of things, just your basic, general preventive
maintenance, just make sure everything worked properly . . .

   I was on flight status . . . I would normally sit on the cargo
deck . . . if they were very nice, the flight crew would [sometimes]
let me up on the flight deck, but most of the time I'd fly in the
back and I would just be a general helper back there. There'd be
a loadmaster and there was an explosive ordnance guy back there
. . . all he did was arm the bomb when we were ready to drop,
that's all he did was arm it. But the loadmaster was the guy who
did the weight and balance thing and my job basically was just to
do what anybody wanted. Sometimes they'd ask me to give them
coffee out of the galley . . . just whatever.

US ARMY – A BATTALION BRIEFING IN THE REAR
How did the infantry units organize themselves in the field and carry out
operations on the ground? James Wheeler, Jr, spent time in the field as
an infantry platoon leader as well as at base camp as the Assistant S-3,
the Assistant Battalion Operations Officer. His duties included briefing
the commanding officers on past operations and helping plan for future
ones:

   . . . One of my principal duties, every morning and every evening,
   I gave the operations briefing for the battalion to the battalion
   commander and his staff [and] any VIPs [when] the commanding
   general comes in . . . I always went the extra mile and I got up
   extra early to commit all my briefing to memory . . . a typical

briefing was early in the morning. The battalion commander would arrive and the principal staff is already there and the commanders and what have you. We just simply went over what had transpired literally [on the ground] . . . For a given morning briefing I would brief following the S-1 [Battalion Adjutant] and the S-2 [Battalion Intelligence]. Of course the S-2 briefed off the map pretty much too because he's the intelligence guy and always had his notes. Like I say I was up an hour or two before anybody else and went into the TOC, the Tactical Operations Center, and really worked diligently, so when I took my pointer and pointed to a site on the map I had: "At 16:30 hours yesterday, sir, Charlie platoon of da-da-da-da made contact with x number of bad guys, enemy and the results were bop-bop-bop." I just did it by the numbers. Of course during the course of the day I'm working with the major and moving forces and evaluating intelligence and making plans for operations, etc, insertions of troops.

THE US ARMY INFANTRYMAN

John McNown, Jr, was an Army infantry platoon leader in Vietnam in 1968 and 1969. He remembers his Company's typical day in the field and what it would do at night:

... Most of the time a typical day would be, we would have dug in the night before, usually late in the afternoon where we'd have plenty of time to dig in fairly well. We were really good about digging in. The Company had seen enough action earlier, having been mortared enough they believed in having foxholes. Some of the companies that hadn't seen as much, they'd try to sneak in and lay up at night. I talked to one of the company commanders and we got into an argument later on. We were out in the jungle and we were digging in. You make a lot of noise when you're digging in and cutting fields with fire and things. We were supposed to be setting up together and he thought that they should just sneak in and lay down so the NVA wouldn't know where you were. My theory was they knew where we were because we made so much noise moving. One hundred Americans loaded down with gear are not a particularly quiet group. There's just no way when you're out in the mountains and you're following trails, looking for base camps or whatever. When you hit somebody earlier in the day they've got a general sense that somebody's out there. Our theory was, we're going to make it worthwhile for them, or make it not worth their while to come after us. If they do, we want to be dug in . . .

Mainly it was a perimeter. We usually set it up as close to a circle as we could make it. We'd literally be a perimeter. We'd find the highest ground we could, dig in on the military crest someplace . . . Then the mortars and the CP [Command Post] would be in the center of the perimeter. You'd have one platoon tying into the other platoon tying into the other and then the shape would be generally round. Then you'd set up the machine guns on the most likely avenues of approach into your area and where they could kind of cover the front of the platoon. Then we would set out claymores and trip flares . . . Everybody carried a claymore and a trip flare. We would set those out and then usually had two men, sometimes three if we had enough people to a position. The size of the perimeter often depended on how many men we had in the field unless we had an area where you had to spread out a lot wider to cover the likely avenues of approach. We liked to be as tight as we could . . . We varied . . . we had as many as 125 men in the field . . . Then we'd be down. We were down to as low as 50 several times . . .

We would normally find a good spot and dig in at 4:00 in the afternoon or 5:00 depending on when it was going to get dark. Usually start digging in about two hours or so before dark. So we could have a good hole and set up and put out . . . listening posts, sometimes which would be usually two men out on the perimeter someplace on each side in likely avenues of approaches. A lot of times that would be the whole company there. A lot of times what would happen is we'd dig around with one platoon around the CP and the other two platoons would split up and go out on ambushes. We'd put out sometimes as many as ten or 12 small ambushes every night. Spread all over a whole area when we were down in the coastal plain. That's pretty much what a lot of what we did down there. Then we'd get back together in the daytime and then patrol as a unit, kind of spread out. Put two platoons in front searching an area, sweeping through an area and one kind of in reserve, pulling in from the rear. With the CP in the middle. Usually spread out over a half a mile or so in width. Following the rice paddies they told you never to walk on the dikes. That's one of the things they taught you. Of course we always walked on dikes, because try to walk in a rice paddy with 80 pounds on your back. The second thing . . . [is that] the Vietnamese were walking on the dikes, so it was usually if you were down in a populated area, if you'd seen Vietnamese walking in an area, it was probably safe. We'd hit a booby trap occasionally . . .

In the daytime you were hot and miserable. You felt better because you could see. We didn't have all the night vision devices that they have now. Of course there was a lot more cover than there has been the last two or three wars [in Kuwait and Iraq]. The fields of fire weren't as good. So you're moving at night and it was just kind of like a cat and mouse game. We were out trying to set up ambushes and we knew they were doing the same thing. They were moving at night . . . You used to hear that thing about 'Charlie rules the night' . . . We didn't move as much at night but we ambushed a lot at night. We never felt that they were any better at night than we were. They just knew where they were. The big advantage they had was knowing the terrain. That was an advantage they had down in the coastal plains. Up in the mountains nobody knew where they were . . . I think in the mountains [we] were pretty much on equal terms, we just were moving around a lot more than they tended to. So we'd blunder into them. I hate to say blunder since most of the time we didn't know where they were. We'd just go out and look for them and sometimes you'd run into them. Often the NVA would have Viet Cong that would lead them to the coastal plains so they knew where they were going, where they wanted to set up and we were out just kind of wandering or looking for somebody to run into.

SUPPLIES

One of the things many individuals discuss about serving in the Vietnam War was their ability to secure items that were not available to them but they needed and wanted for a variety of reasons. The infamous Vietnam barter system, the ways that individuals obtained what they wanted, is humorous and at the same time very revealing of the ingenuity of people stuck in a bad situation trying to better it. Sumner Clayton, an adviser to the South Vietnamese Navy between 1970 and 1971 stationed near the DMZ at Qua Viet, discusses what he did to obtain the items that he wanted:

Well, we ran out of ammunition for M-16s one time. We were down to about 1,000 rounds and couldn't get any, couldn't get them from the Army for some reason or another; couldn't get them from the Navy . . . We put together a team. They were good. Somehow or another they confiscated four cases of M-16 ammunition out of the armory on the South Vietnamese base we were at. And we could go to the Army base in Dong Ha . . . sometimes you'd have to go there for supplies . . . We wound up somehow, I won't say how, with an American Marine Corps jeep. The numbers were changed on it. It wound up with a new paint job . . . When we would go to the US Army bases, we couldn't get on there with a Vietnamese jeep. We could get on those bases with this particular jeep. I think it came from Da Nang somewhere. Anyway, we could drive over there with an empty trailer. We needed sandbags one time. We couldn't get any sandbags anywhere and they had many of them over there [Da Nang] . . . So I went to a signal supply place. I went to the Army Engineers place first. He said, "Yeah. I'll tell you what I need though; we need quite a bit of garden hose," . . . I'm not too sure what that reason was either, but he needed about 500 feet of garden hose. I said, "Okay, I'll trade you the garden hose for two pallets of sandbags. And I need them trucked over there to Qua Viet." He said, "No problem." This is the Army Engineers. They could fix our jeeps, by the way – we would take the mechanic by the liquor store on the base and he would be paid pretty good. We'd take him back. We'd trade a couple of fifths of good whiskey and they could overhaul the jeep, no problem at all. Coffee grounds were [also] good trade material . . .

I didn't have 500 feet of garden hose, not even close. I didn't even have a garden hose. So he shipped me the sandbags. I took one pallet of the sandbags and traded them to an Army Signal battalion who just happened to have a lot of garden hose. Then took it back, gave it to the Army Engineers about a week later and everything was just fine. You were Americans and you were in a foreign country and the 'Saigon warriors' [Americans stationed in Saigon] could get anything they wanted. Everything came in at Saigon. Something like a simple American soft drink. There were no Coca-Colas at Qua Viet. Da Nang you might see some. By the time the supply train, so to speak, got to Qua Viet, you were looking at probably a cheap brand of Sprite or a grocery store brand of some cola. But you could go out in the fishing village right outside the gate, pay somebody ten dollars American money and buy a case of Coca-Colas. I never did but I know people that did a bunch. If you ordered beer, we got Schlitz and Falstaff. Saigon and everybody else was getting the good stuff. And the whiskey was just about the same shape. The farther north you got the more scarce it got. But anyway, I also found out that I could go in any shop in any Army base and just act like I knew what I was doing. I could walk off with whatever we needed half the time.

Michael Sweeney, a Marine infantry company commander, recalls a problem he encountered when trying to obtain a re-supply of food. His men were due for a meal to be delivered to them out in the field, on a hilltop near the Laotian border. They had not eaten a decent meal in a number of days:

> [T]he helicopters pulled out he [the pilot] said [to me over the radio], "Well, we got chow. Which would you like, chocolate, vanilla or strawberry?" I said, "What do you mean?" He said, "We've got 150 gallons of ice cream up here, and that's it." Somehow they'd hooked on[to] the helicopter the wrong load. It was dark by then and our food re-supply consisted of chocolate, vanilla and strawberry ice cream. Of course, the troops hadn't had anything like that in a long time. The top of that hill is still pink and brown and white as far as I know. They were all sick and all of them had the trots and all the rest of it. It was a rotten deal all the way around.

UNIFORM

The typical American uniform varied from branch to branch and from job to job. Mike Bradbury, a US Marine, describes what he would wear in the field:

> Well we would have our jungle fatigues on, which had side pouches on the hips for carrying . . . whatever you wanted to carry with you. You had your flak jacket, you would have your helmet, and of course your mosquito repellent, you would have your cartridge belt and in your cartridge belt you would have your first aid kit, your bayonet, and I would usually pack three or four grenades, the old M-26 grenades, you would have your pack, and you wouldn't have everything in it because you're only going to go on a daytime patrol so in your pack [you'd]

A US Army platoon sergeant takes a break during a "search and destroy" mission northeast of Cu Chi, South Vietnam, in 1967. American infantrymen wore a uniform that blended well with the features of the Vietnamese terrain and was able to hold all of the gear they would need for fighting and life in the field.

have extra ammunition, and you would have some C-rations because somewhere along there you're going to stop and have chow. Then you would have, in my case at the time, an M-16 and I had three or four magazines loaded, and of course your water, canteens.

US Army infantry commander James Wheeler, Jr, remembers what he would wear and have with him while on patrol:

Fatigue-wise it was just the basic old jungle fatigues that you know and have seen. We got to change clothes every so often. There was no regularity to when we changed clothes. I probably started out with my own shirts. Then once you threw them [away] you just wore whatever came in from the big wash . . . So your clothing came in just like C-rations and everything else. When you got a change of clothes you were just happy to get a change of clothes. They were just fatigues in a bag that you grabbed and put on . . .

We just as a rule didn't wear underwear because in the dry season you were wet so much of the time from pure sweat . . . In monsoon season you were [constantly] wet. I assume we considered the underwear something that would perhaps chaff you. Just an extra something there that didn't need to be there under the conditions . . . Socks were very much more important, of course. Both seasons as well. Even though you're not in the wet season, obviously you need dry socks. In the dry season you're perspiring so much that you've got to enforce and you use your medic . . . but [it was] very important to keep the feet clean and well because that was our traveling [means] . . .

[You had] your basic jungle boots. You always had your towel. Towel around your neck was imperative because, again, you're just constantly wet either way. So the towel was a major part of your rucksack. Your rucksack of course being your pack. I've never weighed my rucksack. But the average numbers that I've heard . . . was around 80 pounds, 60 to 80 pounds . . . Not everybody carried a razor . . . You did everything you could to simplify and lighten your load . . . With your rucksack, you had your personal toiletries, as limited as they were, and certainly your C-rations . . . Aside from that you couldn't carry enough water. Everybody was required to carry . . . two or three canteens. We even went to two-quart bladders at some point . . . you couldn't carry enough water especially during the dry season. More than once I've gone to a blue line on my map to get water only to find it's dried up. Then you wore your bandoliers, your M-16 5.62 magazines. Again you're required so many. [If] you wanted to carry more, that was your prerogative. Certainly on your pistol belt you had your standard ammo pouches for that. Generally we carried them in bandoliers. Your ammo pouches were used to carry something else . . . a little snack or something. Of course, you had your first aid pouch there, definitely . . . the helmet liner, steel pot . . . Most everyone of course carried the M-16 rifle no question. We had . . . the grenade launcher, the M-79 was carried as well as the M-60. The M-60 machine gun and . . . the assistant gunner had to carry extra ammo as the assistant gunner for the M-60 . . . I carried the AR-15, the Car 15 which had the folding stock. It looked like an M-16 but it was a much smaller version . . . You always had it over your neck, always in the ready position . . . We had . . . grenades . . . [T]he M-26 fragmentation grenades and smoke. We always carried smoke, various colors, purple, yellow, what have you. Red is only for a bad time.

Jim Ray was a Marine tank platoon commander. He describes what he carried on his person, on his command tank, and the ingenuity of men in the field:

> I'd say being a tanker, we were far better off than the infantry. We could carry luxury items so to speak. A lot of C-rations and Dr Pepper's and things like that on our tank. You know, the infantry couldn't do that. I would say we had far fewer impediments than the average Marine. I'd say we were far better off than most of the people actually out operating in the field . . . Most of us by that time had the standard jungle utilities. They weren't camouflaged, but they were jungley [*sic*]. There were the big flaps on them and those kinds of things. Those were very handy for carrying your maps and compasses and anything else that you had to have. Your small camera that you carried with you, that sort of thing. The only weapon that we [the officers] carried was a .45-caliber pistol . . . The tankers carried inside the tank . . . what we called a grease gun, which was sort of a little automatic weapon, and that's the only weapons that we carried personally . . . which is why we stayed on the tanks . . . We had no need to carry anything with us other than our weapons . . . [W]e wore helmets . . . the purpose of the helmet was essentially it had a radio in it [and a] speaker where you could basically communicate with everybody in your tank. In theory, you could communicate with the infantry and aviation and other people out of that, but it really didn't work that way. The radios inside . . . the M48 tanks in that era were not very good radios. We ended up taking the infantry radios which were . . . the PRC-25s, and we would strap those inside the tanks. That's what we used to really talk to the infantry with.

Navy pilot Ken Craig flew the A-4E Skyhawk and A-6A Intruder. He describes the uniform he wore while flying missions off of aircraft carriers in the South China Sea:

... We had ... Marine fatigues on and we had torso harnesses,
a G-suit, which covered the legs, and it had big pockets and
we stuffed them with survival equipment and things that we
might need if we were down, extra bottles of water and things
like that. And then we had ... a survival vest that went over the
torso harness and the torso harness is where your parachute is
strapped to so that if you eject, you've got a full-laced parachute
harness ... and a helmet. I picked up a big survival knife in
... jungle escape and survival training ... [It was a] shortened
version of a machete [made] out of jeep springs, a bowl or two,
and [it was] sharpened real well ... so [it] could cut through the
brush ... I had one of the parachute riggers make me a scabbard
that would attach to my leg and I carried that for all my years
over there ... So, it was quite a bit of gear. Plus, we were issued
... the first 9mm pistols, automatic pistols, that were issued over
there. We had a very inventive survival training officer ... and
he got lugs on our deviation shoes, jungle-type lugs, holes, and
he got all kinds of other things ... so we carried ... extra little
signal flares ... [It weighed] ... probably [an] extra 40 pounds ...
[W]e were seated, so it wasn't uncomfortable, I have all this stuff
on, you get used to having the bulk on you and it didn't detract
much from flying the airplane.

OUT IN THE JUNGLE

Besides encounters with the enemy, there were many other things lurking
out 'in the bush' in Vietnam and many other surprises. Army infantry
commander Frank Vavrek recalls an incident while out on patrol:

[W]e were trying to move to regain contact with the enemy if
we could, so we were walking cautiously, if you can envision
that, and people were spread out and ... we're looking around.
Every little tree, every corner, every rock because ... we've been
hit pretty hard and we knew the enemy was there and was still
there, was still pretty bad. Well, this one guy, he was point man
[leading the unit] and we had held up; [I] told him to move on
ahead and check – there was some like rock outcropping of tall
rocks ... check around those rocks to make sure to keep from
getting us ambushed as a unit. Well, as he looked around one
rock, this monkey jumped up on the rock and screamed. Well,
the poor point man collapsed, his knees bent and he went to the

ground because it scared the crap out of him so bad . . . man, that was about it for him for that day. We had to give him a chance to recover. We never did evacuate him, but whew! It gave him a scare.

Andy Roy remembers stumbling upon two oddities while on point, patrolling deep in the jungle in the Central Highlands:

I was pulling point [out in front] and I looked up and there was a huge wagon with huge wheels on it and there was no trail, no road, no nothing, just sitting right there and I couldn't figure out how the hell it got there and we all kind of looked at it as we went by it but obviously it had been there for years and we continued on.

Later on that day, another surprise: here's a pre-World War II French Renault automobile, again, no roads, no trails, no nothing. Just sitting there in the woods, slowly rusting. It still had a lot of the black paint on it and I remember looking inside and like the engine had been taken out, it had been scavenged for certain things, the wheels were gone, stuff like that, and I remember again being puzzled, how the hell did it get here and I wonder what the story behind it is.

Vavrek describes another encounter his unit had while out on patrol, something that was a common occurrence in South Vietnam:

We were just out on operation just minding our own business, walk[ing] along, and we come down to a creek. It's a pretty nice area in there and we run into this water buffalo and this guy is not happy that we're around, and he's got his nose down and he's snorting and he's pawing at the ground, and they [his men] said, "Okay, what're we going to do?" I said, "Well, we're going to shoot the water buffalo." Well, little did I know when you shoot at them, you got to have a big gun. So [an] M-16 shot at him and all that thing succeeded in doing was making him mad. The bullets would hit him . . . and he just got mad, so he started to charge. So, next thing, our machine gunner opened on him . . . and then one of the guys with the light anti-tank weapon cocked that thing and hit him with that. It killed him. It stopped him from charging into our troops.

It was inevitable that infantry units would cross paths with the animal life of Vietnam while in its natural habitat. Andy Roy describes the multitude of wildlife that he encountered on his three tours:

> [I saw] mongooses, an orangutan once . . . some snakes . . . when I went over there I thought there'd be a snake around every corner . . . They had some pretty poisonous snakes there. They had bamboo vipers which are probably the equivalent of a rattlesnake, they weren't real bad . . . Cobras I saw once . . . You didn't want to shoot it usually because you didn't want to make the noise. It might get chopped with a machete . . . I've found out since then that down in rice paddies on the average there's two cobras for every rice paddy square, but you never saw them because we're considered too big [for them to eat]. I'm sure there were a lot that just plain got out of the way when they heard us.
>
> One time [in the] Tuy Hòa area we were coming out of a forested area out into savannah lands and right at the line there was this little break opening . . . and I was about in the second platoon back and all of a sudden all of this firing broke out, out front, out in the savannah lands, about 50 meters away or so, and we all dropped to the ground and everybody, every other man alternates [his position], right and left, right and left, and heard the firing and then nothing . . . and then all of a sudden word coming down the line, okay get up, let's go on. What the hell was going on? Well, we went on forward and I looked down and here's the biggest snake I ever seen in my life, a python twisting and rolling in the grass. Well the point man . . . [was] going through this grass about two feet high and had stepped on this thing thinking it was a log and it moved, so him and the other guy just fired it up for which they got chewed out for, because hey it's a snake, don't worry about it, the head's way up there, you can tell by the size of the body, but that was about the biggest snake I ever saw.

Marine rifleman Bill Hancock recalls an incident with a frequent visitor to the American infantry units:

> The rock apes were hilarious. [They] scared the shit out of you mostly whenever they get the chance. We'd be out an ambush or going out someplace, next thing you know they'd be standing

next to you, you hadn't even heard them or anything . . . Well one time . . . we had a guy that was walking point for us going down to the water point . . . and the elephant grass was like eight feet tall and of course the point man is out as far as he can be where you can still see him and so as he was walking out there a rock ape reached out and grabbed him which naturally scared the crap out of him and he [the soldier] just took off running . . . the other way. We had to catch him. But as soon as this rock ape grabbed him, he yelled, the rock ape yelled, [and] took off the other way.

Roy saw other wild animals while in the jungle:

I saw tigers twice . . . helicopters were flying overhead and they had a dead tiger swung by the paw underneath, and I was really amazed at the size of these things. I've seen tracks a couple times, and then during my third tour I was pulling an ambush next to a stream and there was heavy brush around it and there was a trail running through it, and some guy said, "Do you hear that?" I said, "What?" and I heard something crack, like a little twig or something, and then another one, and it kind of moved around and suddenly – you ever heard a tiger give these real low, guttural kind of [growl] . . . something like that came and boy I'm sorry, you had a squad of guys more frightened than if we had had a platoon of North Vietnamese around us and everybody's sitting there with weapons ready on full automatic in case this thing jumped out of the dark. And it walked around our position on the riverside maybe two or three times and then we never heard it again, but we were concerned for the rest of the night . . . God the tracks were huge . . . these tigers, they were just massive . . .

I've seen elephant tracks, I didn't see any elephants. Like I said mongooses, monkeys, there were deer around, they had bears over there. I didn't see any, they call them moon bears, and . . . some freakish birds . . . they had these little mammals, they used to race around at night when you're pulling guard . . . [Y]ou could tell a little mammal by the little scurrying and a quick stop, just like you could tell if a human being is out there or the size of an animal. This thing about Viet Cong, North Vietnamese going through the jungle like a cat is a bunch of bullshit; no one goes through the jungle like a cat except a cat and chances are you're going to hear it if you're listening.

KEEPING PETS

Besides crossing paths with animals in the jungle, the men and women in Vietnam also associated themselves with other animals during the war. They kept pets, both out in the bush and back in the rear. Roy Riddle recalls his unique pet, a monkey that was given to him, which served him in more ways than simple companionship:

> [The monkey] was given to me by one of the Companies from the 3rd Brigade of the 4th Division . . . They were surrounded and I was covering combat observation, brought in some helicopters to give them some support, and they caught the monkey in the process of that mission and brought it back with them. [They] gave it to me. I called him 'Columbus,' because he didn't know where he had been, he didn't know where he was, he didn't know where he was going. He was a good monkey. He liked to fly. He liked to sit up on my shoulder and fly . . . He loved to fly, but he didn't like [the] Vietnamese. Vietnamese could get within 20 feet of him and he would start yelling. I always knew if a Vietnamese was coming near me. He was my bodyguard . . .

Marine Don Cuneo recalls his experience with an animal as his company was ending a patrol and digging in for the night:

> We were getting ready to dig in for the night. As we were going through the village, I ended up getting picked up by this little puppy . . . he ended up with me so I guess either he adopted me or I adopted him. We were getting ready to dig in for the night, and we were outside of a village . . . [T]his Vietnamese male came walking up the path past us and then about five minutes later came walking back down and he didn't have anything on him. We didn't think anything about it. Shortly after that, we got mortared. What had happened was he had paced us off. Here I was digging a hole, and this puppy was bouncing around and everything and when the first mortar hit and the guys that got hit started screaming, somebody yelled, "Incoming, get down!" My first reaction was I grabbed my helmet and put it over the puppy.

Charles Dodge, an Army platoon leader, recalls the mascots his Armored Cavalry unit had with them:

While serving in Vietnam, some US soldiers kept pets for companionship. These animals were sometimes the only native Vietnamese that they befriended in country. This soldier from the 82nd Airborne Division shares a moment with his pet dog northeast of Saigon in 1969.

We had a little dog. Kind of a mutt named Tanker that rode around [with us]. He had a little buddy that was a real mutt. Totally indescribable mutt that we called Uncle Ho. You might think that we called him Uncle Ho playing off Ho Chi Minh. But the name Ho was actually a contraction of the initials HO, which stood for hood ornament. He liked to ride right under the .50-caliber machine guns on one of the [half-]tracks . . . It was interesting because Ho in a firefight – he was typically the first one to arrive being on the front of the track – he'd stand up underneath that .50-caliber machine gun and just give the enemy fits. Bullets snapping around him. I thought, "That old guy's crazy." I did notice that he and Tanker both lasted longer than all the platoon leaders in our platoon . . . The mascots seemed to do okay. We should have listened to them more.

MUSIC

Music played a very significant role in the Vietnam War. The men and women who were there listened to music everywhere: on a base in the middle of the Central Highlands, in the field on their small transistor radios, onboard ship in the South China Sea, in the administrative offices in Saigon, on patrol on a river boat in the Mekong Delta, in the skies flying missions around the area, and from visiting USO (United Service Organizations) bands sent to entertain the troops. The songs of the day impacted them in multiple ways. The music enabled them to get through the days of their tour of duty, it helped them relax whenever they had the opportunity to do so, and it struck deep emotional and psychological chords within the men and women – so deep in fact that the music of the war is as clear and meaningful to them today as it was in Vietnam in the 1960s and early 1970s. Some songs were signature Vietnam War songs, while others simply marked their time in country. Jerry Benson was an Army infantryman between 1968 and 1969. He speaks to the power of music in a war zone:

> **Tom Carroll was in my company. He was the company clerk before I was . . . Tom made a comment on [our] time . . . over there, [in Vietnam, about] the power of music. When you don't really have much to cling to, music in your life is really, really a powerful thing. Whatever kind of music it is.**

Benson recalls one of those powerful songs for him, one that today catapults him back to Vietnam:

> **There is one song by Johnny Horton, the country singer, 'All for the Love of a Girl'. I remember that we were up in . . . the base camp that had all the rubber trees. We woke up at 4:30 one morning to go out on an operation about 5:00. When I woke up somebody had the radio on and that song was being played, 'All for the Love of a Girl' by Johnny Horton. Everytime I think of Johnny Horton I think of that moment and that song.**

John McNown, Jr, recalls what role music played for him and how it still evokes memories of Vietnam when he hears certain songs:

> **I always think of it as a rock 'n' roll war. Every place you went there was music. I remember going in on a combat assault in a**

Huey and I was wearing a helmet talking to the pilot because I was the acting company commander at the time. He had his radio on the NVA channel, which was where you could pick up the AM stuff. I remember we were going in and the gunships were going by us firing into the LZ. Steppenwolf was on playing 'Magic Carpet Ride'. To this day, when I hear that song I can picture those gunships going down there and us coming in on those choppers . . . When you're someplace special and you hear a song it brings that back. [There was] a lot of Lou Rawls. I think a lot of people [who were there] remember the same songs. I think 'Detroit City' was really popular for a while when I was over there. Janice Joplin, 'A Piece of My Heart'. There was time if you were in the rear area just about any place you went you could hear Janice Joplin singing 'Piece of My Heart'. These people in the rear would have stereos coming in from Japan and it would just be blasting out in the evening there. [There was] a lot of music.

A resounding theme among Vietnam veterans is that, not surprisingly, the music of the day fit the war, some songs in particular. Fred Marshall remembers one song that always struck him:

'Homeward Bound' by Simon and Garfunkle, which was not about the war at all, it was just the line, "I wish I was homeward bound."

Perhaps the most popular song of the war was The Animals' 1965 hit 'We've Gotta Get Out of This Place'. As Air Force pilot Donald Davis puts it: "That was our theme song." Air Force pilot Gary Jackson also recalls The Animals' hit during his time in Vietnam in 1967, 1968 and 1969: "Every time that song was played at the Officers' Club everybody joined in at the top of their voice."

Air Force mechanic Eliseo Perez-Montalvo also remembers this:

'We've Gotta Get Out of This Place' was the number one song regardless of who played it. We had a lot of Filipino entertainers, musicians that would do . . . cover songs [of] American contemporary music. And that one [song] would make the guys stand on the tables and whoop and holler, "We've got to get out of this . . ." Well, we would alter the words, "We've got to get out of this place," became "We've got to get out of this fucking place if it's the last thing we ever do."

Frank Gutierrez also remembers The Animals' anthem as well as other popular songs:

> Of course The Beatles were prominent. Somehow the music fit in with Vietnam. For example, The Animals had one called 'We've Gotta Get Out of This Place'. [I remember The Beatles'] 'Strawberry Fields', Otis Redding['s] 'Sitting on the Dock of the Bay', things like that just brings a lot of memories about actually being there in Vietnam. James Brown music, of course The Rolling Stones, Steppenwolf, 'Born to be Wild', you can just hear it blasting all over the place . . . [T]here was the radio station out of Saigon, KFBM, that was very popular, that we all listened to because it was all rock and roll music . . . all we heard was rock and roll because that's what we wanted to hear . . .
>
> 'We've Gotta Get Out of This Place' reminds me about the replacement station in Long Binh where there's three or four or five hundred guys in one place, all brand new, and we don't know what our destiny is and we're listening to this music and the song fits: "We've got to get out of this place, if it's the last thing we ever do." [E]very day you could hear radios just blasting . . . You weren't supposed to [listen to music in the field]! I remember radios being confiscated, especially at night. Obviously, [this might] bring attention to yourself or let the enemy know where we were at. Transistor radios were not allowed in the field. But, in base camps, you could just hear the stereos blasting all over the place.

Richard Schaffer, who was in country in 1968 and 1969, remembers the 1967 Scott McKenzie hit 'San Francisco':

> [The] music of The Doors was a biggie during that time . . . "If you're going to San Francisco" that was always a tearjerker because most guys when they left [Vietnam] went to San Francisco or near San Francisco as a place to get out the service [discharged from the military] and then head home.

Susan O'Neil was a nurse with several units including the 12th Evacuation Hospital in Cu Chi. She was in country in 1969 and 1970 and used music as a way to help her release her grief and exorcise the demons that accompanied her job:

> Every now and then, and a couple of times a week at least, whenever I got a chance, a little time off, I'd get off a 12-hour shift and there was nothing further [to do], I'd drag my guitar over to someplace where it wasn't likely that I'd be heard, and it might be on the edge of the helipad on a busy day or it might be a hooch that was kind of outlying to the rest of the area and it was mostly used to store stuff in or something like that, and I'd just sing at the top of my lungs and beat the hell out of the guitar, and that helped.

DRUGS AND ALCOHOL

There was alcohol and drug use in the Vietnam War – not surprising since the culture of the US in the 1960s and early 1970s followed the men and women to Vietnam during their service there. The use of alcohol was prevalent in the rear areas as a way to help individuals unwind, let loose, let go the emotions and stress of the day. Alcohol could make the war go away for a little piece of time. Most veterans agree that in Vietnam the drinking was almost always done when they were off duty and not when they were 'on the line'. A variety of drugs, besides alcohol, were also available in Vietnam. The most common and popular was marijuana, followed by opium, heroin and cocaine. Like alcohol, the majority of drug use was relegated to the rear areas and was not prevalent in the field. Army infantryman Andy Roy remembers what it was like during his three tours in Vietnam between 1967 and 1969:

> Alcohol makes people really weird, I mean you can't depend upon them to do anything, they're virtually incapacitated. Marijuana is not quite that bad. In the rear areas [was] where I saw for the first time other drugs being used, [like] opium. I didn't see heroin but I heard about it . . . and then [there was] lot of drunkenness, which has been a bane of military – of armies – for a hell of a long time . . . generally it was always boasted that every soldier got two beers and two sodas a day. Well in the rear that was true, but in the field you don't give soldiers two cans of beer a day, number one for logistical reasons; we only got resupplied every five days and you can't supply ten beers and ten sodas along with all the food, the ammunition and everything else . . . So what happened

was every fifth day then we'd get two beers and two sodas . . . I can remember a couple times some guys would trade off their two sodas for two more beers and then might trade off a favorite C-ration or something for another beer and drink a little bit too much, but that was rare and that was not tolerated at all because you do some really stupid things when you're drunk.

There was some marijuana use in the field but it was only in a very, very, very safe situation, like you're sitting on top of a mountaintop with sheer cliffs and there's no way anybody can get to you, some guys would smoke. There were always a few who smoked quite often . . . once in a while it [marijuana] might make its way to a fire support base. I never saw it in a combat infantry unit or anything . . . alcohol was the one thing that, if that had started to get out of hand the troops themselves would [have] rebelled against it because you're threatening my life when you are not able to function . . . but generally everybody was straight, tired all the time, always hungry.

James Bussey was an Army Communication Center Specialist in Vietnam in 1969 and 1970:

In my company, in 1969, we didn't have drug abuse very much. We had about four or five . . . maybe six, that were the druggies and the rest of us really avoided them . . . I was friends with them but I was never one of them. I tried to be friends with everybody, frankly, but they kind of stayed to themselves and they didn't have security clearances . . . one of them actually spent about six months hard time over at Long Binh jail for drug abuse. They lost their security clearances, so they couldn't be in the comm center, so . . . they filled sandbags and repaired bunkers and built bunkers . . .

We had a little bit of alcoholism . . . but we had a lot of drinkers. We didn't have too many that really abused it very much. I abused it twice . . . the first time I got there and then right before I came home. The guys decided they were going to get the old teacher drunk and they did and it didn't take them long to do it either . . . [B]ecause I had been a teacher and I was a little bit older, the guys didn't expect me to do the gin and sin bit with them . . . I wasn't expected to go [with] the prostitutes, I wasn't expected to drink a lot, they expected me to be a good guy.

Army medical specialist James Calbreath remembers that you could get what you wanted when he was there in 1968 and 1969:

> If you wanted grass, you could get grass, if you wanted heroin, you could get heroin. I was not into drugs at all when I was at the 85th Evac[uation Hospital] . . . I did more than my fair share of drinking but no drugs there. There was quite a large pharmacy [staff] and those guys, we knew that they were sampling their own stuff but they were getting their work done and that's their own ass if that's what they want to do . . . [I]f you wanted to go to the village, instead of going to this bar, you'd go to this bar. This bar over here happens to be a bar for white guys who like to drink and this bar over here is for black guys who like to smoke dope or this bar over here is [for] black guys who like to drink and this bar over here is actually a whore house and you knew what was what and whatever you wanted, there was someplace where you could find it.

RACISM

There was an abundance of racial strife in the US during the 1960s at the height of the American Civil Rights movement. These tensions carried over to Vietnam. Racism was present amongst American troops in Vietnam in varying degrees – some experienced it frequently in one form or another, some witnessed or experienced it from time to time, and some veterans never saw it. The incidents of racism and racial tensions in Vietnam increased in the late 1960s after the assassination of Martin Luther King, Jr, and the rise of the Black Power movement in the US. Gonzalo Baltazar speaks to what he witnessed and experienced during his 1969–70 tour of duty:

> In Vietnam there was a lot of racism . . . I came from a small town. I didn't know what racism was as far as black [was concerned]. I knew what racism was as far as Mexicans [were concerned] because in school I ran into a lot of racism between the whites and the Mexicans, but I never knew a black so I didn't think much of it. But a lot of these guys [in Vietnam] that came from Detroit and Chicago, blacks and whites, well there was a lot of racism between them. Us small-town guys didn't know that. We were learning as we're going along that man, there is a lot of racism here. They're vocal about it, too, because you'd hear the name-calling and all

that. I thought, "Man, we're fighting two wars over here right now," so it wasn't very good . . . [I]t turned out in our platoon [that] we all got along pretty well after some of these other guys left that were causing a lot of [the] problems. So, it turned out that toward the end of my tour over there everybody got along real well.

James Calbreath saw the brutal side of racism during his tour:

The first real live casualty I ever saw was a young black man who came in on the stretcher and he was hanging his head over the end of the stretcher and it was because he didn't have a jaw. He had been in town. He and his buddies were at their bar drinking. A white guy came into the bar and words were exchanged. They beat him up and threw him out, so he went for the Jeep and grabbed his M-79 and he lobbed a round into the bar and this was one of the guys that got hit by it . . . You learned where to go and where not to go.

Most racial tension was limited to the rear areas. Rarely would it rear its head in the field. Gary Smith was an MP Sentry Dog handler at Tuy Hoa in 1971 and 1972. He recalls the bond between black servicemen, the gulf between black and white servicemen in the rear, as well as a racial incident in which he was involved:

There was a lot of racial strife that went unsaid. An example was the 'dep' . . . they called it "the dep" [the extensive, patterned, and prolonged handshake between two individuals] . . . I'm 52 years old and I'm looking back now and it's hard to understand feelings but then I do understand the feelings . . . [T]here is mistrust. When you were out on patrol you trusted anybody that was wearing green, we were all green. [In the rear,] the blacks hung around with the blacks, the whites hung around with the whites and you didn't see two white guys doing "the dep". You didn't see a white guy and a black doing "the dep" . . . You just, whites didn't understand why you had to spend so much time doing a handshake like that and I don't think I ever asked anybody why. I'm sure it was just something for them, you know, identity . . . It was just; there was a separation there. Thank goodness we have progressed a lot further than that . . .

I got accused [of racism once] . . . [It] wasn't real well lit and I was coming back from the club one night and as any drunken soldier can testify, you know there is a time when somebody says something. I had a black soldier who accused me of something. He was angry at me, probably angry at any white person. It was directed at me. It was dark out, I couldn't see even who he was. He had a friend with him. It was another black soldier, [he] says, "You've got to excuse him, he's drunk." He drug him on [carried him away] and I was in no mood to fight. I'm more passive than I am aggressive. I said, "Ok, alright." I think I did try to question him, why are you angry at me type of thing. It just infuriated him more. That was the only racial thing I saw out of my whole time there. I mean the tension was there.

Robert Turk remembers that there were no real problems in his unit at Bien Hoa and Da Nang in 1969 and 1970:

[There were no racial issues] in our squadron overtly . . . obviously we were all very aware of the race problems and you didn't want to get in a situation where [it arose] . . . The only time I could remember is when . . . a bunch of us did get pretty well plastered and we were coming back and two of the biggest black guys I've ever seen were on the way home and one of my buddies said something like, "Hey, Black Power, brothers," and so on and they just laughed at us because we were all so potted. We were sensitive to it [and] tried to not provoke any incidents and, I was . . . kind of proud of the fact that I thought that people . . . if they had personal prejudices whatever, they were able to subdue those. I don't recall any . . . I remember more when I got back to the States than during Vietnam time.

HUMOR

Almost every Vietnam veteran states that humor helped them get through their tour of duty. Most veterans agree that without humor, their time in the war zone would have been much more difficult psychologically. To them, one of the best coping mechanisms was a good laugh or a practical joke.

Steve Vermillion was an Army helicopter dustoff pilot. He and his unit used to indulge themselves in a unique activity – chasing water-skiers on the Saigon River:

There was a reporting point . . . called 'the Keyhole' and it was part of the Saigon River . . . The South Vietnamese had kind of like a country club out there . . . [The water-skiers were] a mixture of guys and gals . . . And every once in a while if we weren't occupied on a mission or if we were just going from point A to point B and we happened to see one of them on the river, we would kind of drop down and play some games with them . . . It's kind of like a cat and mouse thing. They just didn't know they were the mouse. If we had time we would come around, obviously get down as low to the water as we can, and come around the corner if there was bend in the river and meet them head [on] . . . Obviously the people that are watching the skier are not paying any attention to us so we have a visual contact with the driver and the skier. The closer we get to them at their altitude, I mean . . . they are right on the water and so are we. We're just three or four feet off the water, probably going 80, 90 knots. So it's a pretty quick rate of closure. They don't know what we are going to do. They don't know if we're going to run over them. They don't know if we are a gunship so you can see all kinds of panic in their eyes.

North Vietnam broadcast over the radio anti-American propaganda on a daily basis. The American soldiers in the field with transistor radios could pick up these broadcasts and listen. Larry Oswald remembers one of the more famous DRV broadcasts, a female voice the Americans dubbed 'Hanoi Hannah'. She consistently provided light moments for the troops:

We never found out who she was. But if she had been captured and tried like Tokyo Rose I think most of us would have voted for acquittal. Listening to her at night was one of those rare things that actually make the job a little more doable . . . Most units started keeping a scoreboard on the people she said they killed and the bases that were lost. She'd come on [the radio] at night with just ridiculous shit. She'd come on there, and the scary part was she might mention your base and the names of a couple of your officers. By God that was scary. That was truly scary. I don't know how they got that kind of information. She'd come on with things like, "We are now in the third weekend of the Tet revolution. Tonight people's forces over-ran the air force base at Tan Son Nhut killing 135,000 Americans and seizing airplanes that we really didn't want because friends of socialist labor in Russia built better aircraft."

But the part that was so funny, and I guess this is the guitar player in me, was the musical interludes. I looked forward to this every night. She'd come on and she'd do something like this, she'd say, "Tonight's folk ballad is a Vietnamese folk ballad from the 14th century titled 'Crush the Heads of the Running Dogs of Imperialism'." We'd just break up [laughing]. You know and I know that the Marines were not at Da Nang in 1428. Then she'd go on and there would be another 13th century song about 'Invade America and Kill the Families of the Running Dogs'. We used to call that the "running dog session". That always got in there somewhere. Listening to that bullshit was kind of a comic relief. When I was flying home and they went through my baggage they wanted to know what this one reel of tape was. I screwed up and I said, "That's Hanoi Hannah," and they confiscated my tape.

Army infantryman Ted Cook was in Vietnam in 1968 and 1969. He recalls a memorable incident on base that involved a fellow soldier being caught in the toilet during a rocket attack:

[W]e had one of our first rocket attacks . . . he was down in the latrine and the latrines were pretty crude affairs. Little wooden boxes that had 50 gallon drums cut off underneath, and he was down there . . . in a pair of cut-off Levi's and shower shoes . . . [in the] evening . . . and a rocket came out and landed right smack next to the latrine. Scared him to death, and the sight of him coming out of there trying to pull up his pants, running in those shower shoes . . . [T]hen another one landed not too far behind him, but far enough, and he stumbled and fell in gravel . . . and skinned himself up . . . [I]t was humorous, but there's some black humor in there, too.

Army infantry company commander Larry Burke remembers a particularly humorous incident that stands out to him when looking back at his tour in 1966 and 1967:

People probably had too much to drink and we were singing these old Army songs and so on. There were a couple of Second

Lieutenants. I was a First Lieutenant . . . one was a West Pointer, one a kid from Minnesota, and they had too much to drink and they left the Officer's Club, which had big double doors and a wooden stairway that came up to them. They left and went down to the motor pool and confiscated a gun-Jeep. What they told the guards who were on duty, I don't know. They got a .30-caliber machine gun out of the weapons room, loaded the sucker up with blank ammunition, put it on the pedestal mount. Drove up to the Officer's Club. Everybody's in there singing and carrying on. I had just left to go back to my BOQ [Bachelor Officers' Quarters] because I was tired. When I was up there I could hear them singing . . . Then I heard the roar of this engine.

Well, what these guys had done was they drove, these two Second Lieutenants, drove this gun-Jeep up to the Officer's Club. Up the stairs. One jumped out, threw those double doors open, drove that gun-Jeep into the Officer's Club and opened up with this .30-caliber machine gun with these blanks. Bap, bap, bap, bap, bap. You could hear the shell cases hitting the floor. The sound of that. Guys diving under tables. I mean beer bottles crashing. When I heard this long burst of machine-gun fire I thought, my God some NCO has gone berserk . . . if they didn't close, that NCO club sometimes could be pretty rowdy. I thought some NCO's got drunk, gone berserk and killing all the officers. I heard this burst. Then there's this absolute dead silence. I think that these two Second Lieutenants . . . realized, oh my God, what have we done? Here's all these other guys on the floor and everything.

Colonel Troy, he gets up out of there he looks at this. He's just stunned. He looks and sees these guys standing over there. Of course, this is the moment of truth and then he just bursts out laughing. Because to him, you see, he thought this is just the way a couple of good Second Lieutenants in the Cavalry ought to act. They never got into any trouble at all for that deal if you can believe it. I'm sure he said don't ever do that again. Pretty soon I'm sitting there and here's this stunned silence after this machine-gun burst. My God should I get out of my bunk or what? I wonder what I ought to do. Then pretty soon I hear . . . they were all singing. It was wonderful. It was great. Those are some of the things I remember about the Army. People who haven't had that experience they just have no idea what they're missing.

Don Cuneo, Marine rifleman and radioman, remembers a humorous moment in which one of his buddies played a joke on a company officer:

> There were two jets up [above us] and they were doing what we
> called 'haloing' . . . they were just circling around up there, and
> Jeff calls them and asks them . . . if they had a mission. They said
> no, they were just haloing. He says, "Well, could you buzz my area
> here?" The guys say, "Sure." . . . "When I give you the word, would
> you hit your afterburners? I'm going to give you a target." So the
> guy's up there and Jeff basically puts [directs] him over this shitter
> [toilet], and the guy comes down . . . the first one came in, and
> I don't know if you've ever heard a jet when it dives and then it
> goes back up with its afterburners. I mean, it's deafening. There's
> vibration and wind. He had this guy hit the afterburners, and
> the second one comes in and he moved him over to where he was
> going off right by this shitter. The guy comes down and Jeff says,
> "Okay, hit your afterburners." And this guy did, and the shitter
> with this particular officer inside of it just fell apart [exposing
> him sitting there], at which point Jeff hands me the radio set and
> says, "I've got to go." I'm left holding this thing. That was funny. I
> didn't get into any trouble for this. He [the exposed officer] knew
> what had happened. I remember him glaring. He got angry.

BRAVERY

One very common feature of the Vietnam War was the simple daily acts of bravery, valor and genuine care for one's fellow soldier. Vietnam veterans speak often of the intense bond formed between them during the war. Experiencing things such as combat and death together bound them as brothers for the remainder of their lives. Soldiers and Marines out on the frontlines describe multiple acts of bravery and courage that they witnessed on a daily basis – acts that were rarely reported or discussed. Marine Bill Hancock remembers the bravery that he personally witnessed during his tour:

> The corpsmen running through the mortar attack on
> [Operation] HICKORY. The corpsmen and Marines just running
> out to pull their buddies back on [Hill] 117, just tremendous
> with all the stuff going on, it's tremendous acts [of courage]
> that . . . no one ever heard about and they don't even care to talk
> about . . . Just unbelievable acts, but it was their buddies out

there so they were going to get them back. So it was just amazing
. . . guys, as soon as the shooting would start, guys running to be
where the shooting's at so they can help out their friends . . .
worrying more about their buddies than any danger going on,
just absolutely amazing. That's why that, why everybody is so
close knit [then and now] . . . I mean there was just countless
times that that happened . . . you would think that people would
be different and . . . talk about how selfish and stuff people were,
and you see that and you think how unselfish they can be.

Frank Vavrek remembers individuals who demonstrated courage in the
face of death, individuals who would pay with their lives:

Michael Vanessa. He got killed there holding his ground. He
was trying to take out an enemy machine-gun position to help
out and got shot in the process and Michael really didn't have
to be out there. He was due to rotate shortly and he asked for
permission to come out on this operation with us. The other one
was David Jolly, a machine-gunner in my platoon, and he took a
bad hit; got killed. He didn't die outright though . . . Jolly took
a shot through the chest – a pretty bad shot – operating [the]
machine gun and he died sometime during the night. Because it
was dark and stormy we couldn't get him medical evacuation. He
just didn't make it through the night. They did everything they
could to try to keep him alive . . . I think they both got silver stars
. . . Samson, Jimmy Samson, he's another one. He got a silver
star . . . I mean in the midst of all that, he just resisted until he
was shot down. And these guys were instrumental. Each of them
though, they were wounded or killed by holding their ground in
position and by putting the [gun] fire [out], and what they did do
is they broke the enemy positions. They suffered, they didn't back
away, they stayed there, they held their ground, they returned
fire, they did all they could and their actions contributed greatly
to [defeating] the enemy on that hill.

Anthony Borra, a C-130 pilot in 1968 and 1969, describes what he witnessed
one night during a rocket attack upon Tan Son Nhut Air Base:

We were at Tan Son Nhut one night, and there was another
rocket attack, and . . . they managed to find the revetted area.

Once it [the rocket] landed in a revetted area, it didn't matter if it hit the airplane directly or not because it was contained in these . . . high steel walls, and so the glass was contained and so the airplane was history. But they hit an Army intelligence gathering airplane . . . So it was burning. But again, because it was a revetment, it contains it, so it did just what it was supposed to do. And some . . . crew chief . . . it was probably a fairly young kid, called on the radio. He was roving the flight line and he . . . wanted somebody to help him move a couple of C-130s.

It was just interesting that people just left whatever they were doing and put themselves in harm's way. Nobody knew whether another airplane was going to explode. That was the concern because there was fuel flowing around it. Some airplanes just got hit with shrapnel and punctured fuel tanks and people just ran over and did what they needed to do. You know I'm sure in a human drama, as we know from accounts that people did exceptionally brave things on the battlefield, but we weren't on the battlefield like that. And yet in this case it was sort of the same thing and people just responded to provide what needed to be provided to rescue anybody that was hurt over there. It was bravery in the sense of putting themselves at risk for a fellow soldier or airman.

DEATH

Death is indigenous to a war zone. It hangs like a wet blanket over all who serve in a war. Nearly everyone in Vietnam thought about or experienced death in some form, either their own death, the death of a friend, or a stranger, whether an ally or an enemy. How one views death and deals with its heavy repurcussions often dictates one's performance in the field and one's psychological state behind the front lines. How did the men and women in Vietnam feel when death surrounded them on the battlefield, or when they were the ones inflicting the blows that killed? Gregory Burch was an aircraft maintenance crew chief on helicopter gunships, a door gunner, and later worked for Air America in Laos and Thailand. He describes how he felt about his job and the lethality he could inflict upon the enemy:

I always wanted to do that, I always wanted to be a door gunner, since I couldn't fly, it would be the next best thing. And, if you're on a helicopter gunship, you get to kill things and . . . you eventually get to like to kill. I think it's the fact that they [the enemy] are targets, they're not human beings. It's the old fighter [pilot] mentality . . . you get to see them die from a distance. You don't see their faces so it's a different type of killing.

Burch remembers an incident in which he, as a helicopter door gunner, saw what his machine gun could do to enemy troops:

You could see the [NVA] mortars being shooting [*sic*]. We went in and knocked out the mortars, went back, rearmed, they cranked up the other gunships and we were just – fly, dump ammo [on the enemy], come back, load up – and they had everybody down there, we didn't even shut the engines down . . . That's where I actually saw people [the NVA soldiers] fall. I'd see [them] flip in the air, and dust fly up around them . . . They'd fly three, four, five, six feet through the air, you hit them a dozen times, it just cartwheels them . . . [Y]ou were actually seeing yourself kill people . . . We were excited. Man, we were just . . . the adrenaline and the exaltation. We're finally getting to see ourselves kill people! . . . [Y]ou couldn't believe it, we were like a bunch of happy campers, we were doing what we were meant to do. I look back on it; we were having fun . . . I still don't feel sorry about that. It was war.

Anthony Goodrich, a Marine machine-gunner in 1969 and 1970, remembers what he felt after his buddy was killed in a firefight and how that loss affected him the rest of his tour in Vietnam:

The thing that sticks out in my mind is that I lost something that day. I was so damn pissed off. I was so angry about his death and I wasn't able to do anything about it. I still feel bad about it. I still feel kind of guilty because I didn't do anything. I was so scared that I had no clue what was going on. I remember we had several KIAs and several WIAs [wounded in action]. I remember putting WIAs [on the choppers] . . . I remember the choppers came in – we blew an LZ at the top of this mountain to get everybody out that had been hit – about how bloody the LZ was. It was just drenched in blood. I lost my humanity or something that day. I don't know what happened. I got numbed. I numbed my feelings. My anger and fear from that day on is what carried me through Vietnam. That's how I survived it. We weren't ever able to mourn the deaths that I saw there. That was one of the things that bothered me for a long, long time. Somebody would get killed. Put them in a body bag and then you'd forget about it because you had to go do the next thing you had to do. So, I guess I lost my innocence that day or something. [It was] something that's always stuck in my mind. That was a big change in my life that day.

Anthony Borra, the C-130 pilot, remembers carrying casualties and KIAs in his aircraft:

The body bag flights were the most sobering. The first time, and I was fairly new there, we went out and picked up body bags, and they all had to be loaded and we couldn't stay on the ground very long, so we just all got out and loaded . . . We picked up a body bag, my aircraft commander and I, and what remains were in the bag just rolled to the center of the bag and we just looked at each other. And . . . there's something about the smell of death that is just – there's no escaping it. There's nothing else like it. That's the way all of these body bags had that odor . . . and sometimes there would be body fluids that would seep out through a, like maybe where the zipper was or something, and that was pretty awful to think of what had happened to some of those kids that were in the bag.

Then when you did the litter flights, air evacuation . . . you had to marvel at these wonderful flight nurses and medics and doctors that went with us, and how they cared for these kids. In spite of all the rush that had to be going on and everything else, they still cared for them in an obvious loving way and that was quite touching. But it was also to see the fear, the fright on some of their faces . . . the wounded, who were not unconscious. I mean, just understandably scared. I imagine, start wondering what's going to happen to them. What their life is going to be like? How they're going to manage with whatever has happened to them? . . . talk about feeling awkward and inadequate to say anything meaningful. What do you say to somebody that's obviously just lost a limb? Everything's going to be okay? That's so foolish. That's one of the very humbling and real feelings of being unable to measure up to the task. Somehow, I thought as an officer I was supposed to know the right thing to say. And I didn't have any right things to say. Those were pretty hard times . . . I learned to say things like, "We're going to get you to the big hospital as soon as we can. We'll try to keep you . . ." I mean what I learned to say to my passengers on Delta [Airlines], "We're going to do all we can to make this flight as pleasant as possible. We're going to get you where you'll get even better help. The folks here, these are really great nurses and they're really going to care for you on this flight." I mean, those sort of things, just something that was real, something that I could deliver rather than wanting to say something to soothe their anxiety, but all I could do was try to put them at ease for what was coming next . . .

FEAR

Akin to the reality of death, the feeling of fear was also ever-present, lurking on the battlefields and in the rear in Vietnam. Individuals coped with their fears and carried forth with their mission in a variety of ways. The officers who led these men also experienced fear and apprehension and still led them in the face of it. Tom Esslinger was a Marine platoon and company commander in Vietnam. He remembers the challenges of leadership:

> You're tired as hell, but when you're the guy leading you've got a lot more on your mind and you can't think about your fatigue. I think it was the same kind of thing. But the mental aspects of the Vietnam experience were difficult enough at my level, I think for the troops it must have been even worse . . . As long as you were just a smidgen less scared than they were, it was okay. I certainly tried very hard at it because I recognized that they took their lead from me. They were depending on me. If I showed those kinds of concerns excessively at least that it would be communicable. It would be a pretty serious problem. I think my primary . . . duty, my primary responsibility, my primary task was to keep these guys alert and to help them maintain morale.

Richard Hamilton, an Air Force jet pilot, recalls his thoughts on fear in the cockpit and the risks he and his fellow pilots took:

> It's a real lie if anybody said they weren't scared. We all were, but it was the whole idea that you had to be tough was stronger than the fear, and so everybody basically hid it. They all would complain a little bit but, as a matter of fact my wife, who is a

psychologist, basically said that fighter pilots are a sub-culture, that they're all nuts. We kind of did the same thing . . . as a fighter pilot anyway, and I haven't been anything else . . . that's the way I learned. If someone crashes or if someone makes a mistake and does something wrong, you look at what the guy did . . . [Y]ou try and go through it in very logical, piece by piece manner and say where is it he screwed up? And then you say if I ever get there, I'm not going to do it. I might have lived.

Some veterans state that simply doing their jobs kept them from dwelling on the obvious. Andy DeBona remembers that the job of piloting his C-130 airplane provided a needed distraction in combat:

I think after the initial fear came in, I didn't have [time to think about it], I was too busy doing other things to reflect on . . . well, I knew I was going to die.

Frank Gutierrez, an Army rifleman operating in the field in the Cu Chi area, remembers how he and his buddies saw fear and that ignorance could sometimes be helpful:

[T]hat was fun thinking about it, being under fire and firing back, it was exciting. Of course we were scared, but if you weren't scared it was foolish not to be scared. But, all of us were scared; not cowardly, but just scared because you know what is out there. Years later I found out that we're in the middle of the North Vietnamese Army [that day], so that kind of bothers me now because at that time, we never knew how close we were to those guys.

Raymond Merritt was a US Air Force F-105 pilot in 1965 in Vietnam. He was shot down, suffered severe injuries, was captured, and imprisoned in Hanoi until 1973. He remembers what it took for him to get through his many years as a POW, live through the fear of the unknown and survive:

Every individual I feel, in my own opinion, was different. You've got to set some standards for yourself and I like to put it down . . . into what I call [four] beliefs or [four] faiths. One, you're going to get home; you don't know when, but you are going to get home someday and doing then what it is necessary to keep yourself going which involves a lot of interpreting. Second, you've got to have a belief that your fellow prisoners are doing the best that they can do, also to live up to the [military] code of conduct in the standards expected of them as you are trying to do. Third of all, you've got to believe that somewhere along the line, your government is taking care of your family; you don't have to worry about it. You know there are problems and more or less, but you have to believe somebody is taking care of them because you certainly can't. Fourth, you've got to believe that somewhere along the line, there is a God that's helping you, even though you're not religious, you do have to have a faith that somebody's looking after you besides yourself. I'm not professing any strong religion, but just a belief that somebody's there to help me because it certainly can't be other people directly. Those four, I think, probably help you get yourself together and say, "Okay, I'm going to make it through here."

8
THE TET OFFENSIVE

In the early morning hours of 30 January 1968, some 84,000 North Vietnamese and National Liberation Front (NLF) soldiers attacked the South Vietnamese, the Americans and their allies countrywide. The leadership of North Vietnam, President Ho Chi Minh and General Vo Nguyen Giap, realizing that by 1968 the US war of attrition had indeed sapped a great deal of strength from its military forces, and believing that the chances of winning a protracted conflict against US firepower was doubtful, decided that a single great military victory in the South would lead to victory sooner rather than later. The attacks hit US and RVN military and government installations all over South Vietnam and took the majority of Americans in country and in the US by surprise. The American public was especially shocked by the attack as the US political and military leadership, President Lyndon B Johnson and General William Westmoreland, had promised them that "There was light at the end of the tunnel" and that a US victory in the war was imminent.

Ho and Giap hoped that the countrywide attacks, scheduled for a time when the Americans and South Vietnamese would least expect it – on the Tet Lunar New Year when a ceasefire would be in place – would lead to a general uprising in the South and an overthrow of the South Vietnamese government before the US forces could properly react. Nguyen Phat Le was an NVA infantry officer who had joined the Viet Minh in 1945, fought the French in the First Indochinese War, and then went south in 1964 to fight the American and South Vietnamese forces. He recalls the confusion and disagreement he witnessed before the launch of the offensive:

> There were conflicts between military units and the regional Party Committee because the military units often had better knowledge of the local situation where they [were] stationed, while the regional Party Committee received the orders from the Central Command and carried out these orders without consulting local units. Those who dared to oppose the regional Party Committee's policy were Party members who had been trained in the North.

For example, most of the military cadres did not agree with the Tet Offensive order in 1968, but since it was the Party's order, they had to carry it out. The Party said it had studied carefully the situation and there would be strong support from the people [of South Vietnam], but most of the military of all ranks did not believe in the [probable] success of the campaign.

The popular uprising in the South against the Saigon government never occurred. American forces ultimately destroyed the NLF militarily in the aftermath of the attack. Although a tactical defeat for the DRV, the Tet Offensive was a strategic victory for North Vietnam as the US public became more divided over the war, the anti-war movement strengthened, and promises of an American victory began to ring hollow.

THE FIRST NIGHT

The offensive was planned for 30 January, but DRV officials delayed the attack for 24 hours. Some units did not receive the new orders and proceeded with the plan. On 31 January 1968, 89 cities and towns and over 50 hamlets were hit by NLF and NVA forces. The fighting was intense, bloody and prolonged. The US personnel who were involved in repelling the attacks never forgot that first night. For many it was a surprise and made for a long and deadly first few hours.

Robert Fischer was a C-123 pilot and was stationed at Bien Hoa air base:

> I don't remember what time it was. It was probably about two o'clock in the morning, and boy the rockets started coming in. The siren went off, we all hit the bunker as usual. We didn't know there was anything different, and then it was intense. I mean it was a lot more intense than what we were used to. Usually we'd catch a couple rockets coming in and when it was over you'd go back to sleep, but this night it continued and then it caught fire. [Our] hooch caught fire. The bunker caught fire because the sandbags caught fire. All the sand started pouring out so it was no protection at all.
>
> We ended up in a ditch, and I remember I had my M-16 and lying in the ditch in my flying suit and we were there all night, and finally daylight [came], and I guess they captured a number of people that were trying to overrun the base . . . I think most of us were okay and we went right back to work that morning . . . I truly lost everything I had [in the fire]. I didn't have anything left.

Robert Smithee was part of the Army's 58th Medical Battalion at Long Bien when Tet erupted. He remembers that first night as a time when things were very intense, frightening, and confusing:

> So, we're sitting here across the street from a very large evacuation hospital, a couple hundred beds, and nobody ever tells the medics anything, and all of a sudden . . . and there was a lot of people there that had been there the whole war, the whole time of their tour, and they'd never heard a shot. They'd never heard anything. Then, when these start going up, massive explosions and things like that, they had never heard anything like that. For some of the people that had been out in country, you could tell right away that this was a big deal. [This was] not just an isolated mortar here. This is a big deal. Of course as the information kind of filters through . . . "Well, the base is under attack. Tan Son Nhut is under attack. The [North] Vietnamese are overrunning Saigon." You didn't know whether you were talking about 1,000 troops or 10,000 troops or 100,000 troops. So, it was scary . . . because that's the first time anybody asked what is going to happen here? Are they going to come across the wire and take over this base? Because that was what the intent was, I'm sure. As it turns out, it was a lot better protected and prepared than anybody thought at the time . . . that was the first time when they [the enemy] really came back and struck the heart of the US command structure at Long Binh. It was pretty scary. A lot of people spent the night in the bunkers. I did.

Fred Marshall was a member of the US Army 525th Military Intelligence Group and an Adviser to the 5th ARVN Division. His unit was stationed near Lam Son Village in Binh Duong Province. One of his duties was to interrogate captured enemy soldiers. He recalls how the news of the offensive slowly trickled in to him:

> We got up one morning and we were told that the North Vietnamese and VC were attacking all over the country. We put on extra guards. We didn't get any sleep for about four days. We had a lot of interrogations of captured prisoners over at 1st Air Cav[alry] and in our own unit down at National Police. Our movements at night were very limited even though we did have to do some driving at night, that was always fun. We had [a] big

battle right outside of our wire. I was in Phu Cuong City about four miles to the west, the provincial capital. There was a lot of action on the other side of the river with the jets coming in and dropping napalm. Our recondo platoon barracks were about a kilometer south of our unit. They got attacked. We spent every night out in our bunkers or down at the IPW [Interrogation] Center. We didn't sleep hardly for four days. We just kind of cat-napped when we could. It was [a] very scary situation too. We'd get reports coming in from all over the country. We heard about the butchery up in Hue. The American Embassy had been attacked in Saigon. There were North Vietnamese tanks coming into Saigon and this kind of stuff. Are we going to be cut off?

After a few days, things subsided pretty quickly. It became pretty apparent over the next few days as we got reports in from around the country that the Communists had just suffered overwhelming losses . . . They had a lot of success further north especially around the city of Hue where they massacred several thousand people . . . It was an intense time.

Michael McGregor was an Army artilleryman with the 1st Cavalry Division dug in at a night defensive position when the attack hit:

. . . I had to go to the bathroom, so I was out [of my bunker]. Of course, I didn't have my weapon with me; I just left the bunker . . . and all of a sudden, "Hawoom!" This thing blew up and everybody starts shooting on the perimeter and all that, and I said, "This is a really smart thing," like "Oh, here I am, on the ground, right next to the piss tubes. I have nothing. The only thing that I have to defend myself with is my belt." That was the first night . . . I was really scared. I said "Oh, I better get back quick" . . . I didn't want to go back because some rounds were landing behind me, so I just crawled to the edge by the perimeter in an infantry position. I mean, I went down in there, and [they] said, "What the hell are you doing here?" [I said] "Jeez, I was taking a leak." So a guy gave me a pistol and I said, "I don't think anything's going to happen, but here we are."

Charles Conn was an Army Military Police Sentry Dog handler stationed at Chu Lai. He recalls what he experienced that first night as the VC broke through the base defenses:

. . . We kind of knew something was coming, but we didn't know exactly what. We knew they'd hit us because it was a holiday . . . I am in bed and I remember this as clear as the day. They [the VC] came through [the perimeter]. They killed one of our dog handlers and got into the ammo dump. There [were] . . . 180 pads of ammunition, which would be big piles of ammunition. They blew up only five of them. I thought the atomic bomb had gone off. We looked up and there was a big mushroom cloud [that] came from the ammo dump. We figured we lost all kinds of [dog handlers] because that was where our guys were. Well . . . by morning and [when] everything sifted out we only lost one handler. They [the VC] went right through and killed him and his dog. That supposedly was the first Sentry Dog handler killed in Vietnam. We found out later on there [were] others. [I knew him] . . . He was in the next bunk.

Larry Wasserman was a C-123 mechanic at Bien Hoa Air Base, just north of Saigon. The first night of Tet for him was particularly memorable. The attack at Bien Hoa came in the middle of the night:

That night it was about 1:00 in the morning and all hell broke loose. It was January 31, 1968. We were coming under severe attack. They started blaring the horns . . . I guess about 2:30 or 3:00 in the morning we were out in a field on a perimeter of the base with our rifles . . . three of us were there . . . dug in on the side of a hill, watching all this going on. We'd see tracer fire coming at us and going out from where we were. Wherever we saw that other people were shooting we'd shoot. Every once in a while you'd get a bullet that would hit right above the hill that you were hunkered behind. Just getting up and firing anywhere you were taking chances. I guess we stayed there. That was a long night and into the morning. I guess it was about six or seven hours that this kept occurring. At the same time there was rocket fire all over. You know, grenades going off. Things like that all around. It was a scary place. I would shoot – I never knew if I hit anything. It was impossible to see. It was pitch black. I guess it was about between 8:00 or 9:00 in the morning before we finally heard that the advancement of the Viet Cong was over. They wanted to overrun the air base. They were trying to take out the base completely and stop its operation . . . There were fatalities at the base.

Afterwards we couldn't just go back [to our barracks]. We were assigned to body bag detail. So that was not pleasant at all. [It was] terrible . . . We'd have to put the dead people in body bags and take them back to the temporary morgue facilities. It was really bad. I saw one guy that got hit on the side of his head with a bullet. Apparently the bullet just exploded in his head. The other side of his head was just completely gone. You could see the brain matter. That was the worst thing I've ever seen.

Chuck Carlock was a helicopter pilot based out of Chu Lai during Tet. His first night of the offensive was full of action in the air and watching the base burn:

Tet '68; I was . . . one of the few helicopter pilots in the air when that thing started . . . they attacked . . . but they staggered their attacks on different days . . . they attacked up north of us so we went up to sink their boats . . . Well that night we didn't sink anything, but they had us up there flying [and] trying to catch them when they were retreating out and we just didn't see anybody and we turned around and looked down at Chu Lai and it's probably 30–40 miles down there . . . we thought they'd hit us with a nuclear bomb . . . The complete ammo dump went up. They got lucky and put one right in the middle of the ammo dump and that thing went off. It blew down our bunch of hooches. My friend Hannah, it was his turn to go after beer [from the bunker]. When you're in the bunkers you took turns over who went after the beer. He went after the beer. When it went off, it blew the refrige[rator] over on him and they gave him a Purple Heart, then they took it away from him once they found out what had happened . . . then I remember we couldn't land. We were up in the air and we called every place that had refueling capability. We had different little firebases around there. They were all under attack so we landed at a place called Hill 35 and we set there until they pumped us full of fuel.

I was in a minigun ship which took a while to rearm it . . . We put an attack in [at Tam Ky first] because they [the VC] were up in the perimeter there and then we went back and we couldn't find a place to land, [and then] went to Hill 35 . . . [There] they were hitting mortar rounds around us, and . . . I remember being in a panic running out of fuel.

. . . So years later . . . I called my crew chief up and I said, "What did we do?" and he said, "Well you dumb shit, you ran it [the fuel] all the way down and we decided we didn't have enough to get to Chu Lai so we landed in Tam Ky and they were shooting across the strip and we sat down there." And he says, and I vaguely remember this, that they stopped firing. Both sides stopped firing. He ran out, he said he only pumped for about two seconds, just enough to get the light to go off. He said he was looking at it and when the light went off. At the light you've got like 15 minutes and he said he knew 15 minutes would get us back to Chu Lai and he said when the when the light went off he said, "Go!" you know, and off we went. He said the war started again once we took off and that helicopter got shot up on coming out . . .

Ngo Quang Le was the son of an ARVN officer and who later joined the ARVN himself to fight the NVA and VC. Le recalls his first experiences of seeing American soldiers in action as a young high school student. He had returned home from Pleiku, where his father was stationed, to Saigon to visit his grandmother. The first time he saw Americans in action was in Saigon during the Tet Offensive:

I was a student, high school student. I came back to Saigon to play, around the [Tet] New Year. So, [around] midday, I play[ed] in the Saigon area . . . and I hear the noise, [and it] look[s] like a lot of fire. [I] say, "Oh, a lot of fireworks." So I come back [home] nearby the American Embassy. I saw the jeep parked in the middle of [the] street. I said, "What the hell. Maybe they're drunk." So, I got my motorcycle nearby, one soldier came out with a gun, a Colt .45 [and] point[ed it] right at me . . . I scream[ed], "No, No! I am student! I speak very little English!" [He said to me] "Go home. [The] VC come here anyway, go home!" So, I run quick, go to the house and say, "Oh, the Communists come already." My grandma says, "You [are] lying, you go home, you come back and made up a story!" I said, "Grandma, listen to me. I know because . . . I know" and I talked with her [told her that] the soldier point[ed] a gun [at] me. The next day, the radio start[ed] talking about [the action] and she called someone, took me back to the airport, shipped me back into Pleiku where I live[d] with my father . . . [At] this time in Pleiku is [a] very, very big fight. And a couple days later we see a lot [of] Communists die. This [is my] first memory: I see American soldier, [and] also I see how men die in the war.

On the other side, NVA infantry officer Nguyen Phat Le remembers his unit's mission the first night of the Tet Offensive:

I belonged to the 'Quyet Thang' regiment and our target was Tan San Nhut [air base] but we did not have [our local] guides and therefore had to stop in Go Vap where my unit was destroyed by rockets. We did not fight our way to the final target. The regiment deputy political officer, Mr Tran Van Ha, later surrendered to South Vietnam regime under the 'open arms' [*Chieu Hoi*] policy . . . Most of the soldiers did not believe in the success of the campaign but since it was the [Communist] Party order we had to carry out. Before the battle began we were very confused. I belonged to the main force regiment. My unit was ordered to break through [the] Saigon defense system, [and] then the . . . 9th Corps would follow us to occupy Saigon. When we moved into Saigon's outskirts . . . [we] tried to break through the defense[s] set up [there and] in three days . . . [we] failed. We expected the 9th Corps would come to help us break through the defense to occupy Saigon; but the 9th Corps never came. We had to stay there waiting to be killed. We were ordered to stay in silence, to wait. Many people became impatient, they surrendered . . . I withdrew back and waited.

THE SIEGE AT KHE SANH

One of the focal points of the Tet Offensive and its aftermath was the siege at Khe Sanh, a US Marine base located in northwestern South Vietnam, about 14 miles from the DMZ, and some six miles from Laos. In 1962, a US Army Special Forces camp was located at Khe Sanh to provide for border surveillance. In 1966 General Westmoreland ordered the Marines to set up the base to interdict the infiltration route. The base overlooked Route 9, the main east–west road in this area and one of the Ho Chi Minh Trail Complex feeder roads leading from Laos into the RVN. American artillery could reach into Laos from Khe Sanh, interdict the Trail and Route 9, as well as provide a jumping off point from which US Marines could patrol into the strategically important surrounding area. John Hargesheimer, a Marine armorer, rifleman, and machine-gunner, describes his arrival at Khe Sanh before the siege began, when things were relatively quiet:

... We flew in a C-130, and we got out, and you just stand there and look around. There was only a few hundred Marines up there then. It wasn't the big one that it ended up being. It wasn't nearly as populaced [*sic*]. It was just like a little outpost. Basically, it was a jumping off point for one battalion of Marines. They came in there and from Khe Sanh they would get in the helicopters and go out into the mountains and engage the enemy and then they would come back. And there was hospitals and stuff right there. So, it was kind of like the rear area for out there.

But it was beautiful country, God, it was beautiful. There was a plateau, but when you first got off the plane, you looked around and you looked at the mountains and that was all pretty ... everybody was living in tents and it was just mud. It was just dirt. It wasn't monsoon then so dust was flying everywhere and you're looking around, "Good God." But then again, "Well, this may not be too bad." Because you're not in the rear so there won't be inspections or anything like that, so this could be okay.

By 1967, the base size was at regimental level. In the spring of 1967, the Americans at Khe Sanh fought and defeated NVA troops for the strategic hills located a short distance from the base. By the fall of the year, the NVA cut Route 9, thus reducing the resupply of Khe Sanh to air delivery. The US reinforced the base with personnel, including an ARVN Ranger Battalion. All told, by the eve of the Tet Offensive, there were some 6,000 Americans at Khe Sanh. They were surrounded by three NVA Divisions, nearly 40,000 soldiers, determined to capture the base. The official siege of Khe Sanh began on 20 January and continued through the launch of the Tet Offensive elsewhere in South Vietnam, and ran on until 8 April. It lasted 77 long days.

On a daily basis during the siege the US dropped huge quantities of ordnance on the area around the base to kill as many of the enemy as possible, to protect the American and ARVN forces, and to deter an all-out NVA/VC attack. In total, the amount of ordnance dropped around the base was the equivalent of ten Hiroshima-sized bombs. The US also placed Marines on the strategic hills surrounding Khe Sanh to protect the approaches to the base. Bill Hancock was one of the Marines dug in on one of those hills. He describes the air strikes on enemy positions not far from his bunker:

Oh, lord it was [a lot of ordnance dropped], I wouldn't want to be under it. We had B-52s and ... helicopter strikes and F-4

Phantom strikes, it was just continuous day in and day out. I
mean there were so many large areas of [enemy] troops, plus
they were digging trenches up towards the combat base that we
could see them digging, and so they [US artillery] were constantly
shelling them and the B-52 strikes were just awesome, I mean it
was just amazing. It was close enough that if you were laying in
your fighting hole the concussion from the strike would bounce
you out of it . . . a couple of feet . . . when you see a [B-52] strike
far away from you, you could actually see the concussion going
through the air and I mean the concussion was so great . . . It had
just bounced you out like a, I guess it would be like being in a
huge earthquake or something, just knock you right of the hole.

Hancock goes on to describe where his unit was and its mission:

We were on Hill 558 along with . . . three companies from the
2nd Battalion, 26th Marines there . . . Echo Company was sent up
and they were on Hill 861 Alpha. Hill 558 was just north of the
combat base, maybe a mile or two . . . it was in a valley between
Hill 861 and 881 on one side and Hill 950 on the other and
there was a river that ran through there . . . [if] large forces were
coming through, they were going to come through that valley
. . . We were placed to block off any troops coming through that
valley . . . Well we thought it was . . . real important and we were
prepared to defend it no matter what it took but . . . it was kind
of nerve-wracking because we knew we were outnumbered. If
they wanted to overrun any one of the small areas and if they had
really taken a notion . . . to hit some of the smaller bases it would
have been tough for us to defend them. I mean they would have
took [sic] terrible losses but I don't know for sure that we could
have held them off if they would have attacked full force.

Hargesheimer recalls how those at Khe Sanh knew something was amiss in
the days leading up to the siege:

. . . This is how you could tell that it was getting bad because
the Marine recon[naissance] unit, when they would go out, we'd
watch them get on the helicopters and they'd go out. Usually they
went out for like two or three days and do recon on the area. Well,
they were out there. You could see each time they went out [they]

The North Vietnamese and Viet Cong 77-day siege of the US base at Khe Sanh in 1968 became a focal point of the post-Tet Offensive fighting. Daily the NVA and VC would mortar the base to break the will of its defenders to force the base's capitulation in hopes of turning the tide of the war, much like the Battle of Dien Bien Phu in 1954.

seemed to be making contact a lot sooner. And they would have to send a helicopter out to extract them. And that's how you could tell something's not right. Of course, we're peons [slang for personnel at the lower end of the chain of command]. We're not officers or anything so we don't get the story. We're just going by what we can see and what we think's happening and anything that's passed down to us. So you could tell it wasn't good because it got to the point where reconnaissance would go out and they would only be out there like an hour and they would have to extract them. They were making contact that fast. So that meant there was a lot of NVA out there. We knew there was a lot of NVA and it was starting to build up quite a bit. But before that, you never even wore flak. You never wore flak jackets. Half of the time you didn't carry weapons. You didn't wear helmets. It was just like a really nice place. But then we knew something bad was going to happen.

Then one night, I believe it was January 2nd, '68, that's when . . .

there was a Marine patrol out in front, I was on guard duty that
night and I was facing the mountains . . . where I was [there] was
kind of a rise and then right in front of me about 100 yards in
front of me was elephant grass. And there was a Marine patrol out
there . . . I was sitting there in my bunker . . . smoking cigarettes
and shooting the bull [talking] and the sun was starting to go
down . . . and they started popping flares, mortar flares . . . they
just kept popping them and we knew something was wrong. So I
got in the bunker . . . this Marine patrol had come in contact with
. . . five NVA . . . and what this NVA [squad] were [sic] doing was
going around, they were taking reconnaissance. They were going
around the base and they were making maps of all the bunkers
and what weapons were in each bunker. Well, they ended up
engaging them in a firefight and they did it right in front of my
bunker . . . all I knew is all of the sudden, here come a bunch of
bullets flying in on my bunker and I had no idea if they were the
enemy or the Marines or what. The enemy was caught between
the Marines and my bunker. So we opened up not knowing what
in the world was happening. All we knew is a lot of rounds are
coming out of the elephant grass at us, so we started shooting
out there and come to find out, we almost shot our own guys . . .
they killed five of them . . . at least two were Chinese, were Red
Chinese, and so they got all the documents off of them . . . that's
one of the ways they found out there was going to be a big siege.

The NVA had 152mm Howitzers set up in Laos just a few miles away that
could reach Khe Sanh. On the first morning of the siege, one of those guns
took out the main ammunition supply facility which contained about
1,500 tons of high explosives. Hargesheimer was on the main base when
the siege began and witnessed the massive explosion:

> . . . This is when the . . . "shit hit the fan" . . . I was manning a .50-
> caliber machine gun on the line . . . So me and two other Marines
> got stuck on a bunker . . . not on the outside perimeter but the
> ones closest to the perimeter manning a .50. And there was an
> M-79 to my right and a rifle to my left. I guess about every 20, 25
> yards, there was a bunker and it was always manned . . . I guess
> it was like 5:30 in the morning. It was before sunlight . . . and all
> these rounds started coming in from, it seemed like they were
> coming in from the north and the west [from Laos]. And you

could just hear the incoming coming, just come roaring in there and that's when they blew the ammo dump, and a lot of guys in the center of the Khe Sanh base – that was the headquarters – were caught sleeping in tents and stuff, so a lot of guys died on that one.

They [the NVA] weren't concerned with us on the line. They were concerned with trying to get as much of the central part of the base as they could. So we just sat there and listened to them go whistling over us and watching all the explosions . . . when the ammo dump went up, it was just unbelievable. You could just see fireballs going everywhere . . . I was scared to death. Of course, we always learned, we were always taught, that before an infantry attack they hit you with the artillery and the mortars . . . we were waiting for the infantry to just come roaring in there . . . we were down there waiting with our guns and everything . . . Luckily nothing happened on that one . . . that lasted for several hours.

Marine infantryman Mike Bradbury remembers the NVA assault against the hills when it finally came:

They were just swarming up the hills . . . General Giap, he was there, the gook division Commander and the whole idea was just to overrun us. They must have had a couple 300 of them out there just on our hill . . . We didn't actually know they were out there until late that night, I think it was 20 January, this is when the whole entire offensive started on all the hills and everything. South side of the hill, our hill, got hit with [an] RPG . . . it must have been around midnight or something, and it killed a couple of guys and then they dropped some mortars in. It's a good thing everybody stayed put because the idea, I think, was to draw most of us over on that side of the hill but the real attack came from the north side. They sent a sniper team over apparently on the other side of the hill, held fire on us from over there, but everybody stayed put and all of a sudden there are all kinds of mortars coming and here they come . . .

The Marines held the hills, and as the siege wore on, resupply became vital to the survival of Khe Sanh. The pilots had to navigate their way through the mountains, through the ground fire on approach to the base, and then, upon landing, they were mortared on the runway until they departed, only to navigate the gauntlet again. The workhorse resupply aircraft was the C-130. Donald Davis was one of the pilots who flew the C-130 into Khe Sanh to bring supplies to the besieged base. He recalls the experience:

It was a bit hair-raising because there was a lot of ground fire up there. I landed a few times up there, pretty early during the Offensive. They [the American commanders eventually] stopped letting us go in there in the C-130s . . . Because the runway was getting beat up. They didn't want to take a chance on losing an airplane. Also there was a lot of incoming. We frequently did get hits on the loading ramp and out on the ends of the runway . . . We did what they called speed offload. You just stopped, dropped the ramp and then accelerate the airplane and then drive right out from under the load. You just lay it right out on the ramp . . .

I did several [airdrops]. We had a drop zone, which was up off the west end of the runway. I don't know how many, maybe a half a dozen or so airdrops I flew up there . . . when the weather was bad the Marine Corps had [a] GCA [Ground Control Approach] unit. We'd fly GCA approach. GCA operator put us over the end of the runway. Then the navigator would navigate from there to the center of the drop zone. We got pretty good at it, keeping stuff confined to the drop zone . . . [We would carry] mostly food and clothing, ammunition. The last time that I landed there it was a pretty tense operation because there was a lot of ground fire. We landed and took off almost immediately. . .

Bradbury remembers the unique tactics the NVA used around the hills near Khe Sanh:

Their common tactics were to wait for nightfall . . . if they could catch you out in the open and then drop a few mortars in there, but they liked to infiltrate at night to see how close they could get and on occasions they would even slip by a trip flare, but if they would hit one of course then they would light off . . . They had a lot of psychological stuff too . . . I will never forget this: they had these little whistle reeds and . . . they [would] 'toot toot' at night and you would hear way out there somewhere, and then you hear another guy do the same thing 90 degrees on the other side . . . and they would do that occasionally during the night . . . [and] early in the morning, and they just move around and blow these

The resupply of Khe Sanh was vital to its survival. Daily flights into the base proved to be extremely harrowing as the transport planes were sitting targets for enemy mortars. Here, US Air Force and Navy jets are laying down a line of defensive fire against enemy units seen moving into position to destroy this C-130 as it was about to depart.

whistles and just keep on your nerves. Where are these guys? You got somebody sneaking up here? . . . and they would do a different number [of] whistles each time to make you think they're whistling in code. Maybe they were, I mean who knows, but you would only hear them at night and it was clearly human but you couldn't see them and they would move around, there would be two or three guys out there, different places and they . . . probably weren't going to do nothing anyway but just keep the Americans on edge, make you lose some sleep, make you wonder what is going on and that was kind of a psychological thing. I remember that, some things stick in your mind forever.

Tom Esslinger remembers how he and his Marines lived on Hill 881 during the siege:

Most of the troops lived in sort of square sandbag bunkers that were fairly sizeable. Inside they might have been 10 by 10 [feet].

There would be six or eight guys in there and that's where they'd sleep. They'd man the trenches during the day . . . this was just really hard clay, almost like rock. Digging was really difficult. You'd bend your E-tool trying to dig this stuff up. Well, [Hill] 881 started taking incoming almost immediately before anyone realized there was a Tet Offensive. We were getting these mortars and rockets that were landing up there. It was just terrifying. I remember we were just scared to death . . . We quickly figured out that . . . we were obviously under observation. Anytime anybody moved on the hill they would shoot at them . . . We had a number of . . . casualties. It became obvious immediately that these sandbag bunkers were death traps. So the word went out. We were moving into the trenches.

Well, under impudence [*sic*] of enemy incoming the dirt got a lot softer . . . I'd say within a week we were living in the trenches. Troops would live in there and [in] the interior wall of the trench they would scoop out a hole. That's where they would sleep . . . moving around during daytime was an invitation to death or worse, death or injury. So during [the] daytime we just stayed in the trenches and kept a look out. At nighttime we'd have a more aggressive lookout. We would put out listening posts, at least initially a few ambushes, but not very far out . . . We quickly settled into a pattern of staying underground and out of sight during the day and doing whatever we needed to do at night. You sort of got tired of that. You started feeling like a rat particularly since it was sort of monsoonal up there and it was foggy and rainy and cold a lot of the time

One day in mid-February it was a nice sunny day. One of the first we've had. I'm sitting outside my bunker . . . on top of this sandbag wall sort of drying out and looking around and soaking up the sun. By this time most of what the enemy shot at us was 120mm Russian mortars, which were pretty devastating. You could hear them come out of the tubes. You could hear the thump. We had figured out that you had 26 seconds from the time you heard the thump until the round landed, a high trajectory. So I'm sitting up there and I hear this thump and I'm saying to myself, you know, these guy[s] are watching me. I'm not going to scurry into my hold like a rat. I'm just going to sit here. So about 15 seconds go by and I . . . know this could be pretty dumb . . . so slowly, showing my disdain, slowly I got off the hill and sort [of] ambled in through the door in the hooch. Just as I get through the door the round lands, and it lands right on the sandbag wall and blew me through the trench, up against the far wall and filled the back of my legs and my butt with shrapnel, the small pieces . . . I really wasn't very badly hurt. I was shook up a little bit but I wasn't really hurt at all. But I often reflect on the potential devastating effect of [my] false pride [then].

The media picked up on the importance Johnson and Westmoreland placed on holding Khe Sanh. Newspaper and television coverage of the siege was unprecedented in the war, as people around the world followed the day-to-day events at Khe Sanh. Esslinger remembers sensing this importance and the psychological strain the siege had placed upon the Khe Sanh defenders:

When this first started I remember just being so scared. It was almost like paralysis. I just was convinced that Khe Sahn was the focus of the free world. President Johnson and everybody between him and me was doing everything they could to get us out of there or to do something. It turns out I wasn't that far from correct. I discovered later Johnson did have a mock up of Khe Sanh in the basement [of the White House] and would prowl around there at night offering suggestions. But if you had told me on the first couple of days that we were going to be up there for 77 days, I don't know what I would have done. I might very well have shot myself. I don't think I could have taken that. It was hard enough to take it hour-by-hour or day-by-day. But then within a couple of weeks you adjust. I mean it was just amazing how resilient human beings are . . . For one thing you sort of overcome the fear. It's hard to believe that sitting there getting mortared and rocketed you can adjust to that, you can accept it, but you do.

Anthony Borra piloted resupply missions into the base in his C-130. He remembers well what he saw – images that mark the agony and devastation of the siege:

You'd look out the window, here I was all excited to be flying over there, and I'd look out and look at those Marines and realize, just look at the expression on their faces, and especially the ones that were not getting to board my airplane to leave there you know, and understood that there was a seriousness to this that I didn't understand . . . Khe Sanh is what I was most impressed with from Tet because I really could see in the faces of the Marines, I interpreted [it] as, "What am I doing here, take me away from here? I want to be out of here."

Borra returned to Khe Sanh over 30 years later as a tourist to Vietnam. He visited the former base:

When I went back, I have a photograph of myself standing on what used to be the runway at Khe Sanh. It's really interesting to hear the birds singing in the bushes and see the greenery and the peacefulness and then think of . . . how stained, if you will, that soil is with American and Vietnamese blood, and how many lives were either destroyed or shattered there. Today, it's just like any other place that is after a conflict – it was peaceful and quiet. Flowers were growing and birds were flying.

The 77-day siege was lifted by a force of US Marines and Army Air Cavalry troops that reached Khe Sanh by ground on 8 April 1968. Two hundred and five Americans died defending the base and an estimated 10,000 NVA soldiers were killed attacking the base. It was a major American victory in the war and prevented the US from suffering a Dien Bien Phu-style defeat. Only two months later, in June, Westmoreland's replacement, General Creighton Abrams, ordered Khe Sanh abandoned. On 5 July, the Marines closed the base for good.

Another area of intense combat during the Tet Offensive was the battle for the city of Hue, South Vietnam's third largest city and its ancient capitol. Hue is located about 45 miles south of the DMZ on the eastern coast. The NVA and VC forces attacked Hue with a vengeance during the Tet Offensive. They successfully seized part of the city and occupied it for three weeks. Alfred DeMailo was an Army helicopter pilot who fought in Hue. He was one of the first into the city to discover the NVA infiltration:

I do believe I flew the first gunship into Hue . . . I flew lead ship . . . We took off for Hue from Phu Bai to pick up this crane. We were flying down Highway One because the weather's bad and we're using that as a navigational route. It's just a dirt road up there. We notice that there's not a lot of people around.

Not like we normally saw from flying up there for a couple of weeks. Nobody's around, everything seems kind of quiet and we mentioned it to each other in the ship . . . We just didn't fly around fat, dumb and happy. We were pretty observant. Here came the tree line of the city of Hue. As soon as I hit that tree line, and I'm right on the deck just clipping the palm trees because the weather did not get any better. As soon as I hit that tree line, all hell broke lose. They shot my ship up. There were bullets coming through that thing. I don't know how we all weren't hit. My door gunner was hit. He got hit through the . . . thigh real good. It got an artery because as soon as he said, "I'm hit!" and the blood started spurting. His heart pumped, the blood started spurting to the windshield. I hollered at the crew chief, who's a door gunner when we're flying I said, "Get a bandage on that damn thing or we're not going to be able to see out the windshield." I called back to Freeman [the other helicopter]. I said, "Break! Don't come over the city, I'm taking fire." The chief started putting rockets right underneath me as I broke. I said, "I'm going for the road. In case I go down, I want to go down on the road and not the trees." . . . I moved my pattern off the road as we hit the tree line because we didn't want to fly the same straight course down that highway. If anybody was waiting, we wanted to be off the highway. Anyway, as I broke over the highway, there's [sic] enemy troops all over the highway.

Those troops took over part of the city and held out until destroyed by American forces. Many believe this to be some of the most intense combat of the entire Vietnam War. To retake the city, US ground forces, combined with close air support, fought street to street against the NVA and VC. Robert Scott Dawson and his Marine infantry company made their way through Hue as part of the US force that was to retake the city. He remembers action at the heart of Hue, around the ancient citadel fortress:

My squad was put to the left of the bridge going across the river and looking across . . . you could see the citadel and a main gate entering the citadel from the bridge side and there was a huge NVA flag on top of that gate. We were put there and Golf Company . . . was given the order to go across the bridge. It was just madness. What we had met coming in and then a bridge, almost about 150 meters across, funneling a company of

Marines, going across there just seemed asinine at the moment. It's one thing to go charging the front when you've got a wide front, but when you've got to put all your people in the space of about five meters and charge when you're talking about automatic weapons, that's insane. They went across. We were laying down a base of fire and then the whole side of the river, the other side just disappeared in the smoke from the gunfire, [the] RPGs and then supporting fire from our side of the river . . . [We were] trying to tear up the walls and anything else or anywhere else that the fire could be coming from. That lasted until the evening. I would say they lost probably 80 percent if you think killed and wounded. That soured me because there was no need for that loss. The people who ordered the attack . . . okay, we're Marines, that's what we do, we did it. But, we don't want to be wasted and that was a waste . . . I guess it had to be tried but it just was too set. It was an ambush, a classic Nelson "crossing the T" type situation. It wasn't a matter of having a fighting chance; it was just a matter of shooting fish in a barrel . . . [T]he orders are "Go," you go. Nobody hesitated. There are no resistors. So, off they went and many of them didn't come back . . .

I remember one night being at an LZ by the river. It was either the first or the second night and you could hear all sorts of shouting and shooting and it was bright on the other side of the river inside the walls of the . . . 17th-century French-style fortress . . . That night we watched them celebrating. Well, they were inside the walls of the citadel and they were enjoying their victory I guess the same way we would have . . . if the tables had been turned, "We have survived, we have prevailed," and . . . for them it was even sweeter because Hue was a symbol of their nationhood and the citadel was a very important part of that concept.

The NVA and VC marked the Tet Offensive in Hue with terror, as they rounded up all those who had aided its enemies in any way and brutally executed them. It is estimated that the NVA/VC murdered between 2,800 and 10,000 civil servants, soldiers, educators and anyone else with connections to the RVN or the Americans.

The American media coverage of the Tet Offensive was unprecedented. The US public received a large quantity of coverage straight from the battlefields of South Vietnam. The print media and the television crews brought the fighting of Tet home into the living rooms of America

A Marine carries a wounded Vietnamese child from the rubble of a home in Hue, the ancient imperial capital of Vietnam, where US forces fought street to street to retake the city. The fighting during and after the 1968 Tet Offensive was some of the heaviest of the entire Vietnam War and Hue was particularly hard hit.

where individuals could watch the shocking and deadly events unfold on television. This coverage made the war seem more real to the viewers and more controversial to those who opposed the war. Watching the US Embassy in Saigon be overrun by VC sappers or mortar rounds dropping in on Khe Sanh or graphic images from the urban warfare of Hue on one's television was unsettling to say the least. The American public had never experienced a war like this before, unsanitized and in living color. The effects of this coverage were vast. There were some veterans, such as Fred Marshall, Army intelligence officer and ARVN adviser, who did not like how Tet and the war was portrayed in the media:

> The Tet Offensive [was] hailed as a huge Communists' victory.
> They got slaughtered everywhere in the country but that got
> turned into a big victory by the media and nothing else. The
> butchery [by] the North Vietnamese in Hue, going into the city

with lists of people and taking them out and executing them
with a bullet in the head by the thousands, burying them in mass
graves. I didn't see any protests and demonstrations over that.

Marine infantry commander Michael Sweeney describes an incident in
the aftermath of the Tet Offensive, when he encountered the media on a
hilltop in the mountains of South Vietnam:

[W]e had eight Marines killed with one round there. Damnedest
thing I ever saw . . . They were brand new kids and the squad
leader had gathered them up and had them scattered out. He
had done everything right. There were six new ones and a squad
leader and one of his old guys. And an .82 mortar round hit in
the circle and killed outright every one of them. I mean you could
drop a nuclear weapon in there and not do that . . .
    After that incident we had the eight dead Marines on the
ground. I tried to get them out, couldn't get them out, and
finally a helicopter came in and there was a television news crew
aboard it. They got in the way and, of course, the helicopter drew
fire as they always did. We only got four of them aboard, four
were still with us. I remember the news crew was taking pictures.
One of the kids' hands had fallen out of the poncho he was
wrapped in. They were taking pictures of it. I just turned around
and told the correspondent, "I hope you don't think you're
leaving with that." He said he could do whatever he wanted to. I
told him that I'd leave him for the North Vietnamese to talk to.
We had a sort of heated discussion. Finally he agreed to destroy
the film. He told me he was going to put me on report to the
highest authority. I said, "What are they going to do? Cut my hair
off and send me to Vietnam and put me out here 25 kilometers
from the nearest friendlies?" How the hell are you going to scare
a guy in that position?
    So it was kind of laughable really. In fact I remember the old
gunnery sergeant from Mike company turned around to this
guy – he's well known, you could see him every week – [this]
correspondent and saying, "You'd better listen to him mister.
He'll do that, he'll leave you here." That was that. We got them
out of there on the next helicopter along with the four dead
. . . Then we flew on into An Hoa, made sure we had everybody
aboard. Everybody was out . . . The general's jeep was sitting there

waiting for me . . . the CG, commanding general of task force
. . . General's driver says, "The General will see you." Went and
reported in . . . I knew him very well. He knew me very well
. . . I'd known him forever. He offered me a beer and sat me down
and asked how it went and all the usual stuff. Then he said,
"What did you say to that reporter up there?" I told him and he
said, "Why didn't you just shoot him?"

The American and South Vietnamese forces counterattacked in the weeks
after the initial Tet assault. Their mission was straightforward: recapture
all areas lost to the NVA and VC and destroy all enemy forces involved
in the Tet Offensive. The US directed its military operations at the Viet
Cong which had now exposed itself. Through intense, fierce fighting, the
objective was met; the American forces successfully destroyed the majority
of the VC infrastructure by the summer of 1968. The US also inflicted
heavy damage on the NVA. Army infantry platoon leader John McNown,
Jr, describes what he and his men encountered after Tet:

By the time I got there – I got there after Tet of '68 – the Viet
Cong really weren't as big, their forces had been pretty much
decimated in early '68 and mid-'68. So we ran into Viet Cong very
seldom. Most of what we ran into there were very small units,
four or five or six people, booby traps, and snipers, a lot of that.
As far as actual fighting goes I didn't think the NVA had a big
advantage over us. I do think they were better informed about
our movements than we were about theirs.

After Tet, Sweeney took his unit out into the mountains near the Lao
border to engage the NVA. He describes an incident when they were pulling
out of an area after engaging the enemy:

When we were going to pull off the hill, we had all kinds of
unexpended explosives and artillery elements and powder and
all kinds of stuff. We imported some more and we just wanted
the whole hill to blow up [when we left] because we had semi-
bunkers. It was the simplest way to dispose of all the stuff. We
had that whole hill set to become Vesuvius II. When the weather
finally broke a little bit, we ran what was then called a mini-
gaggle with [an] A-4 [Intruder aircraft] smoking the hillside. I
remember an OV-10 [FAC] pilot overhead yelling at me, "Get

out, get out, they're [the NVA] coming up the north side, they're coming up the south side." And a [Chinook] 53 [helicopter] comes in and of course the mortars start. I've got this corporal standing there with a five-minute fuse igniter on a five-minute fuse to blow the hill up. I'm counting Marines aboard as they run aboard this 53. Of course this [helicopter] crew chief is counting them too. When we get over 40 his eyes get big. We know it's going to be a hell of a load, and finally I got 50. That leaves . . . the corporal and I. I pointed at him and told him to pull the fuse. He pulled the fuse and covered up his ears and just stood there. He was like 20 yards away, and I had to run over there and grab him by the flak jacket and throw him on the damn helicopter. The pilot's eyes are as big as saucers. The CH-53 is shuddering and shaking. Of course he doesn't know we've got five minutes. He's trying to get out of there. We shuttered off the hill after about three minutes. We hadn't gotten 200 yards when the thing let loose and the whole hillside, hilltop blew up.

REFLECTIONS ON THE 1968 TET OFFENSIVE

Looking back on the Tet Offensive, many believe that the DRV succeeded in its initial endeavor of surprise and attack, and in its mission to empower the anti-war movement in the US. North Vietnam failed in its overall mission to ignite a revolution to topple the RVN government. Ultimately, the Tet Offensive led to the destruction of the Viet Cong. Frank Linster served with the US Army in Vietnam from 1967 to 1968 and in 1971 as a helicopter pilot. He reflects on the planning for the offensive and the results for the US:

From history [books] we found out that some of the ARVN units were infiltrated by Viet Cong. Up to 40–50 percent of their strength were VC . . . These guys are trying to take us out because they knew that Tet was coming right around the corner and so the more aircraft they can destroy, the less they got to worry about during Tet and Tet was a big operation. It went on [in] the whole country; from the DMZ all the way down to the end of IV Corps [the southernmost military region of South Vietnam]. Talk about a coordinated attack! . . . The Viet Cong was making rumblings in the Special Forces camp along the borders [of Laos and Cambodia] trying to draw us out away from our base camps and stuff and . . . one of the generals that was on Westmoreland's staff convinced Westmoreland, "Don't send anybody out. Send out minimum force. Use Air Force, use artillery, use B-52s, use Puff [C-130 Gunships], but don't send ground troops out to relieve these Special Forces camps. It's just a ploy to get you away from your base camps." So Westmoreland kept most of his guys at home. The ones that were in the base camps stayed there, and that probably made a big difference . . . The first couple of days it was touch and go whether we was going to be able to turn the tide on that. The way the newspapers reported it, it turned the American people against us, I think. It just turned public opinion against the war, and from that point we lost the propaganda war.

William Anderson was an Air Force helicopter and O-2 pilot in Vietnam between 1968 and 1969. He believes that Tet was a solid defeat of the Viet Cong and a victory for the US:

We were shocked . . . at the extent of the Tet Offensive but then we gradually learned that this was expected and that was a big offensive. Many people consider the Tet Offensive as kind of a victory that turned us around and it really wasn't, it was a defeat for them because it almost completely made the Viet Cong action ineffective. They expended almost all of their resources and were solemnly whipped; it took a little while after the Tet to get them calmed down. But it nearly annihilated all the Viet Cong forces . . . So in effect it was a victory for our forces over there because it was the last time that they really had any effective action against any American troops or the South Vietnamese in country without the help of the North Vietnamese coming down.

Fred Marshall believes that the Tet Offensive was a tactical failure but a strategic success for the enemy:

As a PR move it was pretty brilliant, because quite a few times during the course of the war, at least when I was there we made these rosy predictions – "The light at the end of the tunnel" – all this kind of stuff. That we were making tremendous progress and we weren't for other reasons . . . I think at home we'd been domestically lulled into a kind of false sense of security. We had been achieving quite a large degree of success in the battlefield especially up in I Corps against the North Vietnamese. The government PR kind of led on that we had pretty much pacified much of the country. The Tet Offensive showed at least the enemy could operate and mount a coordinated attack, nation wide. I just think psychologically it was a pretty good coup by the North Vietnamese. Of course it was militarily where they got wiped out everywhere.

For the DRV, things did not seem as though any victory had been achieved. NVA officer Nguyen Phat Le recalls the feeling amongst his men and the status of the NVA after the Tet Offensive and American counterattack was over:

> After the campaign we did not have enough force to fight in [a] big battle but only to attack and run on the enemy's posts. Our morale was very low, a considerable portion of our forces were destroyed. We had to hide in tunnels all day. The news of Americans withdrawing [from the war] was like a resuscitating pill for us. It raised our morale. And again the Party argued that due to the victory of our . . . Tet Offensive campaign, the American forces had to withdraw. When the US and the RVN forces carried out a military operation into Cambodian territory [in 1970], all the local VC in the area where I lived [in the RVN] had dispersed and sought sanctuary in Cambodia to avoid the mopping up operations. We belonged to the main military forces and had to split up to reinforce for the local organizations.

South Vietnamese Ambassador Nguyen Xuan Phong was a Cabinet-level official in the RVN government. He held various positions during his tenure and was *Chieu Hoi* Minister, the head of the 'Open Arms' program, at the time of the Tet Offensive. Ambassador Phong went on to represent the RVN at the Paris Peace Talks. He describes what the Tet Offensive meant to the people of South Vietnam and the NLF forces, the *Chieu Hoi* soldiers during Tet, and the overall effects of Tet '68 on the RVN, the US and the DRV:

> The Tet Offensive . . . it didn't last very long . . . I think they [the South Vietnamese people] had the impression that the Saigon government, with the American troops there, were more than able [to] push back the guys on the offensive. I don't think that in the minds of the Saigon people, they thought the Communist forces or the Viet Minh forces, or Viet Cong forces, were in any way able

to overrun the town, never had that idea at all. And so probably so in the minds of those Viet Cong too, the NLF, they did not really think that they could overrun the South Vietnam militarily with all the US troops there, never have that chance. It was purely just a show for political purposes . . . But during the Tet Offensive it was very interesting too, because we set up those *Chieu Hoi* centers [places where the enemy troops could surrender and come over to the other side] in the provincial towns, and I had the agreement with Westmoreland to give them heavy arms. At the beginning the ARVN refused, they said it's very dangerous to give heavy arms to the former Viet Cong, but Westmoreland gave the green light . . .

During the Tet Offensive . . . the two highest priorities [were], to take hold of [the] hospital [in each town] to use it as a shield and stay in there and hold the line and give the punishment to the *Chieu Hoi* centers . . . I was in touch with . . . all of South Vietnam during the Tet Offensive and they reported the attacks, they pushed back all the attacks, not one exception, and then Westmoreland was really impressed also by the way they fought because they were former Viet Congs, they knew the ways and means of those guys, the way they fight, so they were very effective, extremely effective [protecting] those *Chieu Hoi* centers.

Ambassador Phong also believes that the Tet Offensive was a major defeat for the North Vietnamese but that it served its purpose in the larger context of the overall effort to defeat South Vietnam and unite Vietnam under the DRV banner:

I was really disgusted with the whole show after the Tet Offensive because it was really a lamentable show, although the Communists were not able to achieve any military gains and victory, on the contrary, they had the biggest beating of the Vietnam War, they sacrificed everything, they're following the principle of fight, fight, talk, talk of Mao [Zedong], and the Tet Offensive was for them to open the discussions with the Americans. Why [did] Hanoi accepted to go there [Paris] and then had to launch the Tet Offensive in order to go there? They always do that before they sit down at the negotiating table, that is to save face, to show their strength politically and militarily. They did that in '54 with Dien Bien Phu, they did that all the time, even after '72 and the Paris Agreement. So that was the principle that they adhered to 100 percent. In the eyes of the people they went to the negotiating table in a position of force. The United States had to sit down and negotiate with them . . . for the ordinary people that was easy to understand. It [the Tet Offensive] was launched completely by Hanoi . . .

The weapons came from North Vietnam. The military leaders and the commanders were really from North Vietnam and then just a few figures militarily among the so-called Viet Cong ranks, but they were not very, very bright, the military leaders. Madame [Nguyen Thi] Binh for example, the military chief of all the [NLF] forces [and] General Giap, so I don't really believe that the NLF had an army to begin with and then had the logistics and supplies to establish in order to do that thing. Of course they [the DRV] used lots of those local Viet Cong people but that would not be sufficient to launch an all out attack against the Saigon [South Vietnamese] army. But I'm sure [that] among the problems that Ho Chi Minh knew very well [was] that the Tet Offensive wouldn't topple the Saigon government or the Saigon army with all [of] those American troops present there . . . Very clearly his objectives were elsewhere. That's why he came to the Paris Peace Talks. [He was playing on the American public] very much . . .

During the Tet Offensive, over 1,000 Americans and 2,500 ARVN soldiers were killed and an estimated 45,000 to 58,000 of the original 84,000 NVA and NLF forces were lost. The Tet Offensive was a major turning point in the Vietnam War. It marked the end of the viability of the National Liberation Front (NLF). The initial attack around South Vietnam was fierce, but the American counterattack destroyed the NLF which had come out into the open to fight for the first time.

Nevertheless, the Tet Offensive was the beginning of the end of US involvement in Vietnam. It shook the American population to its foundation, split the nation even more, drew into question the Johnson Administration's credibility and sparked pessimistic and negative media coverage of the war. For the US, what followed the end of the Tet Offensive counterattack in Vietnam was an overall military effort that was meant to compliment the US and North Vietnamese negotiations in Paris to end the conflict. President Richard Nixon soon began the systematic withdrawal of American forces out of Vietnam and the implementation of the Vietnamization policy. Before this would happen, Nixon launched a series of attacks meant to cripple the DRV before the US left Vietnam for good.

9
THE HOME FRONT

MAIL

Once American servicemen had been inducted, trained and sent to Vietnam, their connections to home narrowed. The delivery of mail became a lifeline, both for anxious families and for homesick troops, particularly those in the field. Many soldiers pined for news of their favorite sports teams, while others wanted to know that their families, friends and lovers were well. As a matter of maintaining morale, the US military assigned the delivery of mail to servicemen a high priority, particularly for men in combat areas. Even so, delivery was chore, and it was not always reliable. As infantryman Marvin Mathiak, who served in Cambodia and South Vietnam in 1970–71, remembers:

> . . . Every three days, hopefully, the log bird [supply helicopter] would find us and if he could set down then we could get out any mail that we'd written . . . When they brought food and water they'd bring mail; they'd drop mail as well. So, we'd get mail every three days when they logged us but we could only get mail out on those occasions when a log bird could sit down and that was much more irregular. That could go for weeks at a time. So, our communication to the outside world was pretty limited, it was pretty much one-way communication.

Writing letters could be difficult as well, and field conditions often put even the best intentions of servicemen to the test. Some found plenty of time to write. For most, including US Marine James 'Butch' Morris, their commitment to writing home varied over the course of their tours:

> It would go in spurts; sometimes you'd write forever and then get on a kick where you don't, but there is only so many times that you can say "the weather's pretty" and "the food's good". I got medevaced one time – for two weeks I was in the hospital with malaria – and when I was in the hospital I wrote a lot of

letters. I'd probably write three or four a day, like to my mom and my sisters.

When writing home many servicemen stayed away from accurate descriptions of the living conditions and battle engagements they experienced in Vietnam. Realistic reports or photos from Southeast Asia could provoke even greater anxiety and fear in family members, according to Stephen Katz, a search and rescue specialist with a US Air Force Rescue Squadron:

> I guess either in Thailand or in Vietnam, I ran across two guys that had been with me at Syracuse [University] and somebody had a camera and they took a picture of the three of us, which we were going to send back to the school. We're wearing our full combat gear, the survival vest and the gun and so forth, and I sent that picture back . . . to my parents, which turned out to be a big mistake. My mother   well, next time I talked to her – she said, "You carry a gun over there?" And I said, "Where do you think I am, a summer camp? You know there are people over here that don't like me. So, yes, I carry a gun, and I know how to use it and hopefully I never will have to." That kind of upset her now that I think [about it] . . . I took it a lot more lightly than [my parents] probably did.

Others, however, were determined that the folks back home have at least a sense of the situation of their sons and daughters serving in Vietnam. Nurse Susan O'Neill was one who, using the ubiquitous Japanese-made tape recorders of the day, made an effort to convey the realities of the combat area to her parents:

> We all had reel–reel tape recorders, but mostly what you sent was cassettes and so we would inevitably bounce the tapes back and forth and I have to admit that I was pretty awful about [it] . . . I'd sit out where it was noisiest and you could actually hear the outgoing rounds and stuff, so that my parents would understand that this was a situation where . . . there really was a war going on over here!

The letters exchanged between lovers, separated by war and geography, could be ironic, angry, passionate or proud, depending upon the state of the relationship, events at home and in Vietnam – and, of course, upon the flow of the mail. Letters arriving late or out of sequence could confuse and confound, while the absence of letters could provoke fear, resentment, jealousy and pain. The separation imposed on young lovers by military service in Vietnam also took its toll on relationships. Some who lost their lovers were glad that they did not get the news while in country, as helicopter crewman Gregory Burch remembers:

> In my case I was glad she lied to me . . . She never sent me a "Dear John" [letter] . . . I was a little upset, didn't want to punch her out or anything. I was just a little upset that my girlfriend now had another boy . . . I remember we had two suicides from "Dear John" letters in my company . . . The guys who took their girlfriend away, and the girls themselves, [were] heartless little bitches . . .

Many of the letters that were exchanged between lovers were honest and authentic records of their emotions and experiences. Some servicemen, like William Giles, a medical aide at the 12th Evac Hospital near Cu Chi in 1967–68 who wrote to his girlfriend in California during the Tet Offensive, simply told their loved ones what it felt like to be in Vietnam on a given day:

> I haven't any idea when things will quiet down. The Viet Cong recently have started with mortar and rocket attacks at the beginning of darkness, and they continue until early morning. Of course, this doesn't help one sleep enough, if at all. And right now I'm so sleepy. I look like a wreck; I haven't showered in three days, or shaved, and I need a haircut, and I feel twice as bad. Of course, through it all, I think of you, and miss you, and long to be with you. I'm sorry I can't alleviate your worry, but "War is Hell!"

For others whose links to family were tenuous before their tour in Vietnam, the mails – however welcome – could also serve as a reminder of the hollow relationships left behind. Army surgeon Jim Evans said:

> I've got a lot of letters that I got from my folks and it's like they had no clue where I was, like I was on some picnic . . . In some ways my folks were very supporting. I did get lots of letters. They sent lots of care packages. They sent cookies and crackers, pizza mix, cashews. When I was in Quang Tri they sent a plastic

Christmas tree . . . So at one level they were very supportive, but certainly not at an emotional level.

Parcels of sweets, nuts and other delicacies, as well as clothing, music tapes, writing paper, books, shaving equipment and other sundries – generally known as 'care packages' – were a popular method of sending reminders and comforts of home to servicemen in Vietnam. Since the US military paid the postage on such packages, parents, wives and girlfriends made the most of the opportunity to make their loved ones' lives easier and more pleasant. Veterans' organizations, churches, schools and civic groups also assembled and mailed care packages to American servicemen in Vietnam. As Marine aviator Neil Whitehurst remembers, servicemen themselves sometimes requested that friends in America send care packages for humanitarian agencies in South Vietnam:

> A lot of us sent letters home and the local churches that we were involved in and organizations gathered a lot of materials, clothing and personal care items and things and mailed the boxes. The US Government shipped them over to Vietnam for us. And we would take these down to the orphanage to give to the sisters in the Sacred Heart Orphanage and to the children . . .

Roy Riddle, a pilot with the US Army, replied to a care package he received from his home town in Texas by asking for another kind of gift:

> They sent me a package at Christmas time. That's all it said. It had cookies and candy and a card, a couple of books, you know, things. I had written back to thank them and I said if anybody had any garden seed left that they didn't use, if they would send it to me. I was going to plant me a little garden at the airfield . . . [The seeds were sent by] First Baptist Church here in Tahoka [Texas], and other churches here in Tahoka. They called [themselves] 'Friends of Veterans from Lynn County.' . . . With seed that we received from churches in the States we taught a couple of [Vietnamese] farmers how to raise vegetables for us . . . We got some radishes, and turnips, mustard, lettuce and onions. Then we got tomatoes and peppers, and [there were] a lot of things that we didn't have very good luck with.

As James 'Butch' Morris remembers, anti-war activists in the US also used the 'care package' format to get their message across to American servicemen in Vietnam:

> One guy got a package and he unwrapped it, and it was a can of dog food. And [it] said . . . something to the effect, "Here is what you deserve because of the animal that you are."

ANTI-WAR PROTESTS

By the time President Nixon took office, in January 1969, the anti-war movement in the United States had emerged as a critical factor in American policy-making toward the Vietnam conflict. It had not always been that way. In 1964–65, for example, after President Johnson's Gulf of Tonkin Resolution had received resounding approval from the US Congress, the few public protests against American involvement in Vietnam were generally viewed as anti-American, and their participants as proto-Communists. As John Lawitt recalls, in 1964:

> I realized I was one of a very few who were protesting the war. I remember going on marches around City Hall in Philadelphia and having red paint thrown on us and people swearing and driving by, trying to run us over and things like that. [It] was viewed as very unpatriotic . . . I didn't understand why it was that people could not see the obvious fallacy of US policy and that they were being fed a bunch of bullshit by the leaders of the country to justify the war. I just couldn't understand it.

One American, a Quaker schoolteacher from Baltimore, decided in 1965 that America's war in Vietnam demanded a reply. In his own homage to the Buddhist priests of South Vietnam, who in 1963 had protested against the Diem regime by setting themselves on fire in Saigon, the teacher immolated himself in Washington DC. One of the students at the Baltimore Quaker school, Dev Slingluff, who later served in the Marines in Vietnam, remembers the event this way:

> Friends, [or] Quakers, are the main part of the anti-war movement at any time, any place. One of my teachers, a math teacher . . . went to Washington and burned himself to death . . . I mean you're pretty appalled by just the concept of burning oneself to death. I'm still pretty appalled by it. It was discussed a lot and you know we talked about the dedication that somebody

must have to a particular ideology or outlook in order to do that, to draw attention to it. As a teacher I always thought that he was pretty weird . . . He was marching to a different beat. He was a good teacher, everybody seemed to like him, but to me he was a little bit strange. I don't mean strange in a bad way, I mean, just, he was different . . .

At that point, the anti-war movement was really confined to a small group of people, of which the Quakers were one group. I mean they were standing out on the streets with signs, "no war", and all the rest . . .

In the mid-1960s, not many young people in the United States were exposed to such anti-war ideas as a part of their high school experience. Increasingly, however, matters were different on college campuses. As the number of men deployed in Vietnam rose sharply in 1966–67, the specter of military conscription and service in Vietnam became a central feature in the lives of America's young men and spurred the broadening of the anti-war movement. College campuses were the first to see large-scale anti-war demonstrations. The University of California's Berkeley campus became widely recognized as a haven for anti-war radicals, but Midwestern schools also saw large anti-war protests. Marvin Mathiak recalls how, as a student at the University of Wisconsin-Madison in the mid-1960s, he saw the protest movement there grow:

At Wisconsin there were a lot of demonstrations that were going on. Wisconsin was an extremely liberal campus and there were a lot of characters who thought it was a lot of fun to demonstrate. I think probably 1 percent or 5 percent of the people who were demonstrating had serious convictions and the remainder were just out for fun. There were a lot of sit-ins, particularly in the chemistry building where I spent a lot of time because at that time, there was a lot of antagonism against Dow Chemical for producing napalm. I remember I had to step over and around and on people to get to my classes. There was a very stressful, very nasty time as the years went on . . . Wisconsin was one of the most active schools. I think Wisconsin and Berkeley were probably the two most active schools in terms of anti-war protesting at the time . . . To me [the protests] were a nuisance and a distraction and I was there trying to get an education. I was very serious about that . . . As far as I was concerned, they were just interfering with my rights to try to get an education by interfering with my mobility and generally being obnoxious. Now as things evolved, I became more and more unhappy with the war and became quite strongly anti-war, and in fact to this day I think it was a big mistake. But in any event, as time progressed, I guess like a lot of the population in this country, I gradually became more and more against the war.

Campus unrest was compounded by the American civil rights movement, which created greater public awareness of race-based social inequities. Some of these inequities were directly related to American involvement in Vietnam, including apparent racial bias in the composition and decisions of draft boards, whites' utilization of National Guard service as a means of avoiding the draft, and the relative under-representation of blacks in deferment-earning categories such as college enrollment. The impression was created that blacks were being disproportionately conscripted into service in Vietnam. Civil rights leader Dr Martin Luther King, Jr, generally refused to overtly challenge American policies in Vietnam, and he was, for the most part, successful in urging African-Americans to pursue peaceful paths to rectify the injustices they saw in America. However, in April 1968, Dr King was assassinated in Memphis, Tennessee. Thousands of African-Americans, particularly in the cities, took to the streets in spontaneous demonstrations of grief and anger. In some places, like Washington DC, violence and looting occurred over several days. As Lou Walters, then a young resident of McLean, Virginia, remembers, US military units were called out to end the violence and secure the capital:

> I at that time picked my dad up in DC, I don't know for what reason. I must've had the car or something, and when the riots broke out in DC and we came out, we had a brick thrown at the car and they shut DC down and they blocked – they had tanks on the bridges and everything.

Seldon Graham, a West Point graduate and Army reservist who was working at the Defense Department at this time, echoes Walters' observations:

> The most vivid recollection I have is the burning of Washington. I was on my two weeks of active duty in the Pentagon and I would always stay at Fort Myer, which was a simple walk over to the Pentagon, but when Martin Luther

King was assassinated, there was great havoc in Washington. And I remember standing out there on Arlington Ridge and counting the number of fires where I could count the blazes above the rooftops. And there were several dozen fires burning all over the city of Washington . . . A friend and I had arranged to go over to the airbase, I think it's Andrews, and he and I drove over there during all these riots and every burglar alarm in Washington DC was going on. No one was paying attention to it and there was looting going on. It's a wonder we did all that safely because we drove through all of this as it was transpiring. It was very upsetting to see your capital burning and being looted.

The impact of the assassinations of King and of Robert Kennedy – who was killed in June 1968 – upon the anti-war movement is impossible to calculate. It was clear, however, that former Vice President Richard Nixon, a Republican, saw in the domestic disarray his opportunity to finally ascend to the Presidency, buoyed by a plan to withdraw 'with honor' from Vietnam. Nixon directed his appeals to America's 'great silent majority,' the tax-paying middle class that despised and feared radicals, anti-war protests and the violence that sometimes accompanied them. It was a successful vote-getting formula, and it produced Nixon's election victory in November. For those who still faced service in Vietnam, however, the events of 1968 had proven deeply disillusioning. As Jim Evans, a doctor who was later drafted, remembers:

I guess the feeling I had in '68 was there was this hope bubbling around and promise and then everything turned sour . . . with Kennedy's assassination, Martin Luther King's death, I mean there was all this violence. There was hope for change and then it was like it was smashed because of the violence . . . It was sort of like watching a revolution get smashed. It was just stunning to watch it happen.

The early years of the Nixon Administration saw the rapid expansion of the anti-war movement in the United States. Many young men began to contemplate the possibility of fleeing the country to avoid being compelled to serve in Vietnam. Lou Walters, who grew up near Washington DC, was one of those who had decided to go to Canada, if he had to, in order to 'dodge' the draft:

Driven by opposition to the draft, civilian protests against America's military involvement in Vietnam grew into a national movement. The best-known demonstration was this May 1970 protest at Kent State University in Ohio, where National Guard troops fired on demonstrators, killing four students.

> Quite frankly, I was going to go to Canada if I had been drafted, I wasn't going to go into the draft. My sister, Jenny, was living in Canada, and she said, "Come on up here." So, that's probably what I would have done. I wouldn't have gone in. In retrospect, I would do things differently, you know. Hindsight's 20/20 . . . but at the time I was just going to leave.

Student deferments were increasingly difficult to obtain, and upper and middle class white males became more susceptible to conscription. In some places, the anti-war movement became more recognizable as an 'anti-draft' movement, as John Lawitt recalls:

> [There] was a demonstration at Independence Hall in Philadelphia [in 1969]. There were lots of people burning their draft cards there at that time. I realized also the only way that I was going to avoid the military was to get a student deferment because everybody that wasn't going to college was being drafted. So, at that point,

I wanted to go to college because I didn't particularly want to go
to Canada or else I would've . . . I realized I [faced] two choices;
either go to Canada or go to jail and I never really had to make the
choice because I had a student deferment and then when student
deferments ended in . . . 1969, maybe 1970, and then went to the
lottery system, [and] I had a very high number [that was unlikely
to be selected] just by the luck of the draw, literally.

The expectations created in 1968 by such 'peace candidates' for the
Presidency as Robert Kennedy and Eugene McCarthy, who had suggested
that an end to the war might be within reach, had been turned upside
down by the election of Richard Nixon. Nixon wanted to bolster the
American position on the ground in Vietnam, and he wanted law and order
at home. New groups began entering the widening protest movement.
Demonstrations that included young mothers and minorities began to
grow. Anti-war groups formed coalitions with activist civil rights, free
speech, and women's organizations to expand their bases of popular
support and to attract larger crowds to their public events. John Lawitt, a
political activist in Philadelphia, recalls the atmosphere there:

In Philadelphia . . . they were arresting people all the time at
that point, whether if you were to protest and you did one
little thing that was outside of what the permit [for a legal
demonstration] permitted or if you marched without a permit,
they were arresting people . . . The Student Non-Violent
Coordinating Committee was not non-violent, and we began
to be guarded by a group called the 'Deacons for Self Defense'
[which was] an armed group of black people who would protect
protesters and would protect speakers, who were sort of like
bodyguards for the civil rights movement. I became aware
of them because of the fact that so many people were being
arrested and that the protests were getting more and more
violent . . .

While some college campuses, notably several in California, Michigan,
and New York, had been wracked by student anti-war protests for
years, other less prominent schools now began to experience larger and
more radical protests as well. John Lawitt recalls the atmosphere during
the 1968–69 school year at the University of Bridgeport, an urban college
in Connecticut:

Then I went to the University of Bridgeport and of course, at that time . . . everybody was very concerned about the war because we were all of draft age and we all knew people that had been killed and we all knew people that had gone [to Vietnam], both voluntarily and involuntarily. Everybody had a consciousness, whether you believed in the war, you didn't believe in the war; whether you believed in the draft, you didn't believe in the draft. Everybody was politically conscious because everybody was faced with having to deal with the issue one way or the other . . . I then became involved with the Black Panther Party, so my political beliefs were moving to be more and more radical . . .

Even at the University of Oregon students engaged in campus protests, sit-ins, and demonstrations. James Mogan, then an Army ROTC student at the University, remembers that:

[At the teach-ins there was] basically a lot of rhetoric, some hand-outs, very repetitious, over and over again the same themes: "The war is wrong"; . . . "Victory to the Viet Cong"; [and] your typical chants: "1, 2, 3, 4, [we don't want your fucking war]."

While protests spread across the country and grew more radical, Washington DC remained a focal point for both local and nationally organized demonstrations and protest vigils. West Point graduate Seldon Graham, who served in the Pentagon regularly during this period, remembers:

It was routine during the two weeks [I was in Washington each year] when the Vietnam War was going on, for the protesters to be waiting on the steps of the Pentagon every morning and usually they would have some kind of crazy uniform on or a skeleton . . . You would step over them in order to get into the front door. And at one point, someone had put a bomb in one of the men's latrines [in the Pentagon], which exploded and probably did a lot of damage, but it didn't hurt anybody . . . [The demonstrators] tried to be there as everybody entered. They'd try to insult you . . . I never did hear anybody argue with them or try to even reply. The best thing to do is ignore them . . . I think they probably did [try to block access to the Pentagon] once and it didn't work, or the MPs [military police] let them know that people do have to get to work and

cannot be denied access to their building. But as far as I ever
observed, they never tried to block, they just tried to insult . . .

In the early 1970s anti-war activists believed that the Nixon Administration
was as mired in Vietnam as the Johnson Administration had been, and as
Seldon Graham has noted, in Washington frustrated protesters began
focusing their demonstrations on the many military installations and
offices located throughout the city. Dev Slingluff, who had returned from a
tour in Vietnam, remembers his experiences with protesters in Washington
at a Marine Corps dispensary:

> I had to drive through them every morning because my Duty
> Station at the Dispensary was right across the street from
> American University. There is a [traffic] circle when you come
> up from Georgetown towards American University and that
> circle happened to be where they had their demonstration every
> day . . . So therefore going to work every morning, all of us who
> were driving in to work . . . were the targets of their verbal, and
> sometimes attempted physical, abuse. When I was coming to
> work, I was in my uniform . . . It was kind of irritating. You
> would try to drive around the circle and they would be in the way.
> You would have to stop your car. They'd start bouncing the car
> up and down occasionally and . . . then they would have their face
> up to the window and they would be screaming something at you
> about what an evil person you are, how could you do this . . . I
> mean it was all the same college BS, you know, "Baby Killer"-type
> stuff. "Murderer!" "How could you do that?" "You should be put
> in jail"-type things . . . We just called them a bunch of idiots. You
> know, "The idiots are out there again."

News of the American military incursion into Cambodia in May 1970
provoked a new round of anti-Vietnam War protests nationwide. The
mostly infamous was the student demonstration at Kent State University
in Ohio, where National Guardsmen fired on a crowd of protesters and
killed four students; a short time later two students at Jackson State
College, a historically black institution in Mississippi, were shot to death
following protests there. Between the Cambodia invasion and the killings
of demonstrators, the protest movement reached a new zenith in the late
spring and summer of 1970. Marshall Paul, then returning from service in
Vietnam, recalls how protests were developing even in Austin, the capital

of traditionally conservative Texas, and how conflicted he felt about participating:

> When I came back from Vietnam in 1970, I went straight to Austin. And during the summer of '70, there was a tremendous amount of a protesting going on on campus. And since I was twenty years old and this was my peer group now, my new social set, I started going to protests. And it seemed like a big party, and it was fun. But at the same time, I didn't agree with what we were protesting for. I was just kind of out there, just to be running around in the streets with a bunch of people, and I suspect that most of the other kids were doing the same thing . . . So it had a circus atmosphere, and I was really asking myself a lot of questions . . . "How could so many thousands of people who are educated or at least getting educations have such radical opinions, or opinions radically different from my own? Could they all be wrong? Is there really something I should be questioning about my role in Vietnam and the country's role?"
>
> I went to one demonstration and they were talking about [the] Special Forces going into Cambodia . . . Well, I had gotten a letter from one of my friends that my unit had gone to Cambodia . . . and my stomach just dropped, because I'm standing at a demonstration, demonstrating against the invasion of Cambodia, and I'm feeling guiltier than shit because I'm not with [my unit]. And I remember thinking, "Am I right? Am I smarter than the 20,000 people in this demonstration? Or are they all . . . you know, who's fucked up here, who's wrong? Or is it just two points of view, and neither one of them makes a difference?" I didn't come to any conclusion then, and I'm not sure I have now.

By 1970–71, many of those attending America's colleges and universities were veterans of the Vietnam conflict who had completed their tours and were using their federally-funded GI Bill educational benefits to earn degrees and begin their careers. The social and political dynamics between these veterans and their often overtly anti-war classmates and professors were complicated. A number of veterans who opposed continuation of US military involvement in Southeast Asia became involved in the anti-war protests, and some joined a special protest group composed of veterans, known as the 'Vietnam Veterans Against the War' (VVAW). Donald McBane remembers why he was drawn to VVAW rallies:

When I got back home in Pennsylvania, upstate New York, there were these local [VVAW] chapters that staged . . . local [demonstrations] trying to get news media attention. But there were veterans who were against the war as well as veterans who were in favor of it. Nothing . . . big that got much attention, but it was a way of saying, you know, there are two sides. Not everybody that served was gung-ho in favor of what we were doing there.

Marine veteran Dev Slingluff, who briefly affiliated with the VVAW group at the University of North Carolina at Chapel Hill, had a slightly different reason for joining VVAW activities:

I agreed with pulling out of Vietnam . . . and my reason was not a typical reason. It was obvious to me, at that point, from what was going on, what I was observing, that there was no way that the people of this country had the political will to finish what had been started. To me the wasting of one more life because you want to gradually do it 'with honor' or with whatever was, to me, an absurdity because to me life was more important than whatever pretense they could come up with for not pulling [American troops] out immediately. However, if I had had my [way], I would have wished that we had the ability and the will to finish what we had started.

Susan O'Neill and her husband Paul, both Vietnam veterans, were active with VVAW chapters in Massachusetts and Maine because,

. . . it was a good group, it was fairly active on campus [at UMass Amherst] . . . And we kind of went with them and were part of the fold and that was fine by me. I joined the organization later when we were up in Maine . . . [I joined because] the government [had] condemned [servicemen] to death, if anything. Those of us who spoke out against it were trying to get them out of [Vietnam] . . .

Other returning veterans who were attending college were alienated by the campus anti-war protests and the radical politics of other campus groups, including the faculty. Chad Spawr, a combat interrogator, remembers the atmosphere at Michigan State University in East Lansing, Michigan, which he attended upon return from his tour in Vietnam:

When I got out of the service and went to school at Michigan
State I was in a veteran's club and . . . we provided moral
support to each other. If many of the other students knew that
we were veterans they just, you know, shunned us. We were
[seen as] "war criminals". I took a lot of heat from some of the
faculty members on campus who had been anti-war themselves.
I guess what troubled me early is they couldn't distinguish
between . . . the war and the warrior, and I was bothered by
that. One particular professor at Michigan State made it a
point in class of singling me out. There were two of us in the
class who were Vietnam veterans. [He was] singling us out for
our "criminal conduct" in the war and . . . we eventually had
to have a conversation in words of one syllable about how
inappropriate that was . . .

Gregory Burch, an assault helicopter door-gunner in Vietnam, attended
one of the veterans' support groups that flourished on American college
campuses in the early 1970s. He recalls an incident at Montgomery College
in Maryland, in which he and other veterans decided to confront the local
campus radicals:

I remember at the college . . . we had the SDS, the Students for
Democratic Society, [that] little Commie bunch. [Other veterans
and I] were having a discussion group . . . There was about 12
or 14 of us in this room and one of our group looked out the
window and said "Them Commie bastards are taking down the
American flag." And they were, they were hauling it down off
the flagpole . . . There was about eight or nine of them down
there, and they're all singing some song and chanting anti-war
stuff and are hauling the flag down . . . Somebody down there
. . . was trying to get them to stop, and they pushed him down.
I said "Hey, that's ten to one. Let's go down and even the odds
up." So we all piled out of the room, went down there and we
didn't discuss anything with them, we just went over and beat the
living shit out of them . . . They called the cops of course. We put
the flag back up, and [the] policemen came over [asking], "What
happened?" "Well, they were taking down the flag, we wanted
to put the flag up and they attacked us." "Oh, okay," and [the
cops] hauled them all away. That was the last that ever happened
and we . . . informed the SDS that they weren't going to be

allowed on the campus, even though the school allowed them on the campus. We [veterans] weren't going to allow them on the campus . . . They remembered, and we never saw them again.

ARRIVING HOME FROM VIETNAM

Many Vietnam veterans experienced social adjustment problems in returning to their civilian lives, and many of those problems had their roots in the divisions within America over the war in which they had served. For some, confrontations over their Vietnam service began as soon as they re-entered the United States. Among the veterans who recall being met at American airports by crowds of anti-war protesters is Gonzalo Baltazar, a US Army infantryman who returned to the US in 1970:

> I landed at Fort Lewis, Washington . . . Of course you're happier than heck that you finally made it back stateside. Then we're getting off the plane and there was a fence around there and there was protesters out there throwing tomatoes at us, yelling at us, "Baby killers!" and "War mongers!" and I thought, "Man, this is our home country right here." It was pretty disappointing. So, you really got a bitter feeling towards the Americans who were knocking us down.

Arriving at their homes, veterans were not always welcomed by all they knew. Parents could be relieved, but distant friends sometimes did not know what to talk to about, or whether to ask about what had happened in Vietnam. For some, like returning Marine Corps veteran Don Cuneo, the best welcome home came from a faithful childhood friend:

> I saw my folks. My dad had a full head of gray hair, which he hadn't had before. It was kind of a neat time. My dog, who we'd had since I was eight years old, was on his last legs, and I had been told by my mom in a letter not to expect to see him. He was basically blind and yet – he was a little dachshund – and yet he managed to walk right up to me and roll over. I went to San Diego a week later for about a week and he died while I was gone.

Many veterans remember that they had difficulty fitting in with their old friends, and that making new friends was even more difficult. By the early 1970s virtually everyone had an opinion about the war in Vietnam, and those who had served there found themselves pressured to defend themselves, the war, and their participation in it. Young people were the most animated in their rejection of the war. Don Cuneo remembers how the mention of his service in Vietnam ruined a date:

> I drove down to San Diego, and a guy that I had grown up with was going to San Diego State [University] and we went over and stayed at his apartment . . . and John introduced me to some of his friends as they came by the apartment. One of them was this really good-looking lady and her name was Diane. John said, "This is my friend, Don." She gave me a nice coquettish smile . . . [Then] he said, "Don's in the Marines and he just got back from Vietnam," and she just kind of looked at me and said, "Oh, did you kill anybody?" . . . I was dumbfounded. I didn't know what to say . . .

Former infantryman Elmer Hale recalls that the US military offered no assistance to veterans trying to come to grips with the changed political atmosphere in America:

> We [Vietnam servicemen] were brought back into this country and turned loose back into society, as we know it. We weren't debriefed. Therefore when you turn a man loose into civilization, and he's come from a combat unit, it's very tough for him to adjust . . . I was fortunate in that . . . I wasn't spit upon, but I always felt looked down upon by people that didn't go into the service or by people that went to school to keep from going to the service . . . I get to thinking, "I've done my job. I was called to do this. I've done it. Why are they looking down upon me?"

THE WAR DEAD

The US military's management of the war dead, and relations with their families, began in Vietnam itself, where Graves Registration units and commanding officers assembled the personal effects of those killed in action and mailed them to the next of kin in America. The bodies of the dead were under the military's control until released to the families for burial, and they were therefore subject to set procedures that were repeated tens of thousands of times over the course of America's involvement in Vietnam. After being embalmed at one of the medical facilities in Vietnam, the bodies of American servicemen were shipped back to the United States and prepared for military funerals, as Joseph Pizzo remembers:

Let me tell you I had a part-time job [in the Army] . . . It was dressing the bodies that came back from Vietnam, in the mortuary. The ones who had lived east of the Mississippi came through our mortuary at Dover, Delaware . . . We had from 50 to 75 bodies a day come through our mortuary . . . We'd go down to the flight line and pick them up out of the hangar. There'd be a bunch of shipping caskets . . . aluminum-colored shipping caskets. We'd pick them up off the flight line, put them in a truck and take them back to the mortuary and offload them and take them into the actual mortuary room and open up the shipping casket. [The bodies] were in a big plastic bag . . . They were nude in a plastic bag. They'd gotten embalmed in Vietnam if they came from Vietnam; the people who came from Germany were embalmed in Germany . . . We'd put them up on the table, cut the plastic bag off them and their wrists were in gauze so they wouldn't get bruised up. They cut the gauze off of them and start putting clothes on them. We put their socks on them, their underwear, their T-shirts, then their uniform shirt, uniform jacket and uniform pants and socks. We had rooms full of every kind of uniform you could imagine. We had Army, Air Force, Navy, Marine, everything – and I saw I think nine Air Force [bodies] come through the mortuary in the time I worked there . . . I was there '68 and '69 . . . We had one guy that came through [from Vietnam], he was running away from whatever, or he was moving the direction away from whatever got him. He had 102 holes in the back of his body from the top of his head to his heels. It was just like junk, just rocks, nails, just junk stuff they put into homemade bombs and killed him with that.

The bodies were like working on mannequins basically. I only worked in 'viewable;' I worked in the viewable room where the people were pretty much in one piece. My friend Robbie, who got me the job, worked in 'non-view' where there were just arms and legs and pieces of people. I could not do that. It would have been too stressful for me. I worked [with] pretty much whole people. We had one guy who was an E-4 [junior enlisted personnel] who jumped out of a helicopter . . . As he went out of the helicopter [the blades] took off about one inch of his skull, sliced it off really smoothly . . . We put him in uniform too, shipped him off to his loved ones.

We had a Marine come through, he was probably about 56

years old and he was a Command Sergeant Major. He had service chevrons from his wrist to his elbow and then . . . he had stripes from his elbow up to his shoulder . . . We had an E-5 [enlisted man] that worked there with us and the guy walks in after the Marine Command Sergeant Major was dressed and he walked up to him, patted him on the chest and said, "They got you, didn't they, Sarge?"

Meanwhile, the military branches also had to discharge the difficult duty of formally notifying the deceased's next of kin. This process was one that Pauline Laurent, the wife of Howard Querry IV who was killed in combat near Saigon in May 1968, recalls in detail:

Well, it actually began the weekend of Mother's Day . . . I somehow picked up the Sunday paper or some paper, I'm not sure what day it was and literally found this article. It wasn't on the front page or anything, it was kind of way in the back pages of the newspaper and it was like I was drawn, some force was drawing me to this article and I read about it and it was about a battle in Vietnam and it was about my husband's unit. And when I read it, I had this realization that my husband was dead and it was kind of like . . . it was an intuitive thing. It was like I didn't know how I knew it, but I just knew it and I just started sobbing and my mother was in the kitchen. I remember I was sitting outside in the backyard under the sycamore tree and she came out and said, "What is the matter?" And I said, "Howard is dead, I know it." And I was sobbing and crying and she said, "Don't be silly. How do you know it?" And I showed her the article and she read the article and then she just went back in the kitchen and then it was business as usual . . . And then that whole weekend, I was suffering from really bad anxiety.

By that time, I was seven months pregnant . . . And I wrote him a letter every day during this time . . . I was just trying to tell him the trauma that I was going through: "I'm so worried, they're fighting in Saigon. You said you were leaving the French fort, I'm sure you're there." I didn't really say, "I read about a battle and I think you're dead." I just kept writing the letters because I was refusing to accept this feeling that I had that he was dead . . . So I was writing like two or three letters a day during that weekend. Well, he died on May 10 and then on May 15, five days later, my

mother had just gotten home from work [at] the grocery store
and she was fixing dinner. I was standing in the family room
looking out the front windows and my father was watching the
evening news and I saw this green army car pull up in front of
the house and my heart starting racing and pounding and I knew
that they were coming to tell me that he was dead. And I told my
mother that there were was an Army car out in the front and then
the dog started barking and I took the dog and put the dog in
the basement and went to the front door.

It took these guys a long time to get out of the car and come
to the front door. It was like they just kept sitting in the car
and sitting in the car and sitting in the car. And of course, I was
going through a lot of anxiety. Finally, they came to the door
and I went to the door and they said, "We're looking for Pauline
Querry." And I said, "That's me." And then they just looked at
me and they saw that I was pregnant. It was pretty obvious that I
was pregnant. And I don't think I invited them in. I think I just
. . . I started saying to them, "Is he dead or wounded? Is he dead
or wounded?" And they didn't answer me. And finally, probably
my mother invited them in and then they kind of read this thing
to me. They didn't really speak it. They read it like it was a script
. . . "We regret to inform you that your husband has been fatally
wounded" or "mortally wounded." They didn't say "dead", and I
was in such a state of trauma [and] I didn't hear the word "dead",
so I kept hanging on to the hope that maybe he's injured and I
kept saying, "Is he injured or is he dead? Is he injured or is he
dead?" And they wouldn't give me a straight answer. It was just
so frustrating for me . . . They read it again and I don't even
think they ever said "dead," but at some level, my mother said
to me, "Honey, he's dead." You know, she didn't say it that way,
but somehow I got it that he was dead and then I went into this
foggy place of non-reality. And I can just remember bits and
pieces of words like "medals" and "funeral" and "arrangements"
and you know, just words. I remember words . . . and I remember
just sitting there trying to maintain some degree of sanity when
I wanted to just explode myself in emotion and just trying to . . .
hold it together while these guys were still there.

So, they delivered all the information they needed to deliver,
kind of like they were delivering a script to me, and then they
got up and left and it was then that I . . . got my dog and I went

into my bedroom and I shut the door and I said, "Just leave me alone." And I remember throwing myself on the bed and of course, then the baby really started kicking and squirming and . . . I felt like my life had just blown up. Like literally, somebody had just thrown a grenade into the middle of my life and I felt like I couldn't breathe. I did not know how I was going to survive. And then I remember at some point, I came out of my room and my mother had invited all these relatives over. So I had to walk out and be with all these relatives at a time when I really just wanted to be alone.

As the recently wedded wife of a serviceman, Pauline Laurent's name and whereabouts had been misplaced by Army officials, and in fact she was not notified first, as official procedures required. She remembers that her relationship with her in-laws never recovered:

The whole notification of Howard's death happened very awkwardly. The Army couldn't find me, they were looking for me at Fort Jackson, South Carolina, because they thought I still lived there and when they couldn't find me after three days, they called Howard's parents and told Howard's parents that he had been killed in Vietnam, and did Howard's parents know where I was? So, Howard's parents were notified first, and they were instructed not to call me because the Army had to notify me. So, when I called them after I found out Howard died, they already knew and I felt this deep betrayal . . . that they knew and they didn't tell me, and they had known for a couple of days . . .

Official notifications, as Pauline Laurent has described, could be very coldly delivered, and usually family members were given little information on how their loved one had died, or under what circumstances. Sometimes, as helicopter crewman Gregory Burch recalls, it was seen as a matter of duty by others in the unit to communicate directly with a fallen buddy's family:

I remember in '68 . . . one of my crew chief buds [buddies], he had gotten killed like two weeks before I came home, and it was pretty bad . . . Lieutenant Simmons was our platoon commander, and [he] said "Burch, why don't you go by? You're on your way home. Stop at Salt Lake [City], go down and see the family." Nobody else had. "The Army's going to send them that little freaking letter." . . . He'd already sent them a letter because he was a crew commander and he said that's all they've got. So I said, "Yeah, I know, I'll go stop by." And that was pretty emotional, trying to tell them . . . They had just found out, I mean like a couple days before I got there, and they were still broke up and everything. I showed up. They were really grateful – [here was] somebody that knew their son. I can remember the father. I stayed for about an hour or two and I think I had a sandwich with him and that was about it. I remember going, taking the father aside and [I] said, "Please don't open the coffin," because he'd been in the water for about four days. I said, "Please, please don't let his mother see him." I said, "Lie to her, do anything, but don't open the coffin."

They sent me Christmas cards for about ten years . . . I guess they were grateful [that] somebody [came], not just an out-of-touch officer showing up and giving them the telegram. It was someone that knew her son.

Not all family members wished to be protected from seeing their loved ones' bodies. Pauline Laurent's husband's coffin was one of those that the Army had marked as 'unviewable.' She remembers the added grief caused by that designation:

When Howard's body came back from Vietnam, we could not open the coffin. And I was not told why. I was just told that I could not open the coffin . . . We were told that it was non-viewable, which means, "don't look at the body." So, I remember my brother at the time, my youngest brother said to me, "If you want, I will open the coffin and identify Howard's body . . ." He had been in the Marine Corps and I think he felt it was his duty to do it. And I said, "You don't have to do that." But because I didn't see Howard's dead body, I hung on to some ray of hope that possibly it could've been a mistake. So, I went to the funeral; I went to the cemetery; we put the coffin in the ground; and I didn't know that I was doing this, but in retrospect, I pretended he was still alive.

The funerals of US servicemen killed in Vietnam were also attended by military honor guards. Their presence was part of the military protocol of honoring those who had died on active duty in a war zone, and most families probably appreciated this form of recognition of the sacrifice made by their loved one. This was not, however, universally true. US Marine Don Cuneo remembers:

> I was doing PR work for the Marine Corps. I did that for about a month and a half or two months. The downside to that was if you were on [duty] you also had to do funerals. I got to do about a half a dozen of those . . . We did one up in Riverside [California]. This was January of '67 and I had just been promoted to Corporal, and we did the funeral. I was the guy that, when the flag was folded, it was handed to me and I, in turn, handed it to an officer who gave it to the family. After all this was done, this guy's sister who was a really, really attractive lady came up to me and she said, "I just have one question." I said, "Yeah?" and she says, "Why my brother and not you?" What do you say? Again, I was just dumbfounded and that was also the last funeral I ever did.

For many families, the pain of the loss they suffered in Vietnam has subsided, but it remains with them, a point of reference for the rest of their lives. Pauline Laurent still has questions about her husband's death, about how the military treated both her and him, and about the war in which he lost his life:

> I feel like I walked through the fire alone because, you know, Howard was in the fire in Vietnam for two months, but the fire that I have walked through has lasted 35 years. You know, his death, the birth of my daughter, raising my daughter alone, living in denial of my grief; that's the fire and the hell that I have walked through for 35 years. And, at some level on a good day, I can believe that Howard has been there in some way with me, but if he has been, for most of my life, I haven't been aware of his guidance and his support. It's only been in the last ten years that I have felt like there was something that was with me all along that was helping me get through it. As I look back now . . . there must've been some kind of force that was with me in some way. Yeah, but at the time, I didn't feel that there was anyone that knew my pain, anyone that could allow me to cry . . .
>
> When all of his medals came back and the citation with his medal said . . . that "Sergeant Querry, disregarding his own

safety, crossed the bridge to rescue the beleaguered force on the other side" . . . I got really angry. How could he disregard his own safety? He had a pregnant wife at home! How could he even do that? But then I know that the military trains men to disregard their own safety, you know? They train them that they're a unit now, they're not individuals. And that whatever the unit is up to, whatever the goal of the unit is, is what their life is about . . . When he went to Vietnam, I know that he went there thinking that he was fighting Communism, because I know that about him. He was a patriot, you know. His father had served in World War II, and he went there thinking this was his duty; he was going to fight this war, and he was fighting for freedom from Communism. And, you know, [he wrote] in his last letter . . . oh here, I have it: "This war just turns my stomach. It seems like a big political game and I feel that American lives are not to be played with." That's what he said. What he meant — your interpretation is as good as anybody's.

10
THE END OF THE WAR
1969–1975

VIETNAMIZATION

President Richard Nixon assumed office in January 1969, publicly committed to ending the war in Vietnam. Before a truce was reached in January 1973, he would bomb and then overtly send American ground troops to Cambodia, order American air support for a major ARVN incursion in Laos, resume the bombing of North Vietnam, establish a maritime quarantine of North Vietnam, and undertake both secret and public negotiations with Hanoi, all in an effort to secure the withdrawal of American troops 'with honor.'

A key element in Nixon's strategic plan for ending American involvement in the Vietnam conflict was what he somewhat imperiously called 'the Nixon Doctrine'; others, perhaps even more awkwardly, called it 'Vietnamization'. The focus of the plan was the phased reduction, and finally the elimination, of American ground troops deployed to Vietnam, and their replacement by South Vietnamese troops trained and equipped to fend off the NVA threat. Nixon planned to use the transition period to deploy more American advisers to South Vietnamese forces, which would meanwhile receive more sophisticated American weaponry as well as tactical support from American airpower. In the spring of 1969 Nixon began the process of 'Vietnamizing' the war by announcing the withdrawal of 25,000 US troops from the Vietnam theater.

Some parts of the South Vietnamese military were more prepared to take up the mantle of the American troops than others, and some parts of the country were more 'pacified' and prepared to provide support for government forces. Marine aviator Neil Whitehurst recalls that when he arrived in I Corps in 1970, the security situation was generally favorable, and Nixon's plan seemed workable:

> We were pretty much of the opinion that we had solidified
> our area of operations, that we had done about as much as we

possibly could as far as securing the northern I Corps for the
Vietnamese to take over, and that every battle that we had gone
into, every skirmish that we had gone into, we had won decisively
and we actually felt like that even though we like to have a
total military victory – that's what we were all trained for – that
within the limitations that we had, we had obtained or were in
the process or on the way to obtaining our objective . . . Never,
in my wildest dreams, did I ever entertain the thought that we
were leaving unfinished business or we were leaving because we
couldn't win this conflict.

As the Navy's Sumner Clayton, an adviser to the South Vietnamese Navy,
recalls, the process of Vietnamization sometimes included the actual
destruction of American facilities, to prevent their capture by Communist
forces:

At an American Navy base at Cua Viet [in I Corps], they turned
some of the boats, a lot of the equipment, a couple of jeeps, you
name it, over to the Vietnamese Navy which had a navy base just
. . . up the river from the American base. Then they tore down
the American base completely. Nothing was there but the big
[landing craft] ramp.

Although the total numbers of American combat troops on the ground
declined, new draftees and military advisers continued to be sent to
Vietnam. The advisers, many of whom had already served one or more
tours, were the ones who saw at first hand the continuing military
weaknesses in some of Saigon's forces. Marine Andy DeBona was one of
those charged with advising South Vietnam's Marine forces in 1971. He
remembers some of the difficulties he encountered:

The [Vietnamization] policy itself was probably well thought
out but poorly executed. The poor execution came from the fact
that the money that came pouring in, the supplies that came
pouring in, once they reached the hands of the Vietnamese there
was no more accountability. Now this didn't happen that much
with the Vietnamese Marines but it still did. There was just an
endless supply of whatever the Vietnamese, in a sense, would need
– boom! They would have [it] in a heartbeat . . . The biggest thing
they had to develop of course was an air force or air power because

Recalled American troops prepare to embark for the United States after attending ceremonies marking the handover of mission responsibility to South Vietnam's military. From a peak number of 540,000, American troops were withdrawn from Vietnam in increments beginning in the spring of 1969.

this is the Marine concept. The Marine, if you will, division does have its own air wing and it has its own support there. The Vietnamese Marines never had that, even though they tried to, in a sense, [be a] mirror image [of] US Marines but without the air – without the other logistical capabilities. For instance, there, they didn't have tanks, they didn't have amphib tracks until later on . . . and they pretty well fell into disuse because of the maintenance problems with them. So basically what they were was light infantry. Any time light infantry goes up against a mechanized attack like the North Vietnamese had, no doubt who is going to win. Did I think they could do it without US help? Not the way they were structured at that time. Eventually, if in fact they had the time, the money, and the training and I can speak strictly from the Vietnamese Marine aspect or side, they were tigers.

Equipment, organization and morale were all key factors in the implementation of Nixon's Vietnamization plan, but one of the most crucial factors was that of leadership. DeBona recalls an incident in 1971 when the commander of a South Vietnam Marine unit engaged in a firefight with NVA regulars bolted, leaving his troops in the field:

> Any landing zone or any cleared area that we moved to, the NVA were there already . . . so it came down to the point I said, "Well, we are going to have to blow our own LZ," and there was a hill called 410 . . . [The] Air Force ran about, well, at least ten sorties into this hill and just blew the whole top of it apart and this then became our [new] landing zone. The interesting thing was we went up there to Hill 410 . . . we found 25 bodies of the bad guys . . . The very first bird [helicopter] that landed, the [South Vietnamese] battalion commander got on it and left before his wounded, before anybody, and so he is gone . . . [When] the next bird that came in, there was a break in discipline and the able bodied [South Vietnamese Marines] started rushing towards the helicopter, hanging on to skids, things of that nature, and so I went over there and physically removed them and told the bird to take off with the wounded that it had aboard but not the able bodied. [I] went to the [executive officer] and said, "Hey, this lift is going to stop right now unless you can get your Marines under control." . . . The XO [executive officer] got the discipline out and finally we were able to get out almost all of the wounded because it was only a two or three-bird LZ and it was hot, in that they were continually taking mortar fire . . .

For American advisers caught in such situations there was, for the time being anyway, at least one source of comfort. Sumner Clayton, the naval adviser, recalls that while he tried to work with his South Vietnamese counterparts, he did not rely on them:

> You cannot sit there and just tell them line-for-line how to do these things. A lot of it [was] you let them do it, and then they may ask you or you may show them a little trick, and they may or may not take your advice on this deal; [but] we had a field radio with us and we could call our radio operator on the [American] base. If we should need fire support, they always kept a big ship [available]. The battleship *New Jersey* was off the coast for about

eight months, about five miles off the coast while I was there. If we needed fire support, I had the Army grid map and a field radio and I could call in support.

Meanwhile President Nixon had implemented another phase of his plan to enable American withdrawal. For years Communist forces had been using areas just inside the Cambodian border as sanctuaries, and Nixon and his advisers knew that if left intact when American troops withdrew, these base areas could provide the launch point for further NVA strikes against Saigon. At the very least, the security of the entire Mekong Delta region could never be assured while Communist military forces maintained their complexes and caches in Cambodia. Because Cambodia was formally a neutral government, some elements of the Nixon administration's policy were implemented surreptitiously. The President had secretly ordered B-52 strikes against Ho Chi Minh Trail routes in Cambodia in 1969; the bombing continued, and remained secret until 1973. In late April 1970, however, Nixon told a national television audience that ground operations had begun inside Cambodia, undertaken by both American and South Vietnamese forces. Army Forward Air Controller Roy Riddle remembers the day the invasion began:

> It was my last flight in Vietnam. That was the day that the Americans went into Cambodia, the launch into Cambodia, in 1970 . . . We were in an orbit from Bien Hoa, kind of [a] north–south orbit, out of the way of the helicopters and things, the landing zone and artillery, observing the movement in [to Cambodia] and all I could say is that you could see aircraft from horizon to horizon.

On the ground, the operation was less well orchestrated. As infantryman Donald McBane remembers, the objectives of American ground forces were to locate and destroy the Communists' facilities and supply depots:

> [I went] into Cambodia three days after the initial landing when there was a lot of heavy shit. [Our battalion was] 19 miles into Cambodia, which was the second or third deepest penetration into Cambodia of any of the American units. They set us down at a spot which they had thought was supposed to be a hospital complex along the Ho Chi Minh Trail . . . [We captured equipment], some of this was manufactured in France, some of it

was [made] in China, some of it was from the United States
. . . They had sterilization equipment, X-ray equipment, quite [a]
well advanced little hospital complex set up right where we did
our little tour of Cambodia . . . And it turned out it wasn't just
a hospital complex; it was a lot more. It was a training complex.
We recovered little wooden models of airplanes where they were
training . . . "This is the kind of airplane to hide from. This is the
kind of airplane to shoot at; it goes slow enough you can shoot it
down." We recovered all kinds of medical gear, training gear and
tons of rice – all kinds of stuff. The unfortunate thing is [that
our location was] not even in range of the [US] Navy's guns. So,
we were set up on a firebase that was out of range of anyone else.
It was the only time that we were set up that way. You did not
want to be set up in that way, 'cause if you got in trouble there
wasn't anybody that could come to your aid.

Infantryman Marvin Mathiak arrived in Vietnam in June 1970 and was
immediately sent to Cambodia. While protests raged in America, he recalls
that the soldiers on the ground had other concerns:

I was assigned to the First Cavalry Division Airmobile, to Alpha
Company, First of the Seventh, which is [General George]
Custer's old unit . . . [I was in Vietnam, near the Cambodian
border, when] a helicopter came in and sat down . . . and a couple
of guys got out and they had body bags that they were bringing
back [from Cambodia]. So they unloaded the body bags and then
came over to pick us up and we almost immediately got going
into Cambodia . . . Typically, we'd have short-term missions. We
had one situation where . . . we were pulled in to defend an LZ
that was under heavy attack. Other times we'd have to go out
and we'd be going from point A to point B through the jungle
looking for trouble . . . All we knew was that we had to follow the
guy in front of us, really, and that's about it. We just followed the
guys in front of us through the jungle.

According to plan, after destroying Communist bases and supplies,
American troops were quickly withdrawn from Cambodia. President Nixon,
who had anticipated domestic opposition to the Cambodia operation, was
shocked by the intensity of the renewed anti-war demonstrations. Even
so, he would not be deterred from pursuing his strategy. In early 1971 he

approved an important field test for the Vietnamization process, in the form of another incursion into a neutral country designed to disrupt the Ho Chi Minh Trail. Operation 'Lam Son 719', the invasion of southeastern Laos, was less controversial in the US that the Cambodian incursion, in part because it involved chiefly ARVN forces, although with tactical support from US airpower. Marine helicopter pilot Neil Whitehurst, who took part in the offensive, recalls its design:

> During Operation Lam Son 719, the concept was basically to hop from one mountain top to another during the assault phase and set up fire support bases to support the invasion [by] the Republic of Vietnam['s] ground forces. They were basically hopscotching all the way across a great portion of Laos and then they were putting these 105s and 155 [mm gun] houses on board, on top of these mountains, and then they were supposed to be able to cover the ground troops as they made the advance along the Ho Chi Minh Trail. And it sounded like a wonderful idea.

Lam Son 719 was also to be a demonstration of the growing self-sufficiency of South Vietnam's forces. As naval adviser Sumner Clayton recalls, preparations for the operation included virtually all branches of South Vietnam's military, including its navy. Even with new ships and better equipment, however, the threat of Viet Cong saboteurs remained:

> The supply boats were bringing . . . food, ammunition, just every type of logistic support that you could think of that could be brought in by boat and we would bring it. They would bring it to Dong Ha. Then it would be put on either C-130 airplanes, some type of cargo helicopter or by truck and moved inland . . . We tried to get everybody back out in the ocean by dark. We didn't want to leave them sitting there up at Dong Ha overnight if we could help it.

In addition to enemy threats, there were inherent problems with the invasion mission. Naval aviator Ken Craig, who flew over Laos on many missions, remembers a basic problem with the Lam Son 719 concept:

> I think whoever dreamed up that one, I mean, it could've been do-able, but they got to look at that terrain. That terrain is the

most difficult terrain in the world. You're not going to easily send . . . even a battalion-sized group of people into the middle of Laos and do anything significant. The terrain is just formidable and you can lose a thousand people in the jungle. I mean, if you look at some experiences that happened when we were fighting the Japanese in Burma for example . . . those kinds of conflicts were very, very difficult to send in striking groups into jungle territory . . . The jungle could eat up thousands of men and you wouldn't even notice that they were there.

As aviator Neil Whitehurst remembers, the South Vietnamese troops sent into Laos in 1971 were routed, and Americans who flew in support of their allies had little left to support:

The NVA . . . knew what was happening. And they had spies everywhere. But they had pre-registered every single possible fire support base with mortars and rockets. So they would wait until everything was in place [at ARVN bases] . . . and then they would start to pepper them with rockets and mortars. Then when [ARVN would] call in for medevacs, they would wait for all the planes to land and then they would blow them all up at one time. That became a trap and then it became mass confusion, and ARVN units broke apart and then they started running and it just fell apart and it was amazing. Then it became a salvage and rescue operation.

The failure of Lam Son 719 did not portend well for the success of the Vietnamization strategy, since even with extensive and well-coordinated US air support the South Vietnamese were outmatched by their NVA adversaries. Rather than pursuing ARVN troops as they withdrew back across the border into South Vietnam, NVA forces went into a period of relative quietude that lasted through the fall of 1971. Andy DeBona remembers:

[The NVA] were probably getting ready, stockpiling things. [The American command] had moved the [US] Marines out of northern I Corps, they had put in a [South Vietnamese] force probably about 50 percent of what was there before, so the bad guys were probably stacking up their supplies, getting ready for this Easter offensive, [which] they had planned, I am sure, a long time in advance. So they would have, as they rolled south, they would just be able to pick up the supplies along the way and just keep rolling.

US Army adviser John Haseman remembers how Americans' frustrations were building at this point:

> Sometimes my cup was half full, and sometimes it was half empty . . . But I always, the whole time I was in Vietnam, questioned whether the South Vietnamese would win the war. In fact, sometimes when the advisers would have their monthly meetings and we'd have five or six beers and . . . someone would start a conversation about what it would be like to be advisers to the VC side, because they seemed to have their shit together better than the South Vietnamese.

THE COMMUNIST OFFENSIVE AND AMERICAN BOMBING

When the NVA did launch its massive Spring Offensive of 1972, which Americans called the 'Easter Offensive', the primary targets were northern I Corps, the Central Highlands, and the area on the Cambodian border north of the Parrot's Beak. By then, Nixon's troop withdrawals had left fewer than 100,000 Americans in South Vietnam, only a handful of whom were combat forces. Apart from US Air Force bombers, South Vietnamese units were virtually alone against 120,000 NVA regulars. Andy DeBona recalls how the NVA's successes affected the unit he advised, the 7th Battalion, South Vietnamese Marines, in northern I Corps:

> We were at Da Nang until the 29th of March, we were in there playing a game of Vietnamese poker which I was winning . . . At 10:01 [hours] the [7th] Battalion received an order that we were moving north . . . We had a whole column of trucks, lights blazing, and I can tell you I was not too happy about that. Moving at night, no security, anything of this nature. We eventually got . . . just outside of Dong Ha at about 2:00 in the morning and . . . no sooner did we disembark off of the trucks and the trucks took off, [than] we started receiving incoming artillery . . . The orders were [that] the next day at noon we were going to go and reinforce Mai Loc. So the 30th of March came and went with no vehicles picking us up and I am still not in contact with any Americans, I have no idea what is happening.

Eventually my buddy tells me through the Vietnamese Marine Net [radio channel] . . . that this is what is happening: the NVA have started an offensive and they are coming across the lines. On the 1st of April [1972], April Fools Day, we started a motor march into Mai Loc . . . It started out very badly: the vehicle directly in front of me with an ARVN driver tipped over . . . I had bodies all over the place . . . We continued on down the road and all of a sudden everybody stops and we were getting out and the reason why we are getting out is because we can't go through Cam Lo because NVA tanks were reported at Cam Lo.

Things are now starting to get a little bit serious, obviously. So then we started a foot march . . . and as we are going over [to Mai Loc] we can see Camp Carroll to the east of us and there are all kinds of artillery rounds bursting around Camp Carroll . . . We eventually got over to Mai Loc, [and] there are artillery rounds landing everywhere in Mai Loc. I have never seen that intense a concentration of artillery any time . . .

The ARVN Regiment, the 57th I believe it was, at Camp Carroll surrendered en masse. The American adviser, who was at that time an Army Major, [came on the radio] and said, "The ARVN are surrendering and I'm getting out of here." At that same exact moment, fortune would have it [that] there was an Army helicopter bringing in a re-supply of artillery . . . and they heard his call, went over there, and picked him up from sure death or being a prisoner and took him back. We're still over in Mai Loc now . . . and we're getting periodic [artillery] and there are mortars firing 300 meters away from us . . .

Eventually the orders were given over the Adviser's Secure [radio] net that we, the Vietnamese Marines, were going to abandon Mai Loc because it couldn't be held . . . [I'll] never forget, we picked up a French priest, we picked up . . . a Vietnamese Red Cross worker and a couple civilians and so I figured, "Hey . . . I'm home free now, we have a priest with us, there is no way [I won't make it]." . . . It took us 29 hours to move from Mai Loc, with no radio contact with anyone due to terrain and also due to the changing frequencies . . . straight across country to hit Highway One. During this period of time we crossed and re-crossed the same river five times . . . We would find other wounded from the other battalions, and the 7th Battalion Marines would pick them up. Nobody was left behind.

In this terrain it was brutal, it was so steep in some cases that you actually had to grab on to trees to pull yourself up. How they got the casualties up there I will never know. Then, going back down the other side you slid down on the seat of your trousers . . . We found a trail and made it out [to] Highway 1 . . . During this period of time the world was falling to an end and the only people up there were Vietnamese Marines and American Marines.

South Vietnam's President, Nguyen Van Thieu, ordered ARVN's reserves into the field to shore up his own regular forces, while Communist guerrilla attacks near Saigon consumed the attention of South Vietnam's militia and police units. In Washington, the rapid across-the-board successes of the NVA were seen as a crisis that demanded a swift and forceful response. Unwilling to reverse course and send new American ground forces into Vietnam, President Nixon ordered the resumption of heavy bombing over North Vietnam itself. B-52 strikes were launched first against targets north of the DMZ, and then against fuel depots and other targets in the Hanoi–Haiphong area.

In May 1972, at the urging of America's theater commander, Army General Creighton Abrams, Nixon ordered a naval blockade of the North Vietnamese coast and the mining of North Vietnam's principal harbor at Haiphong. The harbor served as an important entrepôt for foreign goods, including military supplies from China, the Soviet Union and Eastern Europe. The mines, laid in the harbor by American naval aircraft, were equipped with arming delays, in order to allow ships already in port a grace period to depart. Six other important ports in North Vietnam were also mined, as were river mouths. (After the Paris Peace Agreement was signed in January 1973, American minesweepers and counter-measure units worked to remove the mines, and Haiphong harbor reopened in March 1973.) A-6 'Intruder' aircraft pilot Ken Craig remembers the frustration of observing from his cockpit how one Chinese ship delivered its payload, even while observing the American blockade:

They had a Chinese ship, it was full of rice and it was parked right north of the border and . . . we started shooting up all the [North Vietnamese] junks that would come up to the boat, but [command headquarters] told us not to hit the [Chinese] ship . . . We'd allow them to get away from the ship and then we'd have at them. Well, then they lost too many of their junks trying to get the rice off the ship . . . It was a re-supply vessel from

China full of rice. So they started floating the rice in plastic bags, they'd float them in to the shore and then they would collect them there, put them in trucks or whatever and then they didn't have very far to go before they were into the network of their supply lines going down south to support their troops. We were never allowed to hit that Chinese ship, number one. We weren't even allowed to get close to it, number two. And to me, this was absolutely idiotic. We should've told the Chinese, "Get that thing out of there or we're going to sink it." . . . [We'd] go up and down the beaches and use machine-gun fire, but you know, that's really stupid, subjecting a million-dollar airplane to somebody with a rifle shooting at you . . . It's just really stupid, but that's what we were made to do, stupid things like that . . . We couldn't go into Haiphong and we couldn't go into Hanoi . . . and it didn't take long for the North Vietnamese to figure that out, that we weren't going to go in there on recces [reconnaissance missions] because [our leaders] didn't want to hit something that was sensitive or hit another ship from another nationality [while it] was sitting in Haiphong.

Although many bombing restrictions remained in place, Nixon was determined to make good his private threats that 'the bastards [in North Vietnam] have never been bombed like they're going to be bombed this time'. He approved a broad list of targets in the North, including some airfields. Pilot Ken Craig remembers one of the bombing missions he flew over North Vietnam in 1972:

Dave Kelly was flying the other A-6 and I flew the lead airplane and . . . we flew very close to one another and then separated and I went very low and made a run on Phuc Yen and I'd studied the target. I knew that [their] revetments were for . . . the ready airplanes that would go out the next morning. Then they had other airplanes way back into hardstands and every place like that, but I wasn't planning on trying to get those. But I also knew that they probably had a lot of refueling equipment, so . . . we made a really good run on it and they gave us [bombs] for that mission and I spread my [bombs] . . . right at the taxi runway area, right where I thought they were probably servicing [aircraft] . . . SAMs [surface-to-air missiles] were searching madly for us [but] because we were so low . . . they couldn't acquire us and the other thing is when we got over to Phuc Yen, the triple-A (anti-aircraft artillery) just opened up like mad, but we got the [bombs] right in there and got some fires going. I didn't know if we got an airplane or whether we got fuel trucks or what, but we got a huge fire going and we got the heck out of there because it was really hot. Well, that evening, [the North Vietnamese] flew all the jets to China . . . That was the intelligence reports. So, they didn't even bring them back for a couple of days, so I don't know what we did, but we got them concerned anyhow, let's put it that way. And that's what I wanted to do, that was part of the job, was to get them concerned.

During April and May 1972, as the NVA's Spring Offensive grew, the number of American B-52 bombers operating from Thailand rose to over 200, almost half the total US B-52 fleet. B-52 strikes against targets inside South Vietnam as well as near Hanoi and Haiphong continued through October, averaging 30 sorties per day. In the second week of May the Operation LINEBACKER bombing campaign began, with aircraft based in Thailand striking targets in and around Hanoi itself. For the next three months, the aerial onslaught against the North continued, regularly employing the new generation of laser-guided 'smart bombs'.

In July 1972 actress and anti-war activist Jane Fonda traveled to North Vietnam, where she toured anti-aircraft missile sites with Communist officials and recorded appeals to American servicemen which were broadcast over North Vietnam's official radio station. In her statements she condemned American military policies and the damage being inflicted on the North. Many Vietnam veterans at the time and subsequently took umbrage at her action, viewing her as one of the principal villains of the Vietnam war era. Air Force veteran Tony Borra, who flew C-130 aircraft in Vietnam, notes the range and complexity of the many perspectives on Fonda's actions:

With Jane Fonda, I still have . . . one of those awful pictures of her in a Vietnamese gun emplacement and my buddy wrote on it, "I wouldn't walk across the street to piss on this girl even if she was on fire." And that sort of summed up the way we all felt. That was reprehensible. I gladly fought to protect the right to voice opinion. But that doesn't mean you go and fraternize with an enemy that we're fighting with. And I

Infantrymen of the ARVN First Division's First Regiment are airlifted into battle on a mountain top in Quang Tri Province. Beginning in 1969, the 'Vietnamization' program assigned increasing battlefield responsibilities to South Vietnam's military, which was supported by American equipment and advisers.

came to respect elements of the protest movement because I didn't believe that we should be there either. And that's what America is all about. We're a democracy. You're supposed to voice your opinion.

The massive American bombing of the North had several effects. First, it provided some respite and encouragement to South Vietnam's forces, which during the summer and fall of 1972 began to recover from the drubbing suffered during the Spring Offensive. An ARVN counter-offensive in I Corps recaptured much NVA-held territory. According to military adviser Andy DeBona, improved ARVN morale and the US bombing campaign, along with new US equipment deliveries, seemed to be turning the tide:

That is when the Vietnamese Marines started their counter-offensive and just rolled back the bad guys and they even had plans to invade North Vietnam . . . which was because they always wanted . . . to march north, to go make the amphibious assault up there. My thought was hey, you know, they are going to definitely hold them this time, the NVA are not going to come rolling on down and taking over everything, the resistance has stiffened, American air power is back in full swing. You know, we had B-52 strikes coming in for us, we were directing B-52 strikes where we wanted them, which was unheard of before but this was just a full out-and-out "You want to mess with us? Watch out!" type [of] thing. Also the TOWs [anti-tank guided missiles] came in then to take care of the NVA tanks . . . Naval gunfire, offshore, just broke up columns of NVA tanks, just decimated them. So as long as [South Vietnamese forces] had the heavy fire support there, which I thought would continue on forever or how long forever can be, there was no way that the South Vietnamese were going to lose then.

Nixon's bombing program also pressured the North Vietnamese to renew their pursuit of a negotiated settlement with the United States. The summer's heavy bombing, plus the expectation that Nixon would be re-elected by a large majority, making him more powerful at the bargaining table, prompted Hanoi to seek a deal earlier rather than later. During fast-paced talks in September and October 1972, the US and North Vietnam reached tentative agreement on the outlines of a peace settlement. South Vietnam's President Thieu objected strenuously to the terms, which included allowing North Vietnamese troops to remain in the South. With Thieu's opposition, the opportunity for a rapid settlement seemed to disappear.

NEGOTIATING A SETTLEMENT
The Paris Peace Talks had begun in 1969, and had dragged on for years, making little substantive progress but providing ample opportunity for set-piece exchanges, propaganda and posturing by all participants. South Vietnam's ambassador to the negotiations, Nguyen Xuan Phong, recalls the atmosphere in Paris:

Year after year, every Wednesday morning . . . we were very tense . . . There were about a thousand press people outside each Wednesday . . . Usually after the speeches we had the break for lunch and then we returned. [The session] was used mainly to

make accusations: "Last week you killed so many people" or
"You assassinated the village chief", things like that . . . After the
reading of the speeches there were dialogues, so that was the time
to prepare things and then we tried to respond, but mostly it
was for throwing insults to one another . . . The French provided
lunch, a light lunch but a very good one . . . but they gave wine
too, French wine. Everybody had a free go at the wine, so when
they came back [from lunch] very excited, that's [when they
started] the insults.

The frustrations accompanying these sessions were particularly acute for
Ambassador Phong, who as the representative of the Thieu government
was usually left out of the secret back-channel contacts between Nixon's
National Security Adviser, Henry Kissinger, and the Communists'
representatives. Phong recalls that most days, the delegates welcomed any
respite from the mind-numbing dullness of the negotiating sessions:

> . . . Even during the break, we had to go out – there was only one
> big door [in the meeting room], so all delegations had to squeeze
> [through] to get out for lunch or for the break time . . . Yes, we
> went to the johns [together] and we were over there with the
> Hanoi [representatives] . . . We['d] all mix there, first men first,
> try[ing] to get in there. [After] hours sitting there listening to
> the speeches, we all rush to the [john]: "My god, at least here we
> know what we are doing!"

President Nixon, re-elected by a landslide in November 1972 over his
opponent, anti-war Democrat George McGovern, still faced the problem
of working with a Congress that had long since tired of voting military
appropriations for the Vietnam war. Nixon decided that to obtain maximum
leverage and quickly conclude a peace settlement, he would have to pressure
both South and North Vietnam. First, Nixon strong-armed President Thieu,
offering him $1 billion worth of American military aid and a promise that any
renewal of Communist aggression after a peace settlement would provoke
direct US retaliation against the North; but Nixon also warned him that the
US would sign an agreement with Hanoi even without his approval.

At the same time, to further weaken the North's war-making capacities
and force Hanoi to make concessions at Paris, Nixon ordered a new, even
larger bombing campaign. The December 1972 'Christmas Bombing',
codenamed Operation LINEBACKER II, included massive B-52 strikes

against the North, including the city of Hanoi itself. During the attack, which lasted from 18 to 29 December, over 700 B-52 sorties were flown over North Vietnam, while other aircraft from the Air Force and Navy flew more than 1,200 other bombing missions.

One of the key goals of US diplomacy had always been to obtain the safe release of all American prisoners of war (POWs) being held by North Vietnam and its allies. Several hundred Americans, most of them Air Force and naval aviators and crew members, were held at various camps in North Vietnam. One of these POWs, Air Force pilot Ray Merritt, was shot down in September 1965 during a mission over North Vietnam. Merritt was held for most of his seven-and-a-half years of captivity at Hanoi's Hoa Lo prison, which the POWs called the 'Hanoi Hilton.' Merritt recalls the day he was first taken to the prison:

> The vehicle moved forward and stopped and I could hear this rusty gate being closed behind me. That was my introduction to the Hao Lo prison . . . because you always came in the same way through this big gate and the rusty door always squeaked and always clanked shut. I was taken directly to a cell in an area that we called Heartbreak Hotel; a small section [that] had seven different small cells [in a cell block]. Eight cells; one of them converted to a shower room. I was put inside and told to be quiet . . . There was a guard there patrolling around the outside. I didn't hear anything. This was very early in the morning. Later that same day, I could hear an American talking . . . "Hey, new guy, what's your name?" in a soft whisper. So, I climb up on the bed board with difficulty and [looked] out and I can't see anybody, but this voice calls again and says, "Hey, new guy, say your name." I look around and there's no guards in the hallway of this section, so I said, "Ray Merritt." The voice on the other end says, "Hi Ray, this is Ron Byrne. Welcome to Hanoi."

The POWs were under constant surveillance by North Vietnamese guards, as Merritt remembers;

> At first [there were] very few interrogations, or 'quizzes,' as we call them, very few. Then they got on a kick of wanting propaganda from us and what we thought of the war and these kind of things. Some of the ground rules that we [POWs]

operated under were the code of conduct that says, "I will resist to the best to my ability answering anything beyond name, rank, serial number, date of birth." . . . They wanted you to condemn the US war, praise the Vietnamese people . . . They wanted you to talk over their little camp radio, [which] probably [would be] taped and played all over the world. Not very often did they take pictures, but they did take pictures for propaganda value. Until they really started wanting something . . . and [I] would refuse to answer, they weren't that terrible. They're no fun, but they would threaten and brow beat you and everything else: "You must talk now." . . . Some of them, they were after something and you could pretty well tell when you got into [a 'quiz'] whether [it was] going to be an English lesson for the interrogator, or just a general BS session, or [if] they were after something.

Communication with other prisoners was important to the POWs' self-preservation. Using a matrix arrangement of the letters of the alphabet, POWs 'tapped' out messages to each other on the walls between their cells. Information from home was especially prized. The wives of downed airmen sometimes tried to get secret messages through to their captive husbands. Shirley Johnson, married to US Air Force POW Sam Johnson, recalls some of her efforts to contact her husband:

The Department of Defense called and asked if I would meet with an Air Force officer about the letters . . . He came and asked me if I would participate in encoding my letters . . . I agreed to do it. I would write a letter, send it to them, they would rewrite it, which would be basically the same thing I had written and ask me to send it – copy it and send that to him, which I did. We continued and I guess all the rest of our letters were coded . . . The Air Force [also] sent me a big box of jawbreakers, like a coffee-can size, and would I please send these to him . . . When he got them [the POWs] chopped them up. They took a hammer and just beat them up. He said . . . he was eating them and got microfilm in his mouth and it was the front page of *The New York Times* I think. It was baseball scores, whoever had won the [baseball division] pennant . . . I sent a pair of shorts that were hemmed in code . . . They were horrible looking fabric. It was green print. He . . . only wears white. So, I knew he would notice them . . . He was trying to unhem them. He thought maybe as he pulled the hem out, maybe he could feel something. Like I say, he never figured out how to read it at all.

The POWs' captivity ended after the negotiations at Paris finally produced an agreement known as the Paris Peace Accord, which was signed in January 1973. It provided for the release of all American POWs and the complete withdrawal of all US military forces from Vietnam, although it allowed American civilians and diplomats to remain in South Vietnam. Ray Merritt recalls the day he learned that he and the other POWs would be freed:

[The guards] took everybody out and had a big military formation for us. Our senior officers got us into a semblance of [a] formation . . . and the Vietnamese read the Peace Accords to us. They said there would be four releases starting with the date of the Peace Accords which is 27th or 28th of January to coincide with the withdrawal of military forces from South Vietnam . . . Sure enough, on the night of the 11th [February] . . . they gave us brand new sets of clothes and said, "Tomorrow, you go home." . . . Those [POWs] that were there the longest went out [first], and I happened to get on the second airplane out that day. Everybody was jubilant; everybody was happy. You probably couldn't describe the backslapping and the happiness that everybody felt, it was indescribable . . . We [POWs] as a group said that amongst ourselves, we are not going to show the Vietnamese any recognition that they've done anything . . . other than be very polite, but don't overdo the happiness. As we were still under their control, we were rather subdued . . . outwardly; inwardly, of course we're bubbling like uncorked champagne. It wasn't until we actually got on the [US] airplane [that] all hell broke loose.

In the United States, the release of the POWs was cause for national celebration. Shirley Johnson remembers that after a parade in her hometown of Plano, Texas, local children could not wait to greet her husband, Sam:

All the way home, there were signs along the road and flags . . . We had people coming by to see [Sam] and finally one of our neighbors across the street . . . all the kids were at her house, all the neighborhood children, and they all wanted to

meet Sam. So, she got them all in a line and they knocked on
the front door and they all trooped through the house to shake
his hand and say hello and [then went] out the back door. And
about 30 minutes later I think another group had formed so
they came through . . . They did that about three times. They
had a big paper sign on the front of our house: 'Welcome Home
Sam Johnson.' It was just a big holiday for Plano. It was really a
homecoming for him that day I think.

The celebration in America was not duplicated in Vietnam. Large numbers
of NVA forces remained inside South Vietnam, and the South Vietnamese
troops now had no American ground, air or naval support. After probing
attacks in 1974 to assess South Vietnam's military prowess, North Vietnam
launched a broad offensive in late 1975, aiming at the South's main cities,
including Saigon. In many places South Vietnam's forces quickly collapsed,
but there were exceptions. Bill Laurie, who was an analyst with the US Defense
Attache's Office in Saigon, remembers the ARVN resistance encountered by
the NVA at Xuan Loc, northeast of Saigon, in early April 1975:

The ARVN 18th Division, which had been horrible several years
earlier . . . was commanded by . . . General Le Minh Dao [who]
was widely regarded as an outstanding individual, wonderful
man, honest man, great tactician, true believer, all the way,
very candid in his denunciation of corruption, and everything
else. His troops knew that he was an honest man, a fighter, so
when he was told to hold Xuan Loc, he did . . . Also parts of the
First Airborne Brigade were there as well. And they were taking
absolutely hellacious [*sic*] NVA artillery, just getting pounded.
And then armor came in . . . and basically they held. And word
went out. Somebody from the State Department . . . took a
helicopter up there and went to General Dao and said, "Hey,
we can evacuate you, 'cause if they win you're gonna be in big
trouble," and he wouldn't leave. He wouldn't leave his troops.
And eventually the NVA just simply got tired of running against
these guys and getting blown apart. I think ARVN killed about
37, 38, 39 NVA tanks at Xuan Loc, so it wasn't just a matter of
defending against artillery off in the distance. There were ground
assaults . . . One of my Vietnamese friends that I've come to know
since then was at Xuan Loc with the Airborne Brigade, and some
of the NVA they captured were just kids. They were just cannon

fodder: "Form the human wave!" "Just get the warm bodies up there!" on line assaults, and stuff like that. He felt sorry for . . . these little North Vietnamese kids that were petrified with fear, and crying and everything else . . . Finally, [the NVA] decided that they weren't even going to bother with it any more, and they went around Xuan Loc . . . There were actually two [ARVN] battalions that volunteered to stay and act as a blocking force to allow the 18th [ARVN Division] to withdraw. And they had, of course, no hopes of survival whatsoever.

In late March and early April, NVA troops captured several major cities, forcing civilians and military personnel alike to flee. The US, using CIA-financed Air America aircraft, began flying rescue missions to help evacuate American personnel and Vietnamese VIPs. Jim Overman, a former US Air Force pilot then working for Air America, recalls one flight he made into Da Nang as the city was being overtaken:

We knew it was a very unsafe situation. Those people were frantic. They were jumping on. They were getting in front of the props [propellers] and some of them walked into the props . . . You know, they had never been around an airplane before. It was just a terrible scene. [We had] nothing [on board] but fuel to get out of there. Our sole mission was to go to pick up people.

As NVA troops raced toward Saigon in April 1975, American officials directed last-minute operations there to evacuate Americans, South Vietnamese and other allies. Nikki Fillipi, an Air America employee, recalls the flight operations:

We made the decision that the Marines would handle evacuation from Ton Son Nhut air base and from the US Embassy, and Air America would handle evacuation from these downtown sites, bringing the people out to the airport for the Marines to transport out to the fleet. And that kind of fell apart, too, because everything was so pandemonius [sic] the last day that Air America aircraft were actually going [directly] out to the South China Sea and dropping people and then coming back into town and picking up more and taking them back.

As the evacuation began, a C5-A Galaxy aircraft that was moving Vietnamese orphans out of the country crashed at Ton Son Nhut airport near Saigon. Bill Laurie was among the American officials who, while still trying to organize the larger evacuation, also helped the survivors of the crash:

> It was just utter chaos . . . We were already thinking about the evacuation that was to come . . . Then that C5-A crashed . . . That was a miserable day. We had to haul wounded babies off of helicopters from that thing, and dead people, and all kinds of stuff . . . The strange thing is . . . here's these two-, three-, four-, five-year-old kids . . . they were busted up pretty bad, bleeding, covered with mud, and stuff. We took them on a helicopter. They weren't crying, they were just looking at us, as if to say, "Why is this?" There wasn't a cry, not a scream, just nothing. They were just looking at us . . . At that point it was just a total psychic overload . . . I think your brain just decides to shut itself down to protect the human from short-circuiting altogether: "The guy can't handle this much in one day." . . .
>
> Of course the greater backdrop is that all this effort, all this work, all these people have put so much into [South Vietnam], and now it's all being thrown away . . . The Vietnamese have an expression . . . that you can basically [only] pour so much water into a glass, and then it starts over-filling.

As the NVA drew nearer to Saigon, panic set in. Stephen Katz, a navigator who flew on one of the C-130 evacuation aircraft, recalls the scene at Ton Son Nhut airport:

> I really felt sorry for the people. We were on the ground for a couple of hours, and people were running up and down. Vietnamese civilians were running up and down the ramp trying to sell stuff . . . And just so desperate. [The] people, they didn't know what the future was going to hold for them and there was just an air of, boy – it was obvious that Saigon was going to fall very, very soon . . . We certainly felt that this would probably be the last time that any of us would ever get there, and it would probably be a good idea to get the airplane loaded and get the hell out of there, which we did with our load of refugees. It seemed [a] very hectic time, [a] very exciting time and a tragic time . . . Your heart just kind of went out to [some of] those people, to have to leave them behind.

Bill Laurie, who climbed into one of the evacuation aircraft with a group of Vietnamese he was trying to help escape to the United States, remembers his feelings as he left Saigon:

[We left] Ton Son Nhut on a military aircraft . . . [I] guess 50 or 60 people [aboard]. It was a cargo aircraft, it wasn't like an airliner. You are all just sitting around in the giant bowels of this giant aircraft . . . [I had told a friend], "I'll get [these Vietnamese] out for you," and I was afraid if I didn't go with them they wouldn't get out . . . A whole family of Vietnamese-Chinese – they were just regular normal folks who had some little store somewhere . . . There was one [Vietnamese] guy who . . . had been an interpreter with the Special Forces early in the '60s. His whole life was war. He'd been shot three or four times. Then when the Special Forces left he got drafted into [the] ARVN. His wife and son or daughter got killed in Da Nang in the evacuation . . . There was paperwork all over the place, then in the end they just said, "Go!" "What about this?" "Just go!" . . . I really didn't want to leave . . . I really felt crappy about leaving. My staying would not have been a matter of bravery, or any positive attribute. My staying would have been a matter of my being just a complete bastard. I just didn't like running out . . . I wanted to stay 'til the end.

The end came with Saigon's capture by Communist troops on 29 April 1975. At the same time Khmer Rouge Communist forces were seizing control of Phnom Penh, the capital of Cambodia. American pilots and crews flying for the CIA's Air America were trying to resupply non-Communist units in that city and evacuate Americans ahead of the Khmer Rouge takeover, as pilot Jim Overman recalls:

We were briefed immediately that we were flying food into Phnom Penh . . . I always checked a load before I took off. Guess what was in the back of it? All mortar rounds. So I knew what we were involved in. So I did my mission. I flew it and offloaded it . . . on the airfield. By the way they had just . . . destroyed a civilian aircraft with ground fire on the ramp in Phnom Penh the night before I landed . . . We never shut the engines down because we were being shelled . . . [On another mission into Phnom Penh] we were told by radio . . . that we would be picking

up the [American] embassy people . . . You can hear the mortars
and everything going off around us. Phnom Penh was falling
and I was right in the middle of it! Here come all these civilians
– female, male, some American, some not American – and when
they got on board some of them actually had to come up to the
flight deck and I didn't worry about strapping everybody down. I
wanted to get the hell out of there and so did they!

Gerald Kumpf, another Air America employee, remembers the mixed
emotions of American personnel then at a support air base in Khorat,
Thailand, when Saigon was finally taken by Communist troops:

I was in an F-4 outfit at Kadena and we went down to Khorat to
fly cover for the withdrawal of the Embassy [in Saigon] . . . we
flew cover missions out of Khorat, Thailand, with armed force
and our unit was there. Our pilots all came back, I remember,
off the last mission that night after the Embassy fell. They all
came back empty. There wasn't a bomb or a missile left on their
airplanes. They all wanted to fire the last shot of the war, so
they hit at anything they could on the way out . . . I mean it was
the strangest, strangest night of the war. What can I say? We all
felt super sad, everybody. The town of Khorat down there was
just packed with GIs. Everybody was down there getting drunk,
screaming and yelling and having a strange time. I think we were
not celebrating anything other than maybe the end of an era
and of a time, [the] end of the war . . . We felt somehow that we
let everybody down . . . I felt the same way . . . when Air America
pulled out, [when] we stopped our operation: "We're leaving
them, we're letting them rot on the vine. They're not going to
survive by themselves." . . . We left, that's it. One day we didn't
come back and I can imagine how they felt . . . It was bad. You
know, I still cry about it.

In the United States, many veterans felt as James Calbreath, who had served
as a medical technician in Vietnam, did when he watched the television
reports on the fall of Saigon:

I was pissed, just flat out pissed . . . I had spent a year doing
the best I could to save lives, to save limbs, keep people alive
and we had worked hard at that. We had given everything that

we could possibly give to save people's lives and then what the government did was, what the American public did is that we walked away from it. We threw up our hands and said, "Whoa, I'm tired of this." And as well we should have been tired of it . . . I went into an absolute tirade, one of the few times that my wife left the area. I had come home from work, the TV was on and I remember watching them pushing helicopters off the sides of these fucking aircraft carriers and I was just livid. I went into [an] absolute tirade. I threw things. I went out in the driveway and I yelled at the top of [my] voice . . . At the time I was pissed because the thing for me was a sense of waste. Everything that we had done, all of those lives, all of those limbs, all of that was a waste because [America] walked away.

Veterans of the Vietnam conflict were as divided in their views of the Paris Peace Accords and the fall of Saigon as they were on the issues of American involvement in Vietnam in the first place. Gerald Kumpf, who had served in the Marines and Air Force before working for Air America, was one of those bitterly disappointed by President Nixon's 'peace with honor' policy:

If they'd said we achieved peace, okay that's fine. We got an interim peace [in 1973] but there was no honor in there at all, none at all. We walked out; we left those people hanging on the vine. We make all kinds of promises, [that] we're going to come in here; we're going to do this, we're going to do that. We . . . really never had a chance to win [that] war anyway. I mean it really wasn't a war. What were we trying to do over there, just keep the Communists from taking over the south, right? We don't even go in there and attack [North Vietnam], other than drop a few bombs around Hanoi. You're not going win a war that way!

On the other hand, according to Marine aviator Neil Whitehurst, who served in Vietnam in 1970, President Nixon had been forceful enough to secure an agreement with the North Vietnamese, and if it had not been for the distraction of anti-war protests and the Watergate scandal at home, things may have turned out differently in Vietnam:

[Under President Johnson] we had policies that you couldn't hit Haiphong. You couldn't hit the ports. You couldn't hit

ships that were unloading missiles. You couldn't hit certain
airfields and certain areas because [of] civilians . . . You
couldn't hit the dams. You couldn't hit so many things. You
couldn't go 'downtown' [bomb Hanoi]. You couldn't go after
the [Communist] hierarchy. You couldn't do any of these
things and you couldn't even bomb certain strategic areas
that were main supply routes. When Nixon came in, he said
to heck with some of that but gave the green light to take care
of a bunch of stuff in Cambodia which was a main infiltration
route of NVAs and supplies to the southern part of Vietnam.
Then he also worked out the deal with the South Vietnamese
so they could do Lam Son 719 [the invasion of Laos], at least
try to do something, and reinstituted B-52 bombings of certain
key installations in North Vietnam . . . That finally brought
[the Communists] to the table regardless of whether it was a
great table and a great discussion or not. At least we were able
to do something. I believe that if Mr Nixon had been present
the whole time, we would have actually ended hostilities on a
much better grounds for the United States.

Ex-POW Sam Johnson, who was held in North Vietnam for almost seven
years and was later elected to the US Congress from Texas, sums up
America's difficulties in Vietnam:

I think we totally misread the geopolitical aspects of that war
when we got sucked into it. Kennedy started it and Johnson, I
don't think, knew how to get out of it. But the worst mistake he
made was trying to run a country over here [the United States]
in a peacetime situation and run a full-scale war over there [in
Vietnam]. Henry Kissinger said, and I think I quoted him, the
biggest mistake we made was in not including the people of the
United States in that war; ie, through rationing – gas rationing,
food rationing, whatever – some way, so that the focus was on a
war that we intended to win. The will to win never was there.

CHRONOLOGY

2 September 1945 - the Viet Minh, led by Ho Chi Minh, seizes power in Hanoi, claims independence, and declares a Democratic Republic of Vietnam (DRV)

March 1946 – France recognizes the DRV as an independent state within the Indochinese Union

23 November 1946 – Franco-Viet Minh hostilities begin with shelling of Haiphong

December 1946 – the Viet Minh attack French forces; the First Indochina War begins

8 March 1949 – Vietnam becomes an Associated State within the French Union; Bao Dai becomes nominal leader of Vietnam

1 October 1949 – The People's Republic of China (PRC) is established

7 May 1954 – French forces surrender to the Viet Minh at Dien Bien Phu

16 June 1954 – At US insistence, Ngo Dinh Diem is appointed Prime Minister under Bao Dai

20-21 July 1954 – The Geneva Accords are signed ending the First Indochinese War, partitioning Vietnam at the 17th Parallel forming North and South Vietnam

8 September 1954 – Southeast Asia Treaty Organization (SEATO) established

11 October 1954 – Ho Chi Minh and the Viet Minh take over leadership of North Vietnam

May 1955 – US begins to provide military aid and training to Diem's government forces

23 October 1955 - Bao Dai abdicates and Ngo Dinh Diem becomes head of state; he declares the Republic of Vietnam (RVN)

1956 – Vietnam's reunification elections indefinitely postponed

28 April 1956 - US activates the Military Assistance Advisory Group (US MAAG) in Saigon to direct training of RVN forces

May 1959 – North Vietnam begins sending troops and material to support anti-Diem insurgency in South Vietnam via the Ho Chi Minh Trail Complex through Laos and Cambodia

December 1960 – the DRV forms the National Liberation Front for South Vietnam (NLF), commonly called the Viet Cong (VC)

1961 – Kennedy Administration increases aid to South Vietnam, focusing on counter-insurgency

8 February 1962 – US MAAG becomes US Military Assistance Command, Vietnam (MACV) under General Paul Harkins

August 1962 – Australian military advisors arrive in South Vietnam

May-August 1963 – Buddhist uprising in South Vietnam

12 November 1963 - assassinations of Ngo Dinh Diem and Ngo Dinh Nhu in Saigon in military coup

22 November 1963 - assassination of John F. Kennedy in Dallas, Texas; Lyndon B. Johnson becomes US President

20 June 1964 – General William Westmoreland takes command of US MACV

2-5 August 1964 - Gulf of Tonkin Incidents; first US bombing of North Vietnamese territory

7 August 1964 – US Congress passes Gulf of Tonkin Resolution empowering the President to use military forces to combat Communism in Southeast Asia

13 February 1965 – Johnson authorizes Operation ROLLING THUNDER, a bombing campaign of North Vietnam after US military installations in South Vietnam are attacked; it begins 2 March

8 March 1965 - two US Marine Corps battalions land at Da Nang, South Vietnam, marking deployment of first US combat troops in Vietnam

October-November 1965 - US Army units defeat North Vietnamese Army (NVA) and VC forces in the Ia Drang Valley in the first meeting between US and NVA troops

April 1966 – US Navy begins Operation GAME WARDEN in the Mekong Delta to interdict DRV and VC supply routes

28 February 1967 – US establishes the Mobile Riverine Force in the Mekong Delta

3 September 1967 – General Nguyen Van Thieu is elected President of South Vietnam

22 January 1968 – the 77-day siege of Khe Sanh begins

31 January 1968 – the Tet Offensive is launched; 84,000 NVA and VC forces attack US and RVN forces and facilities throughout South Vietnam

31 March 1968 – President Johnson announces that he will not seek re-election

4 April 1968 – Martin Luther King, Jr., is assassinated in Memphis, Tennessee

3 May 1968 – Johnson announces agreement to hold peace talks in Paris; preliminary talks between the US and the DRV begin on the 13th

11 June 1968 – President Johnson replaces General William Westmoreland with General Creighton Abrams as US MACV commander

5 November 1968 – Richard Nixon elected US President and pledges US troop withdrawal from Vietnam

25 January 1969 – the formal Paris Peace Talks between the US, DRV, the RVN, and the NLF begin

18 March 1969 – the US commences the secret bombing of Cambodia

8 June 1969 – Nixon announces the Vietnamization policy; the US begins withdrawing troops from South Vietnam

3 September 1969 – Ho Chi Minh dies

October-November 1969 – anti-war protests escalate in the US

20 February 1970 – US National Security Adviser Henry Kissinger opens secret talks with North Vietnamese negotiator Le Duc Tho

29 April 1970 – Nixon announces that US troops have been engaged in ground action in Cambodia

4 May 1970 - National Guardsmen shoot anti-war protestors at Kent State University in Ohio; 6 days later over 80,000 people participate in an anti-war protest in Washington, DC

31 December 1970 – the US Congress repeals the Gulf of Tonkin Resolution

8 February 1971 – Operation Lam Son 719 begins, the South Vietnamese incursion into Laos

August- September 1971 – Australia, New Zealand, and South Korea announce that all of their troops will be withdrawn from South Vietnam

30 March 1972 – North Vietnam launches the "Spring Offensive" against northern and central South Vietnam

April-May 1972 - Nixon orders renewed aerial bombing of North Vietnam and mining of harbor at Haiphong

12 August 1972 – the last US combat troops leave South Vietnam

18 December 1972 - Nixon inaugurates the "Christmas Bombing" of the Hanoi area

27 January 1973 – Peace Agreement signed in Paris between the US and North Vietnam

28 March 1973 – last remaining US troops leave South Vietnam

9 August 1974 - Nixon resigns in wake of Watergate scandal; Gerald Ford becomes US President

4 March 1975 – North Vietnam launches broad offensive in the Central Highlands and swiftly moves toward Saigon

30 April 1975 – the NVA seizes Saigon; South Vietnam surrenders; refugees escape with American aid

US Force Levels in Vietnam

1960 – 900	1968 – 536,000
1961 – 3,000	1969 – 475,000
1962 – 11,000	1970 – 335,000
1963 – 16,000	1971 – 157,000
1964 – 23,000	1972 – 24,000
1965 – 184,000	1973 – 0*
1966 – 385,000	1974 – 0*
1967 – 486,000	1975 – 0*

*Americans in South Vietnam were limited to governmental personnel and civilian contractors

GLOSSARY

AO Area of Operations; the area in which an operation takes place

ARVN Army of the Republic of Vietnam, the regular Army troops of South Vietnam

ATC Armoured Troop Carrier

Bird American slang for helicopter

Black Panther Party radical African-American political group founded in 1966 to redress social and economic grievances of black Americans

CIA US Central Intelligence Agency

CIDG Civilian Irregular Defence Groups; US program to conduct border surveillance in the Central Highlands area using local tribesmen

C-rations Military-issued food for personnel in the field

Chieu Hoi Vietnamese for "open arms"; the *Chieu Hoi* Program was an amnesty program that encouraged VC to desert and come over to the South Vietnamese side of the war; the program lasted ten years (1963–1973) and netted nearly 160,000 former VC and turned over more than 11,000 weapons.

Claymore mine anti-personnel mine designed to spray fragments in a fan-shaped pattern about three feet above ground

Cronkite, Walter American television news journalist, 1962–1981, whose coverage of the Vietnam War and assessments of American progress against the DRV/VC influenced US public opinion

DMZ Demilitarized Zone; the area

bordering the 17th Parallel dividing North from South Vietnam after the 1954 partition of the country

DRV Democratic Republic of Vietnam, or North Vietnam

FAC Forward Air Controller; pilot who flew observation and fire control missions; also a ground-based individual used to direct fire on to the enemy

Fleschette arrow- or nail-shaped projectiles packed into artillery rounds, designed to inflict injuries

FNG Fucking New Guy; a term applied to US servicemen recently arrived in Vietnam

Fragging military slang for the deliberate attempt by an individual to kill an officer or Non-commissioned officer

Fragmentation a term usually applied to a grenade which, when it detonates, sprays fragments of serrated steel wire outward in a 15 meter kill zone

GCA Ground Control Approach; term used to describe the landing of an aircraft that is controlled by personnel on the ground

Gook American slang during the war for someone of Vietnamese descent

Gooner American slang during war for someone of Vietnamese descent

GQ General Quarters

Green Beret alternative term for the US Army Special Forces, organized in 1952 to wage guerrilla warfare

Grunt an enlisted infantryman of low rank, usually assigned to combat detail

Gulf of Tonkin Incidents Naval engagements on August 2 and 4, 1964, in the Gulf of Tonkin off of the North Vietnamese coast between the US destroyers USS *Maddox* and USS *C Turner Joy* and DRV torpedo boats in international waters; the sketchy sonar and radio contacts made the incidents difficult to confirm but President Lyndon Johnson used the attacks as proof of DRV aggression and launched retaliatory air strikes against North Vietnam (Operation PIERCE ARROW); the incidents led to the US Congress passage of the Gulf of Tonkin Resolution on 7 August.

Gulf of Tonkin Resolution US Congressional resolution passed on 7 August 1964 in the wake of the Gulf of Tonkin Incidents; it gave the US president the authority to use "all necessary measures" to repel any armed attack on American forces in Vietnam and "to prevent further aggression"

Gurney a hand-carried 'stretcher' or rolling bed used to transport wounded personnel

Hardstand a stabilized or re-surfaced area for parking aircraft, usually spaced at intervals along the taxiway

HICKORY, Operation May 1967 infantry mission using the US Marine Corps and the ARVN to sweep and clear portions of northern I Corps near and in the DMZ in order to prepare for the installation of the "McNamara Wall", an electronic infiltration barrier across Vietnam just south of the DMZ

Ho Chi Minh Trail Complex American term for the North

Vietnamese-built complex of trails and roads that funnelled supplies and men from North to South Vietnam through Laos and Cambodia

Hooch slang for living quarters in Vietnam

Hooch maid a person who cleans a hooch; usually these were South Vietnamese civilian women who were paid by individuals to keep American barracks clean on bases throughout South Vietnam

Hot LZ a landing zone that is under enemy fire

Huey nickname for the American AH-1 helicopter, first used in the war in 1962

Kit Carson Scout nickname (after a nineteenth century trader and Indian agent in the American Southwest) for a defector from the VC who acted as a guide for US forces in Vietnam

JCS Joint Chiefs of Staff, the highest policy-making body in the US military

KIA killed in action

LP Listening Post

LRRP Long Range Reconnaissance Patrol

LST Landing Ship – Tank; a small flat-bottomed vessel used to land troops and cargo on open beaches

LZ Landing Zone; the cleared area where helicopters delivered and picked up men and supplies

MAAG Military Assistance Advisory Group, the headquarters for US military operations in Vietnam 1950–1964

MACV Military Assistance Command Vietnam; the headquarters for US military operations in Vietnam 1964–1973

Mama San US slang, adopted from Korean, for civilian Vietnamese women

MEDCAP Medical Civic Action Project, in which military medical personnel provided medical services to Vietnamese civilians

Mike Force a well-armed mobile unit composed of US and indigenous troops, usually with jungle warfare skills

MOS Military Occupation Specialty; a military job description

MP Military Police; the US Army's military law enforcement branch

Medevac term for medical evacuation, typically by helicopter

Napalm highly combustible jellied gasoline mixed with liquid plastics to ensure adherence to targets

National Guard Reserve branch of US military under the jurisdiction of each state's governors and the Department of Defense

NCO Non-commissioned officer; a subordinate officer appointed from among enlisted personnel

NLF National Liberation Front; founded in South Vietnam in 1960; an organization whose goal was the overthrow of the South Vietnam government

NVA North Vietnamese Army; the title Americans usually applied to the Communists' regular forces; also known as People's Army of Vietnam, based in North Vietnam

NVN North Vietnam; the title Americans usually applied to the Democratic Republic of Vietnam

OCS Officer Candidate School

OJT on-the job training

ONTOS a lightweight, full-track, two-person vehicle armed with 105mm guns

OR Operating room

Order of Battle detailed information on the units, strength, weapons and other assets of a military organization

PAVN People's Army of Vietnam, the main military forces of the DRV; best known to the Americans as the North Vietnamese Army (NVA)

Papa San US slang, adopted from Korean, for civilian Vietnamese men

Poncho waterproof hooded cloak designed to protect soldiers and gear from rain

Punji stakes weapon used by the Viet Cong and NVA as a booby trap; usually these were sharpened bamboo stakes, placed in a concealed pit and sometimes covered with faeces or poison to facilitate infection, sickness, or death

R&R Rest and Recuperation; the vacation time given US servicemen in Vietnam

RF/PFs Regional Forces/Popular Forces

Revetment a wall of earth or other material, often reinforced with timber or concrete, protecting parked aircraft from ground-based attack

ROEs rules of engagement; the formal authorizations for all US military forces engaged in the war

RoKs pronounced "rocks"; American slang for the troops of the Republic of Korea serving in Vietnam

ROTC Reserve Officer's Training Corps; the recruitment and training

system for American college and university students, who after graduation must fulfill military service obligations

RPG rocket-propelled grenade

RTO radio/telephone operator; the individual in an American military unit, usually attached to the commanding officer, responsible for communications

RVN Republic of Vietnam, or South Vietnam

SAM surface-to-air missile; ground-based missiles that target aircraft

SAR Search and Rescue; specialized operations to locate and extract missing personnel

SEATO Southeast Asian Treaty Organization; an anti-Communist multilateral body created in 1954 and pledged to retaliate against Communist military aggression in Southeast Asia

SF Special Forces

Skids pole-like landing gear of helicopters affixed to undercarriage of the fuselage

SOG Studies and Observation Group; joint US-RVN covert operations unit established in 1964 to conduct cross-border missions into North Vietnam and Laos

Stanchion an upright bar, post, or support

TOW tube-launched, optically-tracked guided missile designed to penetrate armour, usually employed against tanks

Two-stepper American slang for the poisonous Vietnamese krait snake, rumoured to have venom lethal enough to sicken or kill a human in the time it takes to walk two steps

USAID United States Agency for International Development, which provided non-military aid

USO United Services Organizations; an American non-profit, congressionally chartered, private organization which provides comfort, morale and recreational services to service members and their families

VC Viet Cong, the insurgents in South Vietnam fighting against the US and RVN forces

WIA Wounded in Action

XO Executive Officer

Zippo nickname (after a popular cigarette lighter) for a US Navy river vessel equipped with special turrets for shooting streams of compressed napalm incendiary onto riverbanks

INDEX OF CONTRIBUTORS

GENERAL INDEX

PICTURE CREDITS

(*Key:* * Douglas Pike Photograph Collection, Vietnam Archive; + Brigadier General Edwin H. Simmons Collection, Vietnam
Archive; † Donald Jellema Collection (Department of the Army Special Photographic Office(DASPO)), Vietnam Archive; Ω
Robert Lafoon Collection, Vietnam Archive)

Title verso VA002335*; *6–7*, maps by Ethan Danielson; *19*, VA000846*; *24*, VA005585, Douglas Pike Collection:
other manuscripts – American friends of Vietnam; *31*, VA003057*; *50*, VA020915+; *59*, VA020846+; *64*, VA029696Ω;
77, VA002550*; *81*, VA003633*; *87*, VA013597, Ranch Hand Association Vietnam Collection, Vietnam Archive; *95*,
VA030880†; *102*, VA030887†; *106*, VA000751*; *110*, VA004061*; *119*, VA005889, Donald L Swafford Collection, Vietnam
Archive; *132*, VA000291*; *146*, VA002111*; *149*, VA020855+;*156*, VA030918†; *174*, VA029698Ω; *182*, VA030560, Bryan
Grigsby Collection, Department of the Army Special Photographic Office (DASPO), Vietnam Archive; *212*, VA006194,
"Burch Collection" of the National Vietnam Veterans Coalition Collection, Vietnam Archive; *216*, VA035397, Peter Braestrup
Collection, Vietnam Archive; *222*, VA006852*; *238*, BE060937, Corbis; *256*, VA002360*; *267*, VA002367*.